Taking Stage: Women Directors on Directing
by Helen Manfull

Professor Helen Manfull taught at the School of Theatre at Penn State University for over thiry years. She is an actor, director, and the author of *The Stage in Action*, which she wrote with her husband, Professor Emeritus Lowell Manfull, and *Additional Dialogue: The Letters of Dalton Trumbo*, a study of Hollywood's blacklist. Manfull received both her MA and PhD from the University of Minnesota, which she attended under a Woodrow Wilson Fellowship. Her interest in British theatre began when she attended Birmingham University's Shakespeare Institute as an undergraduate. She is the recipient of numerous awards for distinguished teaching, a member of Actors' Equity, and a Fellow of Penn State's Institute for Arts and Humanistic Studies. She and her husband recently taught for the University of Pittsburgh's Semester-at-Sea, which took them around the world. Helen Manfull lives in Boalsburg, Pennsylvania.

TAKING STAGE
WOMEN DIRECTORS ON DIRECTING

TAKING STAGE
WOMEN DIRECTORS ON DIRECTING

HELEN MANFULL

with

Sarah Pia Anderson, Annabel Arden, Julia Bardsley,
Annie Castledine, Garry Hynes, Jenny Killick, Brigid Larmour,
Phyllida Lloyd, Sue Sutton Mayo, Nancy Meckler,
Katie Mitchell, Lynne Parker, and Di Trevis

METHUEN DRAMA

Published by Methuen 1999

3 5 7 9 10 8 6 4 2

First published in the United States of America in 1997 by
Smith and Kraus Publishers, Inc.

First published in the United Kingdom in 1999 by
Methuen Publishing Ltd,
215 Vauxhall Bridge Road, London SW1V 1EJ

Peribo Pty Ltd, 58 Beaumont Road, Mount Kuring-Gai
NSW 2080, Australia, CAN 002 273 761
(for Australia and New Zealand)

Methuen Publishing Limited Reg. No. 3543167

A CIP catalogue for this book
is available from the British Library

ISBN 0 413 72790 4

Typeset by Deltatype Ltd, Birkenhead, Merseyside

Printed and bound in Great Britain by
Mackays of Chatham PLC, Chatham, Kent

To women directors and playwrights everywhere, in the words of Di Trevis, 'Just do it!'

Contents

Foreword

The first time I had the opportunity to watch a theatre director at work, I could barely breathe. The experience in rehearsal was intensely unsettling. I had the sensation of watching others make love. The interactions were sometimes tender, occasionally violent, often private, or exposed, at moments wonderful and at other moments, excruciating. In the crisis of rehearsal, everyone is called upon to respond with their entire being. The director must respond candidly, be receptive to the unfolding play, to the unfolding moment, to the text, to the actors, to the tempo, to the spatial composition, and to the incipient truth of the play. She must know when to insist and when to be flexible. The truth is precarious. The tightrope walk is beautiful.

Helen Manfull loves, respects, and is fascinated by the art of directing for the theatre. She travelled throughout the United Kingdom and Ireland to pursue her curiosity and her love. She interviewed thirteen important women directors and wrote this book so that we might enjoy the fruits of her curiosity.

Taking Stage: Women Directors on Directing introduces us to the careers and processes of working women directors who have developed values, opinions, methods, and footholds in the British theatre world. These thirteen women generously describe their lives, their notions about art, their struggles, and their triumphs. Their tales, lessons, and reflections are endlessly refreshing. Their necessary battles, their frustrations and their tenacity are an inspiration. Rather than assigning a chapter per director, Helen Manfull has juxtaposed these women's stories, interweaving the fabric of their experiences into a wonderful read.

Anne Bogart

Acknowledgements

At the risk of sounding like one of the more boring speeches at the Academy Award ceremonies, I am aware of the fact that – although the essence of this book is the thirteen women directors themselves – many, many people contributed to its gestation and formulation. Yet when one begins naming names, one feels almost certain that someone will be slighted or ignored. Nevertheless it is essential to me that I make an attempt to acknowledge all who were so very helpful along the way: first, to C. Gregory Knight, then Vice Provost and Dean for Undergraduate Education, who provided the grant for the Penn State Fund for Research, and Edward V. Williams, Associate Dean for Research, who offered guidance, advice, and encouragement for the project; to the then Dean of the College of Arts and Architecture, James Moeser, for his letter of recommendation; to Carole Brandt, then Head of the Department of Theatre, to the Sabbatical Leave Committee, to Provost John Brighton and then President of Penn State, Joab Thomas – all of whom made the leave possible; to my colleagues, Michael Connolly and Robert Leonard, for sharing their ideas, expertise, support, and encouragement; and to Mark Fearnow, who read portions of the manuscript and offered tremendous moral support and advice on the project; to my students, Debbie Gottfeld and Rosemary Newnham, who were willing to share tips on women directors in London and Manchester; to Rich Tepper for invaluable computer assistance; to Caroline Maude, Manager of the Gate Theatre, who sent a preliminary list of women directors in the UK from which the first contacts were made; to Tony Branch, British and American Drama Academy who helped me with phone numbers and addresses; and to my friend and colleague, Alison VanDyke at Cornell, who put me in touch with BADA in the first place; to Verlana Tkacz, who encouraged me and helped put me in touch with Sarah Pia Anderson; to Professors Rolf Remshardt of Denison University and Elvira Grossman of Penn State's Slavic and Soviet Language Center, for their research assistance; to Helen Cross of the Royal Shakespeare Company, to the literary offices of both the RSC and the Royal National Theatre; to Angela McEvoy at the Abbey Theatre, Siobhàn Bourke of Rough Magic, and Primrose Muir and Gavin Morgan of the Performing Arts Library in London, all of whom were so very helpful with photographs and facilitating details; to Sheckler Photographics in State College, Pennsylvania; to Stephen Wood, Nicola Scadding, Christopher Millard, and Janene Shalom from the Press Office of the RNT, each of whom needed a pint after an afternoon with me poring over and selecting photographs.

Special thanks must also go to Penn State's Institute for Arts and Humanistic Studies for financial support; to Max King, University Scholars' Program, who got us to London; to Bill and Nancy Kelly for exploring Cotswold villages near train connections for us and for accommodations at Goldsmith's College; to Betty and Judd Arnold for sharing their flat; to Bill Wertz and John Farrell for Dublin; to Julia and Nick Irvine, who provided us with our dream cottage in Blockley; to the dour former station-master in Moreton-in-Marsh from whom I finally got a smile when I began to refer to myself as 'his weekly trouble'; to the staff of The Crown in Blockley, who let me make countless phone calls from the pay-phone in the cosy fire-lit lobby, which prevented me from freezing in a red phone box on the street, to Tim Lorah who provided the laughs, the driving lessons, and got me to the stage door at Stratford on time; to Bob E. Gasper for reading and offering comments; to Bendicks for the chocolate-covered ginger (my greatest solace); to my students in the Women and Theatre seminar who listened to long passages from the unpublished manuscript and convinced me that they really did like it.

Certainly I owe a very special debt to the photographers who have allowed their work to be included here, and above all, to the thirteen women directors whom I have come to refer to affectionately as 'my women'. Had any one of them known what she was letting herself in for she probably would have run for the hills. I have begged all of them for time, several interviews, CVs, photographs, responses to the manuscript. I have plagued them with letters, requests, and endless queries, and they have rewarded my tenacity and American pushiness by responding with humour, dignity, great patience, compassion, and understanding. My thanks to each of them is profound. To Marisa Smith and Eric Kraus and their staff, particularly Julia Gignoux, I offer my genuine thanks for believing that this work should be published and for having the courage to do it in America; and to Michael Earley at Methuen for his support, excellent suggestions, and for inspiring me to revise and prepare the work for the British edition; and to the editor, Eleanor Knight, who saw the project through with grace and intelligence. Finally, I must thank my family: Benjamin and Judy who were always with me in spirit and for one wonderful week in person; James who took and helped select photographs and in exchange got himself a week in the Lake District; and, of course, to Lowell who only asked an occasional pint in a pub in exchange for reading the manuscript and making suggestions, my constant excitement about the project, my complaints when things didn't go well, my endless chatter about the women, my syntax and punctuation, my frustrations, and my single-mindedness. But then he's put up with me patiently and lovingly for over forty years, and I don't suppose there were many surprises. For his incredible support, I offer my heartfelt thank you.

Introduction

It has only been in the past fifteen years or so that we have begun to value and credit the enormous contribution of women directors to the world of theatre. I recently taught a course at the Pennsylvania State University titled Women and Theatre. Structured as a seminar, the class was made up of graduate and senior students who explored together the work of playwrights, directors, producers, actors, designers, and theorists who happen – as a result of biology – to be women. The students were constantly amazed by the people whose work we examined; by their courage, their tenacity, their vision, their knowledge, and their craft. But one area of our study seemed sparse and inadequate: the work of women directors. Perhaps there is a good reason for this; the director's contribution to a production is largely anonymous and immeasurable. There is an old saying that if the show is a flop, the director gets the blame; but if it is a success, the actors get the credit. Directors are low profile artists of the theatre. Let me give an example. Not long ago I went to New York to see the stunning actress Fiona Shaw in a staged version of T.S. Eliot's *The Wasteland*. Amid the rave reviews was the sometimes casual mention of the fact that the production was directed by Deborah Warner. Shaw was alone on a stage devoid of scenery. What did the director do? What truly was her task, her function, her contribution to the theatrical experience? The answers to these questions are impossible, for the work of directors is varied and disparate. No two would ask the same questions of their actors or explore the fabric of the play in the same way. Indeed the same director probably works very differently on a Marivaux comedy to one by Noël Coward. Some directors wish to leave their indelible marks on the production while others wish to sweep away their imprint as the production nears its opening. Some believe it is their duty to ask questions, not to answer them, to remain silent rather than speak, to facilitate rather than command. Some think of the director as the advocate of the audience or as the audience of one.

Another reason why we know less about the director's work than that of other artists of the theatre lies in the recent development of the craft. The director is a modern concept. Only when it became necessary to synthesize all of the elements of production – the actors, the lighting, the sound, the scenic elements, the costumes, the choreography – did the art of directing emerge. Today, it is an art of paramount importance to the success and indeed to the very life of the production.

Because it is an invention of the modern theatre, because the role of director varies greatly, and because it is a low profile occupation, we know only of those women who have, in the past, made some particular mark or left a memorable imprint on the profession. We know, for example, that Lucia Vestris (1797-1856), managed first the Olympic and later, in partnership with her second husband, Charles Mathews, both Covent Garden and the Lyceum Theatre in London. Vestris is often credited with being the first theatre manager to employ the box set, thus leading the British theatre towards modernism and realism. We know that Marie Wilton (1839-1921) became a theatre manager at the age of twenty-five when she borrowed a thousand pounds to lease the then disreputable Queen's Theatre, turning it into a bastion of respectability when it was re-named the Prince of Wales. While Wilton is credited with developing ensemble acting, raising the status of actors, improving scenic elements, and creating strong realistic theatre for the middle classes, she relinquished most of her authority when she married Sir Squire Bancroft in 1867.

Had she not been heiress to a tea fortune, perhaps Annie E.F. Horniman (1860–1937) would not have been a key financial player in the establishment of the Abbey Theatre in Dublin in

1904. However, her great contribution to the British theatre lies in her pioneering work in the repertory theatre movement; in 1907, Horniman created England's first repertory theatre in the city of Manchester. Certainly in America we know of the pioneering achievements of English-born Eva Le Gallienne as actress, director, translator, producer, and founder of the famous Civic Repertory Theatre in New York. We know that American women like Margo Jones, Nina Vance, and Margaret Webster were major figures in the development of the American regional theatre movement and that Hallie Flanagan guided the creation and existence of the courageous but ill-fated Federal Theatre Project of the 1930s.

Returning to Britain, in the period following World War II one woman's name became synonymous with a new energy, excitement, and methodology in the English theatre. That woman, still alive and living for much of the time in France, is Joan Littlewood; but she has rejected the established British theatre just as that established British theatre and its critics once rejected her. It seems extraordinary to me that – in spite of her voluminous memoir, *Joan's Book* (Methuen, 1994) – this major figure of the mid-twentieth century, this innovative giant, has not been the subject of significant books and studies about the reawakening of British theatre in the 1950s and 60s. It was Littlewood who popularised the techniques of Brecht in England and subsequently in America, who experimented with a boldly presentational form, who mixed the comic, the serious, the grotesque, and the theatrical to anticipate the eclectic postmodernism of the late decades of the century. It was Littlewood who tried to reach a new, working-class audience and to politicise the British theatre. She was brave, brash, creative, and far ahead of her times, yet she ended her theatrical career not at the Royal National Theatre or the Royal Shakespeare Company, but working with at-risk children at the Theatre Royal, Stratford East and dreaming of a Fun Palace in Lea Valley. Perhaps the next major figure of the British stage was Mary Anne 'Buzz' Goodbody, the first woman to direct for the Royal Shakespeare Company. After searching for intimate venues for new and experimental work, the RSC opened The Place, in London's Euston Road in 1970, with newcomer and John Barton protégée, Buzz Goodbody, in charge. Her first production was *Occupations* by Trevor Griffiths, featuring the as yet unknown talents of Ben Kingsley and Patrick Stewart. In 1974, Goodbody was named Artistic Director of The Other Place in Stratford-upon-Avon which opened with her own *King Lear*. Yet in spite of her apparent success, Buzz Goodbody ended her life in April of 1975 at the age of twenty-eight as she was preparing a minimalist *Hamlet* with Ben Kingsley.

One day in 1988, I remember picking up the *New York Times* and reading an article by Mel Gussow (August 7, 1988) which bore the headline, 'Englishwomen Make an Impact as Directors'. In that article Gussow named four young women (actually one Irish and three English) who directed that season at the RSC: Sarah Pia Anderson, Garry Hynes, Di Trevis, and Deborah Warner. The presence of a handful of women directors making their way on the established stages of Great Britain made quite a stir in those idealistic days of women's activism. These were not women who were necessarily the first at anything: establishing a repertory company, at introducing the box set, or at managing a company. They were simply committed women practising their craft with skill and assurance. Often in interviews they were asked questions like, 'How does it feel to be a woman director?' Never having been other than women, the directors found these questions perplexing and disturbing.

So it was that I became determined to explore the craft of a select number of these gifted women directors. The reader might understandably ask why I as an American devoted my study to British rather than American women directors. My reasons are simple. First, since my first visit to England in 1954 – when as a student I saw actors like Laurence Olivier, Vivien Leigh, John Gielgud, Robert Morley, Anthony Quayle, Peggy Ashcroft, Edith Evans, and many others – I have been hopelessly in love with the English stage, its sense of theatrical tradition, quality, abundance, affordablity, and availability that simply do not exist in my own country. I remember seeing Mary Morris at the Arts Theatre Club in a production of *Six Characters in Search of an Author* that remains one of the most compelling theatre experiences of my life. I wonder if such productions were as remarkable as I thought they were or if it was a question of, as Sir Tyrone Guthrie said, 'We see all the great theatre when we are young.'

Second, the geographic density of Great Britain and Ireland made travel from theatre to theatre, city to city, both possible and attractive; third, personnel of the British theatre are often more approachable and accessible than artists in America. This was never made clearer than on a bitter cold night when a group of students we had taken to a production of *Richard II* at Stratford wanted to meet Jeremy Irons and waited at the stage door. Irons emerged, exhausted, hair still damp from a shower, and spent a good half an hour talking with these awe-struck students from America. In my own country, I could envision calling a regional theatre to speak to a director, being turned over to the assistant to the assistant, scheduling meetings months in advance, and travelling thousands of miles rather than a few hundred. By contrast most of the British and Irish directors I approached were not only co-operative and giving but they seemed genuinely interested in my project. In the ever-increasing emphasis on a world theatre and an international theatre scene, in which directors work from Toronto to Tokyo and Salzburg to Sydney, distinctions and differences blur and become minimal. Most of the directors with whom I spoke work in New York or California as readily as they do in England; many of them are achieving international stature. A great director from any country can inspire and teach all of us working in the theatre.

With considerable correspondence across the ocean, the collecting of photographs, the time needed for the women to peruse the manuscript, and my own teaching responsibilities, the process of preparing *Taking Stage* has encompassed approximately five years and in a number of instances has involved several interviews rather than a single interview. But despite the slow process, it has been an exhilarating experience. Talking with these women over an extended period of time has allowed for a depth and variety in their comments that I could not have imagined on that cold, rainy day in London when I launched my investigation.

I began my quest with a list of directors and a list of questions. Although I had written to six women, I had no responses before embarking on my journey. Since my letters had to be forwarded from theatres, I had not allowed enough time. Then one bleak day in January, frightened to begin, terrified of rejection or failure, and perceiving the telephone to be my natural enemy, I made a call from a red phone box on Fulham Road to Tony Branch of the British and American Drama Academy, who gave me a few phone numbers and the names of some agents. The first director to return my call and hence to launch my work was Phyllida Lloyd. I met her in the canteen of the British Museum where she was doing research for a production of *La Bohème* for Opera North in Leeds. I found her so giving, so intelligent, so perceptive, and so warm that I was not only immediately at ease but fired with enthusiasm for the project as never before. At first I thought it might be an article or a series of articles, but as I met more women directors I became convinced that the scope of the project was wider than I had imagined. The second director to respond was a woman whom I admire tremendously and a woman whose name has become a leitmotif through my entire study. Although she has never directed at the RSC nor until recently at the National Theatre and has never worked in America, Annie Castledine is a director's director. Nearly all of the women interviewed spoke of her as not only a profound force in the British theatre, a director who has remained uncompromisingly true to her ideals and beliefs, but as a woman who, in spite of enormous craft, has never achieved the recognition she deserves.

It was perhaps with this knowledge that my objective emerged with absolute clarity. If the classic volume *Directors on Directing* (edited by Toby Cole and Helen Krich Chinoy, Bobbs-Merrill Company, Inc. 1963) offers insights into the craft of a large number of gifted directors of another generation, then why not a book – designed to offer inspiration to all aspiring and practising directors and craftspeople of the theatre – that defines, distils, and offers insights into the work of our contemporary women directors? I was fascinated by their directorial processes and methods, how they work with actors, how they work with designers, the kinds of scripts that attract them, their attitudes towards feminism, their concern for women in the plays they direct and in the larger theatrical world, their sense of mission and purpose, and their goals and dreams. All of these women have inspired and instructed me; might they not inspire and instruct others as well?

To suggest that these thirteen are the only working women directors in Britain and Ireland would be ludicrous. Late in 1998, for example, Jude Kelly scored a triumph at the West Yorkshire Playhouse with her production of Chekhov's *The Seagull*; Kathryn Hunter brought new life to Brecht's rarely performed *Mr Puntila and his Man Matti* at the Almeida; and Helen Kaut-Howson of Theatr Clwyd mounted a brilliant *Major Barbara* for the Shaw Festival at Niagara on the Lake, Ontario, Canada. In his excellent book, *A Better Direction* (Calouste Gulbenkian Foundation, 1989), Kenneth Rea concludes that in 1988, twenty-seven per cent of all theatre directors were women, a figure that some consider inflated. The women represented here are a sampling rather than any kind of exclusive list. These directors exemplify a tremendous variety. All of them work with professional Equity-affiliated theatres, some in regional theatres, some as freelance directors, some as founding directors, and some as artistic directors. There is diversity in the jobs they do and in the points of view they represent. Some are directors of classics while others are interested primarily in new plays. Some are committed feminists while others seem never to consider the issue of feminism or the fact that they are women at all. Some are working almost exclusively in television and film. Some find the class system, and particularly the hold on the British theatre of those directors with Oxford or Cambridge degrees, more of a difficulty than is the fact of their gender. Sue Sutton Mayo explains it very well when she says, 'I've never allowed sexism to stop me doing anything. I'm very aware of it, and I do believe I've missed opportunities because I am a woman, but I've never allowed it to affect what I do. I don't go out into the world saying, You're going to give me trouble because I'm a woman, I just assume they're not going to until they do. So it wasn't because I was a woman that I didn't go off and direct, it was more to do with class. You know the British theatre has been dominated for centuries by the middle classes. God knows it's not where the heart of our theatre is even today. But the management of our theatre has been dominated by the middle classes, particularly Oxbridge graduates. To succeed one needed to be a man, one needed to be middle class, one needed best of all to be a graduate of Oxford or Cambridge with that perspective on everything.'

At least five of the women expressed this same concern about the British class system. While differences abound, most of the women agree on several factors about the contemporary British theatre. They agree that it is less healthy than it was fifteen or so years ago; that the Thatcher and Major governments, prior to the election of New Labour, have been far from sympathetic to the arts which have suffered financially, aesthetically, and prestigiously as a result of Conservative policies; that Peter Brook served as a primary inspiration to these young women as they found their places in the profession; and that they know one another and respect one another as women, as artists, and as practitioners. Indeed their lives have criss-crossed and con-verged. They need, however, to go a step farther, as Annie Castledine points out in *A Better Direction*. 'Women have got to be far less afraid of being seen to enable their own. And men have got to see that. I do think women are oppressed in the theatre and I think a lot of it is unconscious oppression, not necessarily intentional. I have been enabled by men. There is not one woman in my theatrical history who has so far enabled me.' I asked Castledine at a later date if she wished to reconsider this statement. She thought about it very hard and then concluded, 'No, I wouldn't say I've ever felt an enormous amount of practical support from my women colleagues.'

One final quality was shared by all of the women. Not only do they know of and respect one another but their comments were totally free of gossip or clever little anecdotes about famous theatrical people. Rather they showed astounding intelligence, conviction, and, above all, courage. The reader had best be forewarned that this volume does not contain substantive biographical material about its interviewees. I was not concerned with their personal lives but with their work. Ages, marital status, sexual orientation, lifestyles were outside my domain, although it is interesting that those women who have young children – Jenny Killick, Sue Sutton Mayo, and Di Trevis – spoke frequently about motherhood, all considering it an important factor that does affect their work or working habits. This is a book about craft.

In spite of the fact that these women are all actively involved in furthering their own careers, there is a tendency to freeze them in time, to regard the present endeavour as some kind of pinnacle or ultimate achievement. Julia Bardsley, for example, has done a great variety of work since I first met with her at the Leicester Haymarket Theatre, where she was working as joint Artistic Director with Paul Kerryson. Similarly, Garry Hynes has left the Abbey Theatre and returned to the Druid Theatre Company where her creativity originally flourished. All of these women are involved in careers that are constantly changing and evolving. I doubt that all of them still believe in everything they so passionately espoused at the time of our first meetings. In fact, at times they even contradict themselves; after all, it is human nature that the circumstances in which we find ourselves influence our beliefs and feelings.

While the body of this book will focus on the craft, philosophy, and work of the directors, with examples being drawn from their productions, perhaps a note about each is appropriate at the juncture. More complete biographical information is to be found in the Appendix. **Sarah Pia Anderson** currently spends six months each year in America as Professor of

Dramatic Art at the University of California, Davis, and the other six pursuing her various directing projects in Great Britain and Los Angeles; **Annabel Arden**, who teaches and acts with Theatre de Complicite, devotes much of her time to directing opera; **Julia Bardsley**, a tireless experimenter, focuses her energies on film and visual arts; **Annie Castledine** is a prolific and influential freelance director, while Tony-winner **Garry Hynes** directs primarily for Druid Theatre in Galway. **Jenny Killick** balances the raising of two sons with her position as a producer for the BBC and Channel 4; **Brigid Larmour** set up the Royal National Theatre's Shakespeare Unplugged project and is Artistic Director of ACT – a production development company attached to Associated Capital Theatres, one of London's two major West End theatre management groups. **Phyllida Lloyd** directs for the Royal National Theatre and for national opera companies in Britain and Europe; **Sue Sutton Mayo** is currently producing Channel 4's *Brookside*; **Nancy Meckler** is Artistic Director of Shared Experience Theatre and **Katie Mitchell** was Artistic Director of The Other Place in Stratford-upon-Avon. **Lynne Parker** runs Rough Magic in Dublin; and **Di Trevis** currently divides her directing and teaching work between the UK, the United States, and Cuba.

I hope these interviews will prove to be packed with the perspicacious observations and reflections of these directors' convictions and processes. While the words are chiefly those of the women, my voice will, by necessity, be present as well, primarily to link and focus their insights. It was my decision not to place all of the lengthy quotations in the usual single-spaced form but to let the narrative flow in and out of the women's own statements.

In deciding how to arrange the book, two major plans occurred to me: first, to record each director's comments in a very straightforward and direct way. That would have been the easier technique but would have, I believe, ultimately become tedious and redundant. Therefore I have chosen to select individual responses to various topics – their training, their pre-rehearsal processes, their approach with designers, their rehearsal techniques, their beliefs and projections about their craft, their concerns about women in the director's role – hoping that a balance will be achieved and that each woman will be amply represented, although each will not necessarily be represented in every chapter. There is no hidden agenda, no twisting of the material to make a consistent statement. The women's responses are as varied and diverse as the women themselves. No thesis is intended beyond making the reader aware of the training, work methods, insights and practices of a number of theatrical directors who are women. It is, in short, an investigation and revelation and, yes, even a celebration of their craft.

All of the women are proud of their work and seem confident about what they do and optimistic about their personal futures as artists. They all value a collaborative process; not one of them pre-blocks the action but rather allows it to emerge in the rehearsal process. Di Trevis says, 'Funny this word "block" isn't it? One would think you'd be trying to unblock actors, not block them.' All cherish a certain mystique about the craft of directing and find it very, very difficult to articulate. By the time I had completed my series of meetings with the women, I was keenly aware that the gifts requisite to directing – the eye, the judgement, the leadership, the instincts, the taste, the artistic vision – are innate talents that one either possesses or does not. I was quite amazed at how little actual training most of the women had. If one does not have the basic equipment to be a director, no amount of training, practice, or education will cultivate those qualities. Yet if one has the gift, she or he can be made better, more insightful, more dynamic.

The distinguished director Deborah Warner has warned that no amount of training will turn a dull director into an exciting one and that students must not think of directing as being about mise-en-scène or staging. Certainly no one has ever clearly defined what the director's job actually is; there is no formula. Each individual will approach the work with her own unique approach, methods, and philosophy. I doubt very much that these women sitting together in a room would agree about what the craft is, how they exercise it, and what they hope to achieve.

At all times, however, we would find them unified in passion, commitment, purpose, and resolve. Each in her own way is trying to make the theatre better, more viable, and more meaningful to generations of audiences to come. In her excellent book, *Clamorous Voices: Shakespeare's Women Today* (Carol Rutter et al, edited by Faith Evans, The Women's Press, 1988), Carol Rutter, with five actresses of the contemporary British stage, asks, 'Would things be different if women were directed by women?' Rutter outlines the progress, but concludes, 'Still these appointments are exceptional enough to raise comment.' Can we look forward to the day when women are in a position of supporting and hiring other women? When women are as respected in the profession as men are? When women directors are sought after and valued for their particular perceptions and talents? When women directors are not tokens, or mavericks, or oddities but a genuine part of the theatrical world? The comments of these thirteen women convince me that they certainly merit complete acceptance and respect. Yet I fear we have a long way to go. Speaking from my own experience, I know that I have been a director for over thirty years and have directed over fifty productions. My reviews have been good, actors seem to enjoy working with me, and public response to my productions has been positive. But the directors in my academic department remain a triumvirate of males, and directors are still spoken of as 'he'.

Perhaps what Sheila Yeger is quoted as saying in Annie Castledine's Introduction to *Plays by Women: Nine* (Methuen, 1991) could apply to directors as well as playwrights '. . . forced to exist on the fringes of polite society, a beggar forever at the gate, battering, unheard, at doors which hardly ever open. Although as a woman, I am the same sex as more than half the population, my voice is constantly treated as though it were that of an awkward and unacceptable minority, my opinions, viewpoints, emotions, considered to be of less significance and interest than those of my male counterparts.' May this book, this revelation of craft, in some small way forge a link toward better understanding, appreciation, and valuation of women theatrical directors. I can say with certainty that the words and ideas of these remarkable women have made me a better director than I was before the study was undertaken. I, for one, have learned a tremendous amount from each of them.

PART I

THE PREPARATION

CHAPTER I

Being a director is
saying you are one

As we explore the careers of women directors, it seems
appropriate to begin with their training and with the signposts,
failures, and triumphs that launched and informed their work.
Several of them knew from childhood that the theatre was to be
their lifetime pursuit. Phyllida Lloyd says, for example, 'I was
completely stage-struck from an early age. I was sent to a girl's
boarding school in Malvern. Before my time George Bernard
Shaw and Edward Elgar had regularly played piano duets for the
girls on Sundays. Plays and music really were the thing. The
school's calendar was peppered with its own pagan festivals, and
we used to celebrate them by making and giving plays: plays for
Hallowe'en and plays for midsummer eve and so forth. I always
seemed to end up writing and directing them and having
frightful altercations with the rest of my class who I berated for
their lack of professionalism.' Katie Mitchell launched her
directing career with school plays at the tender age of sixteen.
Similarly, Sarah Pia Anderson traces her developing interest to
getting involved in amateur dramatics in school and to two
teachers who took their students to theatre on school trips. 'We
were exposed to all sorts of plays: London, Stratford.'

To a small number of the women, impulses began even
earlier than school exposure. Sue Sutton Mayo says she knew
since she was very small that she wanted to work in the theatre.
'Family legend has it from when I was five.' Julia Bardsley,
whose mother and great-uncle were actors, grew up in a strong
theatrical tradition. But these same early impulses led both Mayo
and Bardsley to teenage rebellion. 'I come from a working-class
background in Liverpool,' Mayo explains. 'I was the first child

to go to a grammar school in our large extended family. By the time I was sixteen, nobody really knew what to do with me because the tradition was that women got married and raised children. I was a bit of "a brainy bod"; I wasn't your run-of-the-mill, and it was clear to my parents that I wasn't going to do that. However, I did leave school at sixteen because I didn't find that school was giving me what I wanted. I went to work in various jobs and had a wonderful five years, during which I had hardly anything to do with the theatre at all. I didn't do amateur dramatics, I didn't do anything. However, I went [to the theatre] constantly; I watched so much. And I read plays. But after a few years of living this free life, earning a bit of money, and having a good time, I realised that this was not going to be good enough for the rest of my life. I narrowly escaped marrying someone – as I think we all do, don't we? – and again didn't decide I was going into the theatre but decided I was going to teach. I honestly believed I had a vocation for teaching.' Similarly rebellious, Bardsley states, 'My upbringing, and my idea of what theatre was, was very conventional. When I was about fifteen or so I totally rejected it, because all I saw were West End shows – that sort of theatre, those sort of values. I thought that something else in theatre was right for me, but I didn't know what that was, and it wasn't until I moved to London and discovered fringe theatre that I said, "This is the sort of theatre I want to be involved in." '

The majority of the women directors became genuinely immersed in theatre and excited by its potential during their college years. It is extraordinary, however, that very few of them knew they wanted to be directors or even studied theatre as part of their university experience. As Nancy Meckler says, 'I never really had thought that I wanted to be a director. I always wanted to be an actor. I hardly ever got cast in anything and when I did I think I was very inhibited. However, because I love the theatre I always did a lot of peripheral things because I wanted to be in that world. So I developed stage management at the university, and I did some lighting design, and I did a directing course. As a result of doing the directing course –

because my final project went very well (it was a very funny one-act play by O'Casey) – I had a bit of a reputation for being a good director. So I did get the odd invitation to direct, and I would do it from time to time but I always thought I was doing it as a sort of favour. I don't know why it never occurred to me that I might pursue it.'

Almost all of the directors, on the other hand, benefited from the freedom to explore, to play, and to fail that amateur college theatre offered them. 'I think my training for theatre and directing', Meckler asserts, 'was helped by the fact that I went to a small college with a tiny department. This meant the students were given enormous responsibilities for production, and we often put on our own projects as well as the official productions directed each term by a faculty member. It wasn't a question of having to compete with hordes of drama majors to get a chance. And it was great fun as well! One learned so much about every area of production and almost always, one learned by doing.' Garry Hynes maintains, 'I didn't train at all. At the time when I was growing up there was practically no specific theatre training in Ireland. And even had there been, I was, by living in Galway, particularly removed from professional theatre, and so, very likely, I wouldn't have trained as a director. I only discovered about theatre when I went to university and joined the drama society which at the time and still to some extent does function as a provider and channel for young talent into the profession. So I started directing plays at the University of County Galway where I did a BA degree in English and History.'

Irish director Lynne Parker expresses similar joy in her extra-curricular university experiences. 'When I was eighteen, just after I left school and before I went to the university, I joined the National Youth Theatre of Great Britain for a summer season, and that was where I realised theatre was going to be more than just a hobby. And when I came to Trinity, I joined Players' Theatre which is the university drama society. I spent four years learning the craft, doing every and any aspect of theatre from poster design to stage management to directing. I find for myself that was a more useful way of going about it than doing an academic course, because I am not an academic. I mean I have an academic training in that I have a degree and I've been through the school process, but I always find I learn faster and better if I am working practically in a situation under my own control, one that wasn't structured around a syllabus or a curriculum. I also think that theatre is substantially subversive and is about making mischief and being naughty. It's more useful to me to regard it as something I was doing, almost like blowing off my lessons, in order to be in the theatre and just explore what I wanted to do there. The great advantage of Players' Theatre was that it wasn't controlled by the college, it was controlled by the students, and you could paint it pink if you wanted to. In other words, it was completely your space, and it promoted the kind of anarchy which I think is useful at that stage. The advantage is that you have four years where absolutely nobody cares what you do, and you're not doing it for anyone but yourself. No one is judging you; you weren't put on trial until you had succeeded in making a thorough fool of yourself, which I think everyone needs to do in the beginning. And that's the advantage of an extra-curricular university set-up.'

Katie Mitchell comments on the broad opportunities offered her at Oxford. 'I did a whole spectrum of work from radio plays to forming a feminist theatre group called Medusa to assistant directing to doing my own productions on the main stage of the Oxford Playhouse. And I acted, playing Juliet in *Romeo and Juliet*.' Similarly, Cambridge University offered two of the women chances to experiment in an extra-curricular environment. Brigid Larmour maintains, 'I haven't had any training, but went to Cambridge because I wanted to work in theatre, and I did a lot of acting and directing there.' Annabel Arden says, 'My training has been very informal and haphazard. I suppose you could say that it really started when I was in my teens. I went to The Place, which is the London contemporary school of dance for young people. I was completely mad about Martha Graham. I was a schoolgirl and I went three or four times after school and on Saturdays. I didn't acknowledge it for quite a long time, but that actually was the beginning of a training. Then I went to Cambridge, and I read English, and I did a lot of theatre, as one does. And I became interested in experiment per se and didn't do so much the sort of Footlights kind of stuff. I did much more kind of strange little new plays, and I started to devise things. And I met my great friend and colleague, Simon McBurney, at Cambridge. And we found we could work together somehow and talk together.'

Phyllida Lloyd is more reserved about her university experience. 'I decided that I wanted to be a director at university. David Edgar, the playwright, ran a writing course, and I began by directing the new plays that came out of that. Prior to that time I was sure I was going to become an actress. I'm glad I got through that phase. It is very difficult to break into the theatre as a student director. There is almost no investment in training directors in this country.'

Jenny Killick, commenting on the University of London, says, 'There was nothing at my college in the way of drama or a drama society. My interest came out of that void; I started directing the plays and being in the plays. I gave myself the best parts. I graduated with a very unremarkable degree because of all the theatrical activities.' Killick worked only with classic texts. 'I think I'd directed four Shakespeares and was moving on to the Jacobeans, you know, that way of doing things as a student in university drama.'

Whereas most of the directors thought of their college apprenticeship as a time to explore and experiment, Sarah Pia Anderson found her study of English literature at Swansea a period of confusion and loss of confidence. 'I thought I would like to work in theatre but didn't quite know in what capacity. I knew I couldn't act, didn't want to act. I didn't think I could direct; I didn't really have a very high opinion of myself or what I could do. I thought I would be lucky if I got a degree. I don't know, it's strange. I've talked to some other women about this. I suffered enormous lack of confidence at university. I was very confident when I was eighteen. But by the time I came up to the university I had no confidence whatsoever, and I still really don't know why to be honest. I enjoyed it enormously but I think something about it left me feeling inadequate. I didn't like the way drama was taught; we approached it like any other literature. I just thought it was dull, and I think I was a bit rebellious. In a way I withdrew from the academic world. Although I was told I was very bright and that I should get a first-class degree, I didn't. I got a second-class degree. I withdrew from it; I know I did. And sometimes I still feel guilty about it, but there we are. I've always had this thing; I just do things by the skin of my teeth. I'm not very confident about much. I know I give the impression to some people that I am, but I don't really feel very confident.'

Most of the women emphasise the importance of a broad, liberal arts basis as vital to their ultimate pursuit of careers as directors. Nancy Meckler says it succinctly: 'I think a broad education is very helpful, taking courses like history of art, religion, history, literature. The broader one's education the better, really. A lot of the theatre courses I did at university were a bit of a waste of time.'

To several of the women teaching – or a desire to teach – provided the route to directing. Garry Hynes, for example, stayed on at Galway for a year in order to earn a diploma in education that qualified her to teach on the secondary level. But she says she did no work on that degree because she was so passionately involved in the theatre. Sue Sutton Mayo came to Manchester to train as a teacher of drama at what is now Manchester Metropolitan University, then the Didsbury College of Education. 'I found I was on this incredible degree course in which I was one of a number of guinea-pigs. I'd chosen drama as my main option from the beginning. I found that they'd linked up with the School of Theatre at Manchester University. Half of our time was spent learning how to teach, and half of our time was spent learning about the theatre. So I was doing educational drama with part of me and the other half was doing theatre. And I realised in about three weeks that what I wanted to do was the theatre. So I spent three years and I came out with a first-class degree, but it was a fluke because I spent three years directing. I went through the kind of performing thing, and I realised that I just wasn't good enough. It wasn't that I didn't have any talent; I could just see that there were other people better than I was. I did some backstage work which I did enjoy, and then I got a chance to direct a show and that was it. That was all I wanted to do, and I spent three years either with the drama society at the college as a part of my curriculum or I'd just grab people and say, "Do you want to do a play?" Nine times out of ten they'd want to do it. I was so lucky. I was with a very talented group of people, both students and tutors. The lecturers were wonderful; they were very open and had designed this course in such a way that they had everything in play for us. And they supported us. I did *Marat/ Sade*, for example, with a budget of twenty-five or thirty pounds which even then was not a great deal of money. It was just wonderful. And I came out of that, and I still – I guess I'm just a very slow developer – I still didn't see that what I ought to do was go off and direct theatre because – I'll tell you why – I thought other sorts of people did that. I didn't think people like me did.'

Annie Castledine says, 'I didn't train to be a theatre director at all. I came from a part of the country and a class (we're incredibly class-ridden in this country still and particularly when I was growing up) so it couldn't have occurred to my parents, who were fanatical about the theatre themselves and did an enormous amount of amateur dramatics, that I should go into the theatre profession. That seemed to be something that was for aristocrats or Cambridge- and Oxford-educated people. I went to a grammar school certainly – I was very intelligent – but I went to a working-class grammar school in the West Riding of Yorkshire. My father worked down in the pits, and it was a very, very good thing if you became a teacher or if you became a nurse. Those were roles that were suitable for women, and I was therefore channelled into being a teacher. And I became a teacher of drama and went to train in Devon. Then I went to Goldsmiths College, which was a part of the University of London, to take a special third-year intense course in theatre which was an absolute continuation of my two-year training. There I met someone who was crucial to my life and development. She was head of the Theatre Department at Goldsmiths. She's now dead but she was a considerable force in the education of theatre and English in this country. She was a woman called Honor Mathews, and she saw in me, I suppose, this raw, back-woody kind of person who came from the depth of Yorkshire and had a kind of Lawrencian upbringing. That's not being romantic; it's just being accurate. Honor Mathews was an aristocrat, very wealthy, highly educated, academic to a degree, a profound musician, and someone who was very austere. She began, I suppose, a Scott Fitzgerald course of education for which I can only thank her. She took me on the grand tour and taught me about other values and other ways of looking at things; yet she didn't displace my own. She did it very, very thoughtfully. She had done this with quite a few students. And I think there my alternative education began, and that's where perhaps the training to be a director began.

'But I went into education, and I taught for two-years in a comprehensive school and then in a college of further education. Four years after I'd trained – when I was only twenty-five – I went to a college, now a part of the University of Reading, to train teachers to teach drama. Since I was responsible for the training of teachers, I was working with students and began to direct. From there I went to York University and got a further degree. While I was at York as a mature student in my mid-thirties, I continued to work with students, taking the results of our work to the Edinburgh Festival and all kinds of things that students do.'

Besides those who trained for teaching, several of the women trained for work in the theatre other than directing. Di Trevis is unique in being the only woman whose initial career after university was acting. 'I didn't go to drama school, I read anthropology at university, and I started acting from university in fringe groups. I had quite a sixties-type entry into my adulthood, a lot of going off to live in Morocco, and things that delayed decisions rather. But finally I was an actress at Glasgow

Citizens'; that was really my training ground. I was there for several seasons, and then I came to London. I played classical roles, and I did some interesting work in television. It took me a very long time to have the confidence to say that [directing] was what I wanted to do. But really by the time I got into the rehearsal room, I knew that this was really what I wanted to do. And at the end of the first day I had a sense that I could do it. Thank God. I had a real sense and a very profound confidence that this was something I would be able to do.'

Similarly Nancy Meckler attempted to pursue a career in acting but without, she feels, much success. After her post-graduate acting course at LAMDA, Meckler had, she says, 'a sort of personal crisis where I wasn't really sure any more why I was in theatre. It was partly to do with the fact that I was in therapy, and I was questioning why I wanted to be an actress at all. So for two years I really tried to leave the theatre altogether. I worked in a day nursery for underprivileged children in England, and I went back to New York and looked for some sort of arts-related work. But after two years I finally realised that, although I didn't want to act, I really did want to work in the world of the theatre. So I got back to doing more technical things, and I got a job as a production secretary on a Broadway musical.' It was then that Meckler enrolled in New York University for a Master's degree and became involved with an experimental company that was exploring the techniques of Grotowski. 'Once again I didn't really perform but I did all the exercises and experienced acting from a completely different approach; a non-intellectual, highly physical, very intuitive approach. So I was really trying to stay in the world of the theatre but finding it very difficult to find a place for myself, and I came to England on a visit in 1968 and decided to stay for a few months because I had no work to go back to in New York. The fringe was starting up in England, and I got involved with a theatre company that was pursuing experimental techniques. Because of my involvement with the group in New York, I was able to lead them, and the next thing I knew I was directing them. It was "Please, please, will you direct this?" and my saying, "Oh, well, all right, I'll do it just this once." And I suddenly realised that I seemed to be a director and that I wasn't that keen to go on stage any more and probably never really would want to. So in a way directing found me.'

Julia Bardsley's degree at Middlesex Polytechnic was in Performance Art. 'There were young courses there; they'd only been going for about four years. It was a brilliant course for someone like me: I'm very interested in the visual arts, I'm interested in design, I'm interested in performance, I'm interested in lots of different things, and I never thought about directing while I was there. I did a lot of performing, a lot of photography, and it wasn't until my last year that I did my first piece of directing, an adaptation of an Ian McEwan short story called *Cupboard Man*. We took it to the student drama festival where students from all sorts of different backgrounds come together.'

Others obtained their first real experience by stage managing as well. Sarah Pia Anderson reflects on her experiences stage managing at the Traverse Theatre, Edinburgh, 'I thought I wasn't much good at anything else, so I thought I'd better start there [stage managing]. I felt much more confident starting at what I perceived to be the bottom. Then, of course, once I felt I'd mastered the job, I thought I couldn't do it for the rest of my life.' Responding quite differently to her work as a stage manager, Lynne Parker states, 'I went to London [a year after graduating from Trinity] and stage managed at the King's Head Theatre in Islington. The theatre is gorgeous, charming, tiny, but they can do some extraordinary things there. And I think that's a good training for anybody because you can't get more of the mechanics of theatre than by stage managing a show.'

Nancy Meckler concurs on the value of stage management as a significant factor in training. 'Looking back on it, all the stage management I did was very helpful. At Antioch College every summer, we used to have visiting professional directors. I would stage manage for them so I would see at very close quarters how different directors worked. And I wish that, as far as young directors are concerned, they could be stage managers, that that would be considered an appropriate training because you really are the right-hand person to the director. You get a situation where the actors will talk to you if they have thoughts they don't want the director to hear or maybe that they do want the director to hear. You hear the director's problems and fears and aspirations, and you're in on the whole process.'

While stage managing was viable training for some, others found value in serving as Arts Council trainees. After eighteen months as a stage manager, Sarah Pia Anderson received a bursary to train at the Sheffield Crucible. Annie Castledine was attending graduate school at York University when the head of the York Theatre Royal requested her as his Arts Council trainee director. So it was that in mid-life, Castledine began the formal part of her training for the professional theatre. Fresh out of undergraduate school, Jenny Killick, in the heady days of arts funding, got a bursary to work as an assistant director in the distinguished Traverse Theatre. 'For the first year at the Traverse I didn't direct anything. I was able to watch actors or meet writers, to begin to orient myself. In my second year I directed two productions which were pursued by the Edinburgh Festival and got me a lot of attention; at about the same time my boss, Peter Lichtenfels, said that he wanted to leave. He supported my application. I remember thinking that was a joke, but he said, "No, I think absolutely seriously you should get out and do it."' Subsequently, at twenty-five Killick began a five-year tenure as Artistic Director of the Traverse, the first woman to hold that position and the youngest artistic director in Great Britain. Phyllida Lloyd had taken a job with the BBC and applied three times before she was granted an Arts Council Trainee Director bursary which started a four-year roll of work which took her from Ipswich to Worcester and to Cheltenham where she directed twelve productions at the Everyman Theatre. 'I wasn't marginalised to the studio theatre as a lot of more inexperienced directors are but I was alternating my work between the studio theatre and the main house. It was a real apprenticeship.' Sadly, the number of director trainee bursaries offered by the Arts Council of Great Britain has been greatly reduced, thus severely limiting a mode of learning that served a number of the women directors exceedingly well.

Unique among the women because of her American training, Nancy Meckler speaks of her Antioch co-op experience of working at the Hedgerow Theatre in Moylan, Pennsylvania as chief gofer, props maker, electrics operator, costume mender, etc. 'Because I was so enamoured of theatre in its broadest sense, I was always looking for opportunities to observe at first hand. One of the actors was brilliant at make-up and I would sit and watch him applying it each night and take notes. Talk about keen! Another time I asked a director there who I admired if I could sit in when he was doing one-to-one text analysis with an actor. Later when I worked as production secretary on a Broadway musical, I was in on all the late-night and weekend meetings where changes were being discussed by the director, choreographer, designer, etc. I do feel all that first-hand experience was a terrific way to learn. Perhaps it would be good if potential directors could shadow professionals, to include designers, directors, production managers, and so forth.'

There is a certain audacity and boldness of youth. Impatient to direct, tired of waiting for job opportunities to arise, five of the women simply went out and created their own companies. Julia Bardsley formed a company titled dereck, dereck Productions upon graduating from college. From the Edinburgh fringe the company went to the Almeida in Islington. 'It's a fantastic space. In those days, companies like us had access to those spaces. It was possible for us to do the work we wanted to do. Although everyone was on the dole, we could make theatre, and there were places where it could be shown.' Katie Mitchell achieved her first major successes directing for her own company, Classics on a Shoestring, which is still operational. In November of 1994 they presented John Arden's *Live Like Pigs* at the Royal Court Theatre Upstairs. 'And', Mitchell asserts, 'we still have plans for the future!' For the most part, however, as the directors moved on to other projects, these companies disbanded.

Three of the directors, however, are still working with the

companies they created shortly after graduating from college: Lynne Parker at Rough Magic, Annabel Arden at Theatre de Complicite, and Garry Hynes at Druid Theatre Company. Parker considers Rough Magic merely an extension of her extra-curricular work with Players' Theatre at Trinity. 'During that period, Declan Hughes, who is the co-founder of the company, and I directed quite a lot of the shows that Players' was putting on at that time. There was a very company feel to what we were doing. And that's why we wanted to continue that after we left, and we set up [Rough] Magic almost unnoticed, a child of Players', if you like, because we did our first summer season in that theatre. In the first year we did seven plays.'

Similarly, Annabel Arden and Simon McBurney created Theatre de Complicite as a result of their fellowship which began at Cambridge. In the first year after graduation McBurney went off to Paris to study at the Jacques Lecoq School while Arden participated in her theatre collective, titled 1982. Of that experience, Arden says, 'I learned how to book a tour, I learned how to manipulate the avant-garde fringe circuit. It was a year of brilliant productivity; it was about working in a group and it was about ensemble performance. At the end of that little adventure, Simon called me. He'd finished his Lecoq training and he said, "Listen, shouldn't we just put something together?" This was in 1983. It's funny, you see, because I'm talking about my training. And that's when Complicite started. Then I realised I had to pick up on training that I hadn't really done – except that I just went out and did it, did theatre. So I went back to Paris in fits and starts to work with two teachers. One is Philippe Gaulier, who was a teacher at Lecoq, and the other is Monika Pagneux, who was also a teacher at Lecoq. But they had both left. Monika is an extraordinary woman who has created a way of looking at movement for the stage which is completely unique. Philippe is an amazing clown and teaches a great deal about play, comedy and improvisation. I've also done a little work with Lecoq quite recently – I studied his course about space. He teaches with an architect, and it's about the use of space, the movement of space. All of my training has been very practical, and it's been about the body and movement. And it's been a very unconscious process if you like. I've always been a person who turned my hand to whatever was there that attracted me.' For over a decade, Arden worked almost exclusively at Complicite with Simon McBurney. It should be noted that while Arden still acts with and teaches for Complicite, she no longer shares the directorship with McBurney. 'It became clear to me', she says, 'that I really needed to find my own path. I've started directing more and more outside the company. It was clear that Simon was on a creative roll after *Street of Crocodiles* and so it was difficult to conceive and plan projects. It was difficult, partings always are, but I think it is definitely for the best.'

A final theatre to be mentioned is Garry Hynes's Druid Theatre in Galway, which continues to flourish. 'I left the university in June of 1975 and opened the first three productions of a professional company in July of 1975. Basically a group of young colleagues of mine at the university and also amateur actors involved with the Irish Language Theatre, An Taibhearc, came together, and we decided we wanted to be a professional company. Galway didn't have a professional company, so with all the naiveté that can come to a bunch of young people, we said, "Well, we're going to provide it." So in January of 1976 the theatre got its first grant from the Irish Arts Council, and we became the first professional company to be based in Ireland outside of Dublin.' The theatre company remains committed to Irish themes, ensemble acting, and a high level of professionalism. It has toured to Glasgow, New York, and Sydney, and its productions are often co-produced in London with the Royal Court Theatre.

Approximately half of the directors interviewed got at least a part of their training at the prestigious Royal Shakespeare Company. It was when Sarah Pia Anderson worked with Buzz Goodbody as a stage manager at The Other Place in Stratford that she was first inspired to try directing. 'Buzz was a very important female director, the first woman to direct at the RSC.

There is still an award given each year to encourage a young director, the Buzz Goodbody Award. Anyway I was a stage manager at The Other Place when Buzz was there, and she encouraged me in my repressed belief that I could direct. She said, "Just go do it."' When I asked Anderson what made her feel she could direct, she responded, 'I think it's actors really, thinking I could work with actors. I wish I could tell you it was something grand. I don't think it was. It's not that I didn't have ambition, I did; I'm really quite ambitious. Otherwise I wouldn't be doing what I'm doing, but I just loved the theatre, and I didn't know how else to fit into it. And it wasn't much more of a step from stage management actually when I started doing just little bits and pieces. I didn't really take on anything ambitious for a few years. My nature is to sort of ease into things gently. It was a different time then. People were trying all sorts of different things. There was money for experimentation; there isn't that now.'

Annie Castledine, Brigid Larmour, Katie Mitchell and Di Trevis, were all assistant directors at the Royal Shakespeare Company and Sue Sutton Mayo had a job with the RSC's *Nicholas Nickleby*. For Castledine and Larmour, that experience, although valuable, did not lead to directing positions at the RSC. Castledine assisted Ron Eyre and Trevor Nunn. 'I was Trevor's assistant for over a year. [I worked with] *All's Well that Ends Well*, the production he did with Peggy Ashcroft and Harriet Walter. I went with Trevor as his assistant on *Henry IV, Parts I and II* which opened the Barbican. And it was a wonderful time.'

Larmour is more outspoken about the experience. 'I went to the Royal Shakespeare Company as an assistant director, which was essentially my apprenticeship. I was apparently their youngest ever assistant – twenty-two – and I did learn a great deal there, but it was not an unmixed pleasure because it was a thoroughly if unconsciously sexist organisation at that time. Most of the men who run the RSC started as assistant directors and worked their way up. But none of the women assistant directors had been allowed to progress through, and none of the women who have since been given work there has come from within the company. I thought, I've got to say something about it, and I'm going to do something about it. They did eventually offer Di [Trevis] a production but not Annie [Castledine]. I know I helped to enable other women who have since worked there get through the door, but so far they've not been able to create a climate in which many women actually want to stay.' In a later interview Larmour qualified this statement: 'Perhaps the exception is Katie Mitchell who is now an associate director at the RSC and Artistic Director of The Other Place.' Remembering the heady days when Sarah Pia Anderson, Di Trevis, Garry Hynes, Katie Mitchell, Phyllida Lloyd and Deborah Warner were all directing at the RSC, I expressed surprise to the directors that only a few of the women – Trevis and Mitchell, for example – were directing there on a regular basis. In fairness, it was believed that more of the women were invited to direct at the two large institutional theatres but had declined because of other engagements and commitments.

Of her experience as an assistant director at the RSC, Katie Mitchell says, 'It was an extraordinary opportunity to observe the work of a whole spectrum of different directors from different backgrounds and also to see how actors sustained their work over a two-year period, which was often the length that the shows were actually in the repertory. I also gathered together a group of extraordinary actors and we did our own work which we presented on what is called the Stratford fringe. At the end of the year assistants and actors present the work that they want to do in rough-and-ready circumstances.'

It is fascinating that the same assistant directing job could be perceived by two of the women directors in such radically different ways. Larmour reflects, 'When they were planning the tour of *Nicholas Nickleby*, I did quite a detailed proposal of the kind of support work I thought they should do because I had all this experience. But I had absolutely no desire to be an assistant director again. In fact, I was leaving to be Associate Director at the Contact. But to my amusement I got a call asking if I would like to assist Trevor Nunn on *Nicholas Nickleby* for its American tour because I had such clear ideas about the role of the assistant. And I said, "No, of course not. I'm an associate director here at Contact, and I've got productions of my own to direct.'"

Sue Sutton Mayo, on the other hand, tells a delightful story about getting work with the RSC. After college Mayo taught for a year, formed a children's theatre company in the Hulme area of Manchester, got pregnant (twice), and worked for War on Want. She and her husband bought a house and seemed to be settling in to a comfortable domestic pattern. 'Then I went to Stratford with a great friend. We'd brought our children up together, and our kids are exactly the same age. And we were having this weekend away. We watched *Nicholas Nickleby,* and I thought, "Well, that's it, isn't it?" And we sat in a pub the next day having to go back to our families and our homes because I'd been really a housewife and a mother for four years. That's what I had done. I'd never stopped going to theatre but I hadn't practised at all. I hadn't made any theatre for four years. I have to say I have no regrets about anything I've ever done in my life, ever. But I sat in this pub and I said, "I am never again going to sit outside the theatre wishing I was on the inside. I'm going to do something about this." And my friend said, "Well, what are you going to do?" "I don't know but I'm going to do something.'''

So I wrote to Trevor Nunn, and I told him what had happened to me: that I'd been in the theatre and seen *Nicholas Nickleby,* and that he had to give me a job. I posted the letter and I thought, "Well, that's it. Nothing will happen." And two days later the phone rang, and I was there in my dressing gown with the kids around, and this voice said, "Hello, this is Trevor Nunn." "Oh, please, who is this playing games with me?" And he said, "No, this is Trevor Nunn." And Trevor had got my letter in which I had poured out everything I felt, and he said, "Of course, you must come and work for us. Of course you must. What can we do?" I couldn't believe it. And actually I believe in synchronicity. I think Jung was right when he talks about synchronicity. This particular production of *Nickleby* was going to the States, to Los Angeles and New York. So he said,

"Can you be in Newcastle on such and such a date?" And I said "Yes!" My daughter was only eighteen months old but I didn't see that I had a choice really. There was an assistant director travelling with the show, Cordelia Monsey, whom I shadowed. She was really generous and helpful because directors don't talk to other directors very well in my experience. I think we're a bit frightened of one another: the whole thing about work being so scarce and the stakes so high.

'You can imagine what it was like for me because the RSC had been for me – I don't feel the same way now, I have to say – just like gods. And I would sit in the wings on theatre trunks and baskets with RSC stamped on the side, and I would just be in tears, "It's me. I'm here. I'm here." I did all the tea-boy jobs: I checked sound levels, sat up all night doing light checks. My God, what a way to learn your craft. I couldn't believe how much I'd learned by the end. And skipping over all the problems I had with what you do with two children when you're on a six-month tour . . . my marriage nearly collapsed. It really was a nightmare time. It was an ordeal by fire but by that stage I just didn't feel I had any choice. I had a nanny, and I used to come home on a Friday with my wages and hand the pay packet to my nanny. My husband was wonderful. He looked after the children, although he had a full-time job, and of course he'd married someone who was training to teach; he hadn't married this woman who . . .

'Everything that happens to you when you're home for that long, and the way that power balance shifts in a relationship, the best of relationships, because he was going out into the world every day and I was home, and I was with kids, and everything that means societally as well. You're never left in a moment's doubt as to what your status is in society. Of course, I'd poured energy while I was at home into campaigning for children, I'd campaigned for nursery education. It was wonderful, I'm really glad I did it. But all the time I was aware of my status, so to turn around and go from that to touring with the RSC was difficult, very difficult. So I did that with *Nickleby* and then I did stage crew for the Palace Theatre here in Manchester. By this stage I realised that I had to direct. At last I knew what it was I had to do.'

Luck and tenacity continued to figure prominently in the development of Sue Sutton Mayo's career. She got a job stage managing at the Manchester Library Theatre, the same theatre where she later became a resident director. 'We used to have a lunch-time season of shows. It's my dream to reinstate it. Basically there were restrictions on what you could do: they had to be able to fit into lunch-time so they were fifty minutes long, they had to have no more than four actors, and they had to be on a set that would fit onto the existing set for the evening show, and a set that could be easily erected and dismantled within the lunch-time period. And the budget on them was minute. It's thrilling to work on new plays. There I was every day in there working with this director [John Durnin], seeing how theatre is put together, stage managing. I still believe that stage managing is the lynchpin of theatre.'

Mayo created an opportunity for herself when a woman, scheduled to direct on the lunch-time series, decided she didn't want to do it. Not one of the theatre staff could afford the time for the project, so Mayo spoke up and said, 'I'll do it.' With John Durnin's encouragement, she went to Roger Haines, Associate Director of the theatre, who said, 'I couldn't possibly let you do it. What experience have you got?' But Mayo talked her way into the job. The play, *Effie's Burning* by Valerie Windsor, is included in Methuen's *Plays by Women, Volume 7*, where Windsor writes about the experience, praising Mayo's creativity, collaborative spirit, trust and support. Because of its success in Manchester, the project was invited to perform at London's Bush Theatre. 'We were over the moon' Mayo recalls. But the Bush suffered an electrical fire the week before the scheduled engagement. Not to be dissuaded from taking *Effie's Burning* to London, Mayo phoned David Brierley, General Manager of the RSC. Ultimately the one-act play was performed at the National both as a platform production at the Lyttelton, as a studio production in the Cottesloe, and subsequently at the fringe Offstage, Downstairs in Camden

Town which was run by another wonderful woman, Buddy Dalton. 'You understand it wasn't really for me, this; it was the fact that the play was going to go to the Bush, and the Bush is incredibly well respected, and they wanted to do something for the Bush because of the fire really.' But as Mayo concludes, 'So within the first year of being in proper theatre, I'd worked with the RSC, I'd worked with the National, I had a show on the fringe in London. You can imagine I was up in the air!'

Unique among the experiences of the women is that of Katie Mitchell who went to eastern Europe on a travel grant from the Winston Churchill Memorial Trust. 'I went with a brief to study directors' training and rehearsal techniques because although I had had experience both in the London fringe theatre and with the *crème de la crème* of the classical theatre at the RSC, I still felt I needed to learn more. So I went to Poland, Russia, Lithuania, and Georgia for four months where I observed the work of the Stary Theatre in Crakow, the Moscow Art Theatre, the Maly Theatre in St Petersburg, Anatoly Vassiliev, Andrzej Wajda, Tadeusz Kantor, Eiumentas Nekrosius, Gardzienice Theatre Association in Lublin, and the directors' courses in the state drama schools of all the capitals – a whole spectrum of extraordinary experiences. And, of course, there they take director training very seriously. Whereas the courses for actors last four years, the courses for directors last five years and in many cases start with the directors having to do a formal Stanislavsky acting training for a year. So I suppose that's really how I learned my craft: through observing other people doing theirs. And then, of course, by directing my own shows. And I don't ultimately ever think you stop training or learning as a director.'

What strange stories of circuitous routes, grasped moments, and chance opportunities have informed the training of our women directors. Three final illustrations may serve as a kind of summary. Di Trevis states, 'During my time attending what I now regard as rather historic workshops with Peter Gill at the Riverside Studio over a period of about two years, I finally told Peter that I wanted to become a director. Peter organised a workshop for young directors, and he invited me to this workshop which spanned a weekend. I said to him, "Well, actually, you know I'm not a director, I'm an actress at the moment." And he said, "Well, if you come to this workshop, you will be a director because being a director is deciding that you are one." So, I said, "Right. From this weekend's workshop, I'm going to say I'm a director." And he told me to find a new play, buy the rights to it, and get it on.' Trevis followed Gill's advice, took her play around London where it received lukewarm responses, and finally got it produced at the Citizens' Theatre in Glasgow. 'So I was an actress one Saturday and then I went into a room and became a director the following Monday. When I went home that Monday evening I really had decided that I would give up acting absolutely as soon as possible and that directing was the only thing I wanted to do ever again.'

Perhaps Phyllida Lloyd says it most succinctly. 'I think it's really, really difficult because young directors have to carve out their own, there isn't a prescribed route. You've got to get on and direct your own show. So one learns a lot by one's mistakes.' Lloyd, however, expresses a note of warning about the lack of preparedness to focus on one project for a long time or to revisit it again and again when she remembers working with a distinguished director in Soviet Georgia who once asked her how many plays she had directed. 'When I told him, his jaw dropped and he just said that should never have been allowed to happen. He was aghast at the market economy's demands on a theatre practitioner to take so many jobs. In Georgia they might rehearse for a year on a production. He was appalled at the lack of thoroughness of study. To him it sounded as though I had just been churning out productions.'

Can any conclusions be garnered from these varied and eclectic examples of training for directing careers? Perhaps there are several: first, almost all of the training was practical rather than academic; second, while few of the directors decided in formative years to be directors, almost all of them moved forward in their pursuits with a tremendous amount of courage and tenacity once they recognised their own needs and desires, actively seeking jobs, applying for grants and accepting low-paying assistant directors positions; finally, they had some luck, but they all expressed convictions, belief in their own abilities, an awareness of what inner voices were telling them, and an overwhelming passion and drive that moved them forward with their goals.

CHAPTER 2

Revealing the beauties of space

One of the most fascinating areas of the directorial process is the delicate balance and relationship achieved between director and designer. As Phyllida Lloyd points out, in Britain most often the costumes and the scenic design are achieved by one designer, whereas in America there is usually both a scenic designer and a costume designer who must work together with the director. 'In both countries lighting and sound design are created by separate individuals. No two directors will ever approach designers in the same way, use the same vocabulary or the same methodology. Moreover, questions abound: how much should the director give the designer, how close should the collaborative process be? It is an area so subtle and so fragile that whole courses are taught on the subject. In my own experience I have worked in situations where I all but created the designs myself and in others in which the designer offered something that far surpassed my meagre visualisation. Once years ago, I took a pencil and sketched the kind of sleeve I wanted for a garment; the costume designer was deeply offended by my presumption. And therein lies the delicacy of the relationship; it is that point at which several talents and several art forms must merge, cohere, and find harmony. There are very few directors, I believe, who feel totally adequate in this area of the collaborative process.' As Garry Hynes points out, 'I couldn't say that I communicate with *designers* because designers are *people*, and I communicate differently from person to person. I think designers are crucial to the process and that in a sense what you are doing when you enter into a relationship with a designer is this: you are entering into a collaboration on an understanding of the play. The place in which the production takes place, in which the story takes place is crucial to me; therefore, I like to have a close, co-operative, collaborative relationship with the designer. Sharing everything. Anything and everything: ideas, images, thoughts about the play, needs of the play, what it's about, casting, everything; because you're building up effectively a reference book for the production. This is all the material out of which we are going eventually to create the production.'

This collaborative process is poignantly evident in Hynes's directing of the Martin McDonagh trilogy at the Royal Court Theatre with Francis O'Connor as her designer. The interior set is almost the same for each play: a central table, an upstage door, a stove or fireplace, and a kitchen sink. Yet while the audience can recognise these basic elements, the character of each is distinctly different, and the use of detail rich, varied, and individualistic. For example, in each of the plays a source of heat exists on the stage left wall. In *The Beauty Queen of Leenane* it is a stove that has not only seen years and years of service but one that has been neglected, even abused, in that service. The stove alone tells the audience of the despair and hopelessness of the woman who commands that stove. In *A Skull in Connemara* it is a fireplace, less important but certainly a symbol of the somewhat elevated station in life of its single occupant. In *The Lonesome West* it is a stove again – bright red, new, a prized possession and technically rigged for both its destruction on stage and a spectacular display of pyrotechnics. There is an enormous amount of realistic detail: real dirt, running water, and a long rainfall. But these environments are not realistic, for the walls are only partial; a vibrant blue surround of swirling, troubled sky is evident in each play; and a dominant symbol of Catholicism, a religious statue, looms over each place. It is clear that there was an incredible process, both economically and artistically motivated, that brought these two artists, Hynes and O'Connor, to their shared vision that would embrace and support all three plays.

It is often through areas of design that the play will be

unlocked to a specific director. Sarah Pia Anderson finds the key in lighting. To her it is lighting that creates the mood, the feeling, the essential 'soul' of a production. To Annie Castledine it is music which is vital. 'Usually I like to have live musicians, and if one is not in the text', she maintains, 'I like to have one anyway. I did a production of Charlotte Keatley's *My Mother Said I Never Should*, and I imposed on the text a violinist, who accompanies and is a part of the action. I usually love my live musicians to be in the arena. You know, somebody is speaking and somebody is playing behind his or her ear. When the playwright came – actually she was not with us in the rehearsal process – she was absolutely aghast because it was a huge and absolutely amazing imposition. The play started with a violinist coming on and playing some Mendelssohn with muslin wafting, and she said, "I haven't written that musician." But anyway she got to like it, of course; but it did take a little bit of time. And it is true that I would like and do like to use live music in all of my plays.'

Castledine continues her discussion of the importance of music by relating her process of working with a musical director. 'The musical director comes and sits with me in rehearsal, and we work organically and play together. If I've got someone playing the piano and also composing the score, then they will be with me during the first week of rehearsal, probably go away for the second and compose, and then come and work with us just as an actor, playing and weaving the music in and out of the text in rehearsal.'

About her production of *Marching for Fausa* at the Royal Court Upstairs, Castledine says, 'Biyi Bandele [author of *Marching for Fausa*] didn't write music; he didn't write a text to have any music; he didn't think there would be any music in his text. Therefore you have to work very sensitively with the playwright and with the musical director and with the actors, and say, "Well, maybe this particular music wouldn't take us where we want to be and where we want to be is . . . and can we actually find a piece of music or a song or a rhythm that will do this?" And then we rehearse it just as we would a line of dialogue. Yes, that's absolutely right because that's what it is, and then the music begins to grow as indeed an improvised text would begin to grow. It's like an improvised text really.'

Commenting on her production of *Goliath* at the Bush, a study of three neighbourhood riots that erupted violently in the summer of 1991, Castledine states, 'In the second week of rehearsal I invited the sound designer, Mic Pool, into rehearsals. I looked at the sound from the point of view of symphonies, riot symphonies: the glass symphony, the joy-riding symphony, and finally a cacophony of all three riots. I asked Mic to think about the production in terms of three pieces of music which underscored the three movements. He worked in rehearsal and I talked to him continuously as I was working with the actor Nichola McAuliffe. So the soundscape was developed in the same way as the performance. I chose the pieces of music which were English pieces reflecting an idealised and unrealistic concept of England and that became a point of ironic commentary.'

Castledine extended her concept of music to include the nineteen voices that McAuliffe portrayed, in what Castledine calls, 'The music of the voices of this country. I saw those voices in terms of music, and I wanted them represented with dignity, honour, and integrity. That meant an enormous amount of research as far as those voices were concerned – very particular, very individualised, very specific people who were met, interviewed, taped, gave their permission, and were studied. They were represented fairly and accurately.'

While to some of the directors, an element like light or music is vital, to almost all of the directors the idea of environment for the production is crucially important. Several of them emphasise their own sense of design. 'Everything starts with my reading of the play these days,' says Sarah Pia Anderson. 'I physicalise it in my mind. I stage it. I imagine what it would be if it were inhabited. I can't say I see it, but I have a sense of it, what's important about it. So it's a slightly abstract idea of the set. It may turn out to be a naturalistic set but I have a – not as strong as a concept – but a sense of it. When I did *Rosmersholm* at the

National, I had a sense that there had to be quite sharp contrasts in the set, that it needed to have a sense of the Norwegian geography, which is the dramatic nature of the fjords and the mountains and the sky and the water, and I wanted somehow to reflect that on stage. And the paintings that Ibsen talks about in his description of one of the rooms of the house, Rosmer's house, I wanted them to dominate the environment. And so we ended up with a rake which was a wooden floor, like a wooden Norwegian floor. And it also had a sense of floating. Around it was just blackness, and then on what sort of suggested the walls – although there weren't walls – was a row of about thirty-six paintings, real paintings of the Rosmer family, that looked down on this square. Behind, you looked towards a V shape [upstage] which was, of course, a fjord where Rosmer and Rebecca went at the end. It was a terribly simple set: rooms were defined by furniture and this floor. And I used music. Mike Figgis, who is now a well-known film director, did a score for it which was very, very minimal – just sounds, barely audible sometimes, which represented what I would describe as the undertow of the play, which is the unconscious sort of dragging Rebecca West inevitably towards her doom.'

It was a production about which Anderson felt very good, as she did about her earlier production of Franz Xaver Kroetz's *The Nest* at the Bush Theatre in London. 'We set the whole thing in a gauze box which, when lit in a certain way, was totally transparent, and when lit in another way was completely solid so that the scenes could change within the box. And there was a rich use of light. I suppose that's where my love of film and theatre come together – in the use of light in space and how it can transform something solid into something translucent. I'm not very fond of mechanical scenery. It's a silly thing to say really because I'm sure if it fitted the play or the event, I wouldn't speak against it. But aesthetically I just like the way simple things can be transformed simply but perhaps boldly. It was quite a daring thing to do, to put actors in a gauze box. The theatre management was terrified that it was going to alienate the audience. But it had the wonderful effect of drawing people closer to it because the characters were somehow heightened in this box.'

With similar strength of her convictions, Annie Castledine knows what she wants in her theatrical designs. 'Usually my designs are incredibly heightened and expressionistic. I don't like anything built; I like the use of fabrics. I don't like the use of wood; I like the use of metal.' A major feature of *Goliath* was a strong, steel, spiral staircase. 'I don't like heavy ponderous designs; I like very frail, fragile.' She adds, laughingly, 'I usually have lots of wafting material, fans on, material blowing in the wind – whatever the play!'

Like Castledine, Nancy Meckler wants costume and scenic design to be a physical representation of an inner reality. 'For Ariel in *The Tempest*, I wanted physically to represent the idea that her spirit was trapped. I cast a woman and thought of the character as he/she and that it was her femaleness that was not allowed to exist. All the things Prospero asks Ariel to do are very aggressive, warlike, traditionally male actions. They're about deceit, manipulating people, and getting power. Ariel, in contrast, is air and has this gentleness which is about giving and emanating energy rather than controlling and manipulating. The costume was based on a strait-jacket but it also looked like a fencing jacket with long thin arm extensions which brushed the floor. When Ariel was feeling constricted, she flapped her arms and the long sleeves would flap around her head and make a strange noise. When she was finally released by Prospero, she unpinned her hair, tore this garment off, threw it to the ground, looked at her bare arms, and was so amazed at who she really was because she had been a prisoner to Prospero's imagination and needs. The costume allowed her journey to be expressed physically, so that's what we're trying to do – have the physical be an expression of the inner.' The only elements added to the white set were a few ropes. Five large sails, which in the beginning formed the boat, became huge wings for Ariel, or simply served as backdrop. 'I quite like doing everything with a few elements because the audience sees the elements being transformed: one minute they're sails, the next moment they're part of the seascape, then they are wings when Ariel becomes the harpy. The audience's imagination is filling in because they see how it's done. It becomes the magic of the imagination rather than the magic of the prop maker.'

Such a sure sense of design is also reflected in the work of Julia Bardsley who often designs her own productions, a fact she laughingly describes as 'very greedy'. 'Sometimes', she continues, 'I've gone so far virtually in my own mind with a piece that it would be unfair to try to impose that on a designer. If you work with a designer, then I think you both have to start at the same point; whereas if sometimes I get strong ideas about how I want it to look, it would be very unfair not to give designers their creative space.' Bardsley speaks in rich detail about her production of *Macbeth*. 'Initially there wasn't going to be any set; it was just going to be lights. I thought I'd just put lots of things together. It's very simple: an open space with a big wall [like a giant hinge] which works as a kind of pressure which can sweep away any kind of decorativeness from the stage, wipe the slate clean, or put physical pressure on Macbeth. There are metal troughs down front which contain water or liquid of some sort. And then any props are bits and pieces from all of the other shows I've done, nothing made, all from other pieces of theatre – the idea of having things that have a theatrical life because they've been used in past shows.' These objects – a sink, a mirror, a pile of chairs, an umbrella, a sword, buckets, boards – are used to stimulate physical action. For the sleepwalking scene Bardsley has a series of pillows placed on stage over which Lady Macbeth makes her path. All of this is placed in a powerful black void.

In relation to her costumes, Bardsley says, 'The men just have very dull, ill-fitting baggy suits mainly, T-shirts or vests. Periodless, totally timeless, placeless. Time and place happen within the theatre. The place is the theatre, the time is the time watching it. I think *Macbeth* is brilliant in that it allows you to do that. It doesn't have to be a historical play, it doesn't have to be set anywhere specifically. I think it's the most open to interpretation of Shakespeare's tragedies but strong enough that it will not be drowned by a new interpretation.'

Most directors are probably not as sure in their visualisation as Bardsley but may have flashes of insight into the physical world of the play. Brigid Larmour comments on the rare glimpses and more frequent collaborations that make the design process happen. 'The design is a fantastically important determining factor in the production. I like to work in a very open and collaborative way with the designer mostly. Once or twice I have known what I eventually wanted the design to be. In my production of Brecht's *Galileo* I knew I wanted the design to be a terracotta bowl tipped over the edge of the world. And it was suspended only by fly lines so it had a slightly surreal Dali-like quality, and it was tipped over the front of the stage so that you thought you were on solid earth but actually you weren't. And then the designer for that production took that and built an outer ring around it, a walkway, which is like a ring of Saturn with a wooden piece at the back which held all the props. So in a sense it was unusual for me because I said, "I have an image, and I want it to be this" and she worked around that. More typically I would say, as for *Measure for Measure*: "I want it to be a dark and ambiguous world where you don't know where you stand and that owes something to the Vienna of Graham Greene." There's that slightly romantic, slightly sinister use of light and costume. I don't give a designer a brief; I have a conversation with a designer, and I say this is what I think so far. And although I do a lot of academic research, I don't present it in a coherent, cerebral, analytical way. I talk about ideas and instincts and feelings I have about the play, and I try to spark off the designer's interest in the thing. Then he or she will say things back to me, and I'll say, "Well, yes" or "No" or "That's a good idea" or "That opens up this whole area of debate" and the process starts: the sketching, the model, and I listen very closely to those things. Again, I try to keep it at a creative and instinctive level rather than necessarily rationalising too much. And I have a very strong sense of what is right in the design and what is wrong, and I will question at all stages. So I do take a very strong role, I think, in design; I'm very unlikely just to sit back and say "That looks nice".'

In the four productions she has directed for Shakespeare Unplugged with the Royal National Theatre, Brigid Larmour has worked with the designer Nettie Edwards. 'The design process', Larmour says, 'has happened in advance of rehearsals. We've gone through the play and imagined the ways that it might work in a promenade setting. Nettie had much more experience of promenade than I did at the outset of the process, and in any case, we have a working relationship that goes back many years. So her ideas about the play, scenes, and characters are brought into the whole of the conception of the piece. Very collaborative. Then, in the end, she says, "I'll give you an acting machine, and you play with it and do what you want with it" and I go into the rehearsal room.' For *Henry V* it was ladders, scaffolding, and gym equipment; for *The Tempest* a series of richly patterned 'rocks' with magical properties: they were all playable as musical instruments, or could be used to store props, and one was a kind of well with water in it. In each case, it must be flexible, portable, and durable; yet it must be able to inspire the audience's imagination.

Similarly, Lynne Parker recognises the importance of the director's input to the designer's creative process while at the same time recognising the elusive quality of that collaboration. 'Quite a lot of the process is sitting, looking out the window with your mouth open, hoping an idea will come to you. Let's take, for example, the play we're starting on next week. Declan [Hughes] only finished the script last week. But I can't say that was the reason I didn't have any ideas about it until very recently. I was getting close to panic about it because it just wasn't triggering anything visually. Kathy Strachan, the designer on the project, was sitting there making a model, and I was looking at it blankly and thinking, "Hm, that's nice." But I didn't know what to say about it. And last week I had to go out of town and sitting on the train, it just came to me what the whole thing was about, and I realised I'd been thinking in terms of sky, skyscapes, and the whole atmosphere of the sky, and I realised that what the play needed was not a kind of monumental skyscape but much more of a secret, dark, dangerous and sinister atmosphere that was much more like a forest. And I thought of it being set in autumn, and the colours have got to be strong autumn colours. Also because it's concerned with demons and hell, red is what's making the atmosphere. It just snapped, and I realised I'd been stupid about the whole thing. I came back here and went to Kathy, who went er-er-er-er-er, but she changed it completely, and now we know where we're going with it. So there's no straightforward process. You've just got to allow yourself time to keep working, to keep churning it over. I cannot say I have a process, I just have to let it cook in there until I get the idea. And I can't force it.'

The insights about the various ways directors relate to designers has proved one of the most fascinating aspects of this study. Parker continues, 'Sometimes I have a very clear picture, I see exactly what I want; sometimes I don't. Perhaps more important is the way I would relate to the designer, knowing that we're on the same wavelength so that if there is a swift about-turn, the other person can cope with that and respond to it. That's a whole area of building trust. It's not even sitting and talking. You just have to trust each other, to know that you're both pulling in the same direction. If there is a serious rethink of something, you know that's not just arbitrary but it's being done for a very good reason. You have to trust your own instincts.'

Parker is not alone in articulating the subtleties of the director-designer collaborative process. Bardsley speaks of her association with Aldona Cunningham and how, on a project like T.S. Eliot's *Family Reunion*, they would discuss the stimulus to the production, looking at films like *Poltergeist* and *Rebecca* together. 'Then I talk about key words or key qualities or key visual sequences that I think we need to concentrate on. We'd start talking about what the vocabulary was, what the style of the piece was, and she [Cunningham] would go away and do photocopies of very disparate, ugly images. All over the place.

She's very good at finding little bits of inspiration, and she'd have them up on her wall.'

To Nancy Meckler, specificity is probably the most important result of the director-designer collaboration. 'I really like to work with a designer who enjoys collaborating and talking quite a lot about what I think the thing is actually about, having him or her bring something in, and then my being able to tear it apart or suggest things. I find it very difficult if it's an ingenious designer who brings in something quite startling; yet it may not be the right set for the piece. Sometimes when you have a designer who likes to go off and work alone – although the design is impressive – there's something a little bit arbitrary about it, a feeling that that design would do for any number of productions of that piece. Whereas I feel the design should reflect the designer and director who are working on it.'

It is interesting how many of the women directors enjoy their collaborations with women designers. Sue Sutton Mayo says, 'I work with a lot of women because I get on well with women; they see the world the same way I do. I meet with designers as early as I can, and I work with the same people over and over again. Judith Croft has been a resident designer with the Manchester Library Theatre. I adore her. We see things very much the same way. I have another designer, Sue Pearce, who often designs for me. Sue and Judith I'd work with to the ends of the earth. I like designers to be involved as early as possible. I like to have long, often rambling conversations with them about text. We very rarely talk specifically until the last possible moment. All of the women I like to work with do this: we keep the actual physical design on hold until the last possible moment. I love working with designers. I have so much admiration for their eye and the way they are able to make real these images. I'll go up there and say, "I think it's something to do with this and I think . . ." and they'll go "Yes, what did you think about this?" And I'll go, "Oh, God, yes!" They make concrete these things that are just in your head.'

For several years Katie Mitchell has worked with one particular designer – Vicki Mortimer. 'We know each other terribly well, and we tend to work hand in glove.' The two share an intense and meticulous period of research together. 'We are both inside each other's heads, and our designs tend to emerge organically from both of us having researched the text and the context of that text in immense detail. I suppose the strength of the relationship is the fact that we are always prepared to change our ideas in response to what the actors' needs are at any given moment of the play. In the ideal situation the design process is organically developing alongside the rehearsal process. This doesn't often happen, and in most cases one has to finalise the design before rehearsals begin. Even when that is the case, Vicki is present in rehearsals, seeing how the actors are developing their characters and responding to her choices. We're often making quite radical changes in costumes and props in response to what the actors are doing.'

Unlike Mayo and Mitchell, Annie Castledine largely associates with male designers in a collaborative way. Again she stresses the importance of working with a few designers with whom she feels genuinely comfortable. 'I tend to work with designers who are very close friends, and I have a huge pool of designers in that sense, some of the great designers in the country, like Antony Ward. We cut our teeth together. Very talented. He did his first design for me when he came out of college. So you have an exciting journey with designers, especially when you've known them for a very long time.'

Another designer with whom Castledine works is Martin Johns, her collaborator, for example, on *Marching for Fausa* at the Royal Court Upstairs. 'I like working with him because he is very classy in his finish to a design. And I chose him specifically because the Theatre Upstairs is a very tatty space, a very woebegone space, a very difficult space, a shoe box. Sometimes the space is very dirty and very cluttered. I had to have a designer who wasn't messy for that project because of the space. And I knew also that if he chose something it would work. You haven't got a lot of technical help in the Theatre Upstairs so I wanted that expertise on board. I also knew he would make a very good model box. I choose a designer who will actually use the space well, because always I will be interested in working to the space, revealing the beauties of the space, or the unusual features of the space within which I am working. Be it an old theatre like the Greenwich Theatre or the Lyric Hammersmith – whatever it is, the design will fit in the space either deliciously or uncomfortably depending on what I'm wanting to communicate, but always the awareness of the actual external space in which we're working will be paramount. I knew we'd be able to sit and look at the Theatre Upstairs in a highly considered way. Some designers wouldn't have done that. Some designers have so many assistants. Martin Johns is a very famous and a very prestigious designer but he doesn't believe in using design assistants. Those who use design assistants, I think, are not as good because what they don't do is actually rub the space through their fingers. For the Theatre Upstairs I wanted someone who really knew the space as well as I did.'

As with the other directors, Castledine fluctuates between being very specific and somewhat general in her work with designers. While her requests for *Marching for Fausa* were concrete – a fan, venetian blinds, a concrete floor with a gully leading to a drain – her requests for *Gaslight* at the Greenwich were more nebulous, and it was Johns's vision to reveal the back wall, the staircase, the substage that offered tremendous visual excitement. Castledine speaks, too, of an interesting collaboration with Jenny Teramani, a resident designer at Theatre Royal, Stratford East. 'We sat in the upper circle together, and she told me about the space. We looked down on the playing area, and I said, "What's it like when taken to the back wall?" and she revealed the space to me. She was very empowered to do that.'

In her collaborative process, Castledine emphasises the importance of talk, of director and designer not taking one another for granted. The next time she works with Martin Johns, for example, she says, 'We shall talk a long time about images and material and wafting. We shall talk a long time about the use of space, the creative use of space, and how we will manipulate and change the space: on the corner, on the promenade, on the traverse, and that will take a long time.'

37

No one emphasised the importance of true collaboration more than Phyllida Lloyd, especially commenting on her collaborations with designer Antony Ward. 'We engage in all manner of extramural antics at home – and abroad if we can find an excuse. It's all a process of discovering the shape of the play; it's gathering fuel, supplies for the journey. I'm very dependent on that dialogue. It's complete collaboration.' Lloyd maintains that, while she may begin the process a step ahead of her designer, she always expects everything she thought about the piece to change completely by the time the journey has come to an end. Although she often knows specifically what she wants the design to be, she wants the designer to have freedom to go off and create that design. 'I work with people who feel far too passionately about it [the design] themselves, and they wouldn't really respond to that kind of direction.'

In speaking more specifically about the design for Ostrovsky's *Artists and Admirers* which she directed at the RSC's The Pit at the Barbican with Antony Ward as designer, Lloyd says, 'It's very interesting how it evolved. We wanted to play it in the round, and yet [because it is set partly in a theatre] maintain the proscenium.' Director and designer had weeks and weeks of discussion. Lloyd saw the young actress and her mother's world as a vulnerable world. 'They are on a raft in the middle of this shark-infested tank, obviously the most vulnerable image is them plunked in the middle of that little world with us all around them. I was clinging onto that, and Antony was clinging onto the *Artists and Admirers* image [of a proscenium stage] and the more we worked, the more we saw each other's perspective. Then one day he said, "Well, what if we try to do both things: you're able to play your scenes in the round but we also at certain points in the piece reveal the proscenium as well." '

This was achieved on stage by use of a delicate scrim curtain that covered one of the four sides of the space, so that the audience from three sides was witnessing the events from backstage while the spectators on the fourth side saw the events as though from the front of the stage. The round created the intimacy and the vulnerability Lloyd sought, while the proscenium curtain and footlights created the theatrical metaphor Ward desired. 'There were enormous numbers of ideas that were left behind,' Lloyd says, but the important ingredients were discussion, evolution, and compromise.

Just as Phyllida Lloyd emphasises the ongoing evolution of the director-designer process, Annabel Arden, in her work with Theatre de Complicite, employed an environmental approach to design in which the actual design evolves during the rehearsal process while, conversely, much of the staging evolves from design elements that are brought into rehearsal. It was the great director Peter Brook who fully exploited this way of working – in *Carmen*, *A Midsummer Night's Dream*, and *The Mahabharata*, for example – a method that allows for unsurpassed freedom, experimentation, and cohesion.

Arden describes her process of working on Dürrenmatt's *The Visit*. 'We work physically, first and foremost. In *The Visit* it was very important that we did something with those trains at the station in the beginning of the play. I would divide the cast into three groups of two or three people, and I'd say, "I want people waiting on the station platform, I want trains, I want station platform. I want to see it. I want jokes with trains." In other words, how do you indicate a train passing? So we get jokes with newspapers rattling or people falling off of stools. You see, I really want the atmosphere of the trains. There's no sound effects, but soon beautiful things start to happen: somebody reading a newspaper and the paper starts to move, move, move, capturing the intensity as the train comes along the tracks and then the point where the train passes. So they'd spend about an hour working like that, and then we'd look at it all. We'd like this and we'd like that, and we'd record it. I'd make notes of it or we'd take photographs or the designer would sketch; the best filter is to have your designer there drawing it. It's fantastic because the designer's imagination is working right alongside yours.'

'You see', Arden continues, '*The Visit* was never designed until very late, probably the sixth week. We had, as we do with every show, rows and rows of costumes and many objects. We always work with real costumes and real objects from day one because that way you evolve the whole thing, it's organic. And sound . . . we often have our sound designer there and our lighting designer, if we can afford it. They should be there every single day. The sound designer should be playing music.'

Going a step further, Julia Bardsley, in exploring the text for *Macbeth*, chose to keep a strong sense of freedom even in production. She explains that *Macbeth* was 'a representation of where my mind and thoughts were at the time, a reflection of where I think theatre is, and an expression of my frustration with my own work. So the light, created by Christopher Toulmin, and sound, created by Andrew Poppy, were like characters or forces within the piece itself. The music and sound were forces that could disrupt the performance as well as enhance it. What usually happens with the theatre is that the music and lights are there to make a seamless, beautiful piece of work in which the audience is unaware that music and lights are even being used. What I wanted to do was break down the invisibility of those two elements, to make the audience very aware of them as forces. We actually wanted to have the operators down in the auditorium so people could see them and see the stage manager cueing the show, so that the audience was constantly aware of the illusion of theatre. I wanted to re-affect the audience and get them really to listen and see and feel the things that are happening in the play. It's a weird idea but that's the strategy I wanted to use to make the tensions which exist within the play very concrete. The whole piece is about dynamics, opposites – chaos and order, good and evil, illusion and reality, falseness and truth – and I wanted to make them very graphic rather than merely intellectual ideas. So we veered between no music, no sound, work lights and then lurched into something very, very theatrical, so that the production was pushing and pulling all the time.'

Carrying this concept still farther, Bardsley envisions a production so loose that the actors would never know what music or what effect to expect. 'It has a real sort of tension in that they don't really know what's going to be thrown at them.

In a way it's an ideal that could only be achieved if the person who's running the lights, the person who's running the sound, and the person who's cueing the show were a part of the rehearsal process. While I'm not interested in actors being lost or confused on stage, I'd like to push towards that, to create an environment where it isn't really safe. That's the atmosphere I want. It's also about wanting the audience not to know quite whether something is meant to happen. If you're unsettled you're more receptive to what is going on than if you're sitting back and enjoying something in a comfortable, received way. The characters in *Macbeth* are on quicksand, not knowing what's going to happen next, pushed and buffeted. In a way, these actors are trying to do this production of *Macbeth* with all of these forces against them: lighting coming down, sound coming at them, all the theatrical trappings actually being difficulties for them to overcome.' In this way the experience of presenting *Macbeth* parallels the obstacles, the danger, and the buffeting of fate depicted in the play itself.

Bardsley comments on another piece of work of which she was very proud: her *Hamlet* at the Young Vic. In the production, Bardsley and her designer, Aldona Cunningham, literally placed themselves within the production as a magician (Bardsley) and his assistant (Cunningham). Bardsley says, '*Hamlet* is one of those sacred cows. Everyone was saying, "Don't do it; don't do it." But for me it was really important to tackle the piece because it is so much about theatre. It's the play of Shakespeare's that refers the most to the theatre, theatre as a microcosm, the world as a stage. So I could use the play to offer an analysis of and express my passion for the theatre. My version of *Macbeth* was very austere and not interested so directly in the question of theatricality. It was about trying to cut through illusion. My interpretation of *Hamlet* was a celebration of theatricality, all about the glitter, the magic, and, I suppose ultimately, the lie of the theatre.

'So the costumes were very lush velvets and bright colours, and there was a mirror ball, and a glittery little stage in the middle of the space, like a little jewel with a trap, a tiny revolve, and footlights. It had glitter treads leading up to it. It was a visual representation of how we saw the state of theatre; in a way we were saying that the stage, the creative space was shrinking, but at the same time it was intended as a celebration of the potential of theatre.

'By placing ourselves within the fiction as a magician and his assistant, we were saying, in a way, that director and designer conjure up things, and they are also the manipulators of space, ideas, and, to an extent, actors. The magician and assistant were mute, but we were there all the time, passing props to people, handing the knife to Hamlet, conjuring everything out of the space. There was also a deliberate use of the performers doubling, playing with the idea of transformation. Natasha Pope, who played Gertrude, also played Ophelia, and she was in a constant state of transformation, changing her wig and her make-up in front of the audience. Metin Marlowe, who played Laertes, also played Polonius and again you saw him changing. Just as the theatre is about the art of transformation so the actor's art is about transformation. We also had miniature replicas of the characters. In the end Hamlet's little puppet, his miniature double performed the "To be or not to be" speech with the live actor voicing it. We were trying to cut through the preciousness around those famous speeches.'

One of the directors, Jenny Killick, has taught design students in a course of study devised for the purpose of effective director-designer communication. Killick, for example, guided young design students at Central St Martins through a theoretical production of *The Rivals* by Richard Brindsley Sheridan. 'You brief ten or twelve design students on the play and then they go away and design it and you have a relationship with each student, talk about what they're doing. It's very stimulating; you feed them images, and they can chuck them out or take them on. First, I talk enthusiastically about the play. It's curious: I realise that I have seen *The Rivals* three times in my life, and I never remember it. And when I came to read it, I thought, "Why do I not remember this wonderful play?" I talked to them about Sheridan's particular sense of place: two men come on in the first scene and say, "This is Bath." There's an absolutely wonderful sense of story and place. I talk them through the text really and show them the mechanics of how it works and what inspires me about the play. What a wonderful comedy! All the characters come up against death. How do you do that? Enchanted and magical to have death hanging over the end of the comedy . . . a wonderful duel at the end when Lucius O'Trigger forces the issue: "We're going to fight to the death." So I say, "Whatever you do, you must come up with a good idea for the end of the play . . . that has to be magical." So, that's the brief. They all make model boxes and have a final assessment.'

Prior to her directing of *Secret Lies* (*Les Serments indiscrets*) in the United States, Killick again taught a course in the director-designer relationship and explored the Marivaux text with design students, who, she says, came up with all sorts of wonderful things. 'Although an American designer ultimately created the settings, having worked through all the design questions before with these students, I had a thorough grounding.'

Killick maintains that the students are given complete artistic freedom but adds, 'They've got to release the spirit of the play; they've got to get in touch with that. Very open. But I'm interested in their response to the play, and everything has to be justified. They mustn't be lazy and say, "Oh, let's do it punk." They must find an underlying WHY: what is the texture of the play? I like teaching because I'm very interested in finding new ways of making things work, fresh ideas. Students can occasion-ally throw up something absolutely new. I think design is important particularly in a theatre that is preordained as to the way the audience comes to a play. Because people face one way in the dark, ninety per cent of the design is done even before the designer gets there. For the designer, there's only ten per cent left. The British theatre is so confident that the way they should watch a play is by sitting in rows in the dark. Unchallengeable. It's very necessary, I think, to keep experi-menting with relationships between the audience and the play –

otherwise it's really all the same thing. It's like television again. The television sits in the room, and you turn it on, and the pictures change and stories change. But you are inanimate. I think the theatre is sort of lazy. That experimentation is what I want when I'm at my most extreme, but to earn my crust I'm happy to let the audience sit in the dark and watch. But it's what I think about and what I dream of.' And it is this kind of imaginative exploration Killick can pursue with design students.

All of the directors place great value on the contribution of their designers and on the collaborative process. Several of them enjoy the process of technical rehearsals, the intricate cueing and integrating of all the technical elements. None of the directors flounder or back away from the delicate process of working with designers, and none of them dictate or take an authoritarian approach to working with designers. Many of them express interest in trying new things, breaking new ground in their approach to design and their work with designers. Perhaps the beauty of the collaborative process is best summarised in the words of Garry Hynes, praising her work with designer, Frank Conway. 'We share the same perspective, the same aesthetic of theatre. We arrive at a process whereby he absorbs things about the play, and then all of this happens, and I have always been surprised by what I see in the sense that I have never imagined what it is, been able to imagine it visually. I would have imagined something, and what he presents to me eventually in a model is not as I imagined it – is even more than I imagined. That can be wonderful!'

CHAPTER 3

A question of inhabiting the text

There is always in the process of directing a play a certain amount of mysticism. A director may ultimately look at her or his work and ask, 'How did we ever get here?' or at less fortunate times, 'Where did we go wrong?' In my own work, I invariably find that the greatest mistakes, the irretrievable ones, are those made before the rehearsal process ever begins. I remember directing a production of *The Blue Bird* by Maeterlinck many years ago that was over-conceived, over-designed, and over-costumed. I recall looking at the stage in those exhausting and nightmarish technical rehearsals and suddenly being made aware of my own folly. The poor actors seemed but tiny specks in the vast array of spectacle. The play was diminished; the production unsalvageable. The point of this story is simple: what the director does to prepare before rehearsals begin, before the setting is designed, is of the utmost importance. Finding time to prepare is crucial to Julia Bardsley. 'I need, everybody needs thinking time; time when you're not doing anything, when your mind can float around that particular project. That's when the way into the work comes to you, and when that time doesn't exist or is taken away from you, it's difficult to function in the rehearsal situation.' How vital a concept: a time when your mind can float around the project!

Another basic concept – besides the freedom, space, and time to ruminate – is that expressed by Sarah Pia Anderson. 'I think the impressions on first reading [of the play] last for ever. They perhaps last longer than any other feelings. And then as you reread [the text] you discover details, and then you rediscover.

So it's a process of constant discovery of the play and how it actually works. It's one thing to read it and quite another thing to make dramatic action plausible.' When I asked Anderson if she tries to pinpoint or articulate that dramatic action in her preparation work, she explained, 'I think I know if it's not there. I think it evolves really. I've only once been in the situation where I've done a second production of the same text. And there's no doubt that you have a lot of knowledge added which could not have occurred by simply reading the play. I think that's the reason we do plays; they shouldn't be consigned to the way I was taught at university – that reading the play is quite sufficient. They are about *action*; that's why people are called actors.' I believe Anderson is saying that the process of the rehearsal so enriches both actor and director that no amount of reading prior to rehearsal will completely unlock the play. Nevertheless most of the directors agree on the importance of careful, detailed, and repeated study of the text. Jenny Killick advises, 'Read and read and read it. That's all really.' Killick goes on to explain the differences in reading a new play and a classic text. 'If it's a [new] writer, the script may not necessarily be finished. You're often casting on an unfinished script; you're casting on a dream really. So you're meeting actors and talking about this wonderful play that's going to be. Often you don't have the complete text until you're actually there with the actors. But you're always reading drafts of it, and you're very actively involved in the dramatisation of the play. So there's a very fluid sense. You're in a funny situation because you're imagining what will be, but you haven't really got any concrete evidence . . . very different from work on an old play. For example, with *The Rivals*, it's just endlessly returning to the play itself for inspiration and to find out what Sheridan intended, what he wanted. It's a very different experience.'

While most of the women directors emphasise the importance of careful and repeated reading of the text, they also concur that the preparation work will invariably be different for different projects. Brigid Larmour, commenting on the pre-production stage with Christopher Marlowe's Elizabethan masterpiece, *Dr Faustus*, concludes, 'It depends very much on the play. Let's take a classic – *Dr Faustus*. It's a bit like doing a new play because you have to determine your script. So I do a lot of reading of the play, a lot of reading of articles, academic books, books about devils. I went to Stratford to see Peter Whelan's play [*School of the Night*] about Marlowe. I thought it would be good to have a chat with him [Whelan] from the writer's point of view. A lot of time has to do with trying to understand the play, trying to articulate what I want to say in the play because it's a very ambiguous piece of writing, and I'm taking a very strong line on it. Several things that I notice in the play: the things that Faustus does when he's being empowered by the devil are really not very exciting to a twentieth-century person; for example, having grapes in northern Europe in January is pretty commonplace. Even flying through the air can be achieved on a fairly routine basis from Heathrow or even from Manchester. And I thought, "That's interesting; perhaps I should use that, and perhaps I should use the fact that what he's getting is the twentieth century." We talk about the western world having lost its soul. So that led me to the idea of the devil being a twentieth-century character who'd look very extraordinary and strange to the Elizabethan world. And then that took me to the idea that it's all an illusion, that it's all happening in a theatre, so it's all a trick being played on Faustus by the devil; it's all contributing to the theatricality of it. So you hear what I'm saying – I don't tend to start with the grand scheme and then stick to that; I tend to look at the details and the contradictions and evolve the grand scheme out of that. And I think I'm particularly interested in Elizabethan and Jacobean writing where there are fantastic contradictions and complexities. Very often directors attempt to impose a rather over-simplified reading on a play which diminishes its depth because it becomes a celebration of war or an exploration of war or a condemnation of war, in the case of *Henry V*, for instance.'

While Bardsley concurs that the planning is different for each project, she, Lynne Parker, and Nancy Meckler all warn against premature over-intellectualisation. Bardsley states, 'I actually do a lot of preparing. I probably over-prepare in a way. That's just about me trying to focus my mind on the project at hand. It's different for different things. I've read a number of things about the play [her *Macbeth* project at the Leicester Haymarket], but I don't want to be steeped in the wrong sort of information. I work visually, and I try to find visual references: bits out of magazines, exhibitions, a sort of mixture of stuff.' At the outset of her rehearsal process for *Macbeth*, Bardsley confessed, 'I have less of an idea with this than anything else I've ever done. Maybe it's because most of the people I'm working with I've worked with before. I feel much more able not to have fixed ideas about what we're going to do. What I feel about this production is that we have a vocabulary and a big space. I have a number of objects that are possibly going to be used in that space. I have an idea about the light and sound being forces within that space. What I don't know is where those things will happen and the way they will happen. I have no idea, which is quite unusual for me.'

Lynne Parker concurs, stating, 'The longer I direct, the less I do actually. When I was at college I would make diagrams of the blocking and all that sort of stuff. I was always quite shocked to find that actors couldn't bear that – being little tin soldiers. My ideal situation is that everyone is coming to the same known play: that's absolutely the bottom line. You've got to know what it is, but you also have to be able to rediscover and change.' Meckler also says, 'I'm a bit wary of preparing too much because in the early days I didn't prepare at all. I think I prided myself on being incredibly intuitive. Then I began to prepare more, do more research, plan things more, and I realised that I wasn't at my best in that situation. It's one thing to read up on the period, and that I would do, or look at lots of paintings of the period, or read literature of the period; but actually to plan the production is not a great thing for me. It's better when I go into the rehearsal room having no idea what I'm going to do, and it's something to do with what actually happens on the rehearsal floor. So I make myself very familiar with the piece, reading it a lot. When I was doing Chekhov I read an enormous amount of Chekhov's stories. When I was doing *St Joan* I read up on the history, but I wouldn't ever read about how the play had been done before or anything like that.'

Like Meckler, Garry Hynes embraces reading about the world of the play. 'The script work would involve reading the play and reading outside the play, away from the play. And I often find that – if I know the play sufficiently well, which I often do at that point – reading outside to stimulate my thought process is a lot more vital than actually reading the play. I am a reader in any case. If there's a historical context – for instance a production of a play by M. J. Molloy, *The Wood of the Whispering*, which is a very old-fashioned play set in the 1950s about emigration from the west of Ireland – then I will read. The play is very baroque, sort of a fantasy piece of theatre in some sense, but the production of it arose from a book that was a sociological study of parts of western Ireland in the 1950s. It had nothing to do with the characters but gave a wonderful sense of a community and how that community was breaking up. That absolutely inspired the production of the play that eventually evolved. So I will always do that.'

In co-directing *India Song*, Annabel Arden found it imperative in her understanding of the play and of Marguerite Duras's experimental form to read every published work by this gravely misunderstood playwright: her political writings, her diaries, her novels, her short plays. 'You can't just pick up a play and understand her work. Why is she so famous in France? What was this woman's life about? She [Duras] is talking about the experience of love and how it affects people, particularly certain women, and how it can be as devastating as war. She is making the specific link between colonial exploitation and emotional truth. It's not simply a love story. It's about the Vice-Consul of Lahore, a colonial officer in Calcutta in disgrace, because he can no longer stand the French exploitation of the East and has seen the link between his own emotional balance – because he hasn't found anyone to love – and the incredible rape of the East by the West. He finds a match in a woman, Anne-Marie Stretter, who is the wife of the ambassador, who has also seen it. The whole play is about the fact that they have both seen it, yet they're both powerless against imperialism and powerless to make a life together. Duras is really talking about capitalism. It's tragic that people don't see what she's doing.' So Arden emphasises not just the world of the play, but the world of the playwright as well.

Sarah Pia Anderson also emphasises trying to enter into the world of the play and the playwright whether it be *Rosmersholm* or *Hedda Gabler*. 'I read a lot about Ibsen. I picked up Halvdan Koht's biography. I read most of it before I did *Rosmersholm*. I try to understand the writer whenever I'm doing any play – whether it's by Brecht or Frank McGuinness or Robert Holman or Anne Devlin or Shakespeare. My approach is the same really: to try to see how the language conveys the intent of the author. And I suppose if it's Shakespeare, then I've been trained to understand up to a point what he's saying, and I know how to analyse a text, how to understand it, break it down so that I arrive at what I believe to be a clear reading of the play, my understanding of the play. I understand what the words mean, I understand why they're being said, what's motivating them.' When I asked Anderson if her breakdown was like a Stanislavsky breakdown into units and objectives, she responded, 'No, nothing as formal as that. I've never really formalised it. To me it's just a sort of intuitive thing which I then work out with the actors.'

Anderson repeatedly underscores the intuitive part of her rehearsal process. 'I think the way I have always responded to any work of art, whether it's theatre or painting, poem or literature is to absorb it and in some way to surrender to its hidden power. I try to surrender to what people call sub-text, or inner life, or a pulse, something that actually communicates to me strongly. I want to understand the mysterious in something. I'm always attracted to a play if I don't quite understand what it's about. And the desire and the need to make it clear to an audience – not to make it obscure, not to mystify it deliberately but actually to bring something into the light, to take something that's buried somewhere and show it – motivates me and has, I think, in everything I've done. I want to bring something into light with clarity. So while I'm attracted to the mystery, my desire is to clarify it.' In her production of *Rosmersholm*, for example, Anderson reinforced austerity. 'It was very much to do with the Protestant imagination which I think the play is firmly locked into. I find it difficult to think of how to do it without trying to translate that world . . . the darkness, I suppose. It's really a question of inhabiting the text. It does actually come to life in my head.'

If Anderson's emphasis is on the intuitive, then Sue Sutton Mayo's is on the sub-textual. 'I know how to do a literary criticism of the text. Preparing a classic text I always do it [an analysis]. Actually I tend to do it because I find it a very useful way of getting quickly to what the play is about. Even something like *Ghosts*, practically the whole thing is sub-textual. The symbolic life of that play is as enormous as its textual life and actually I think bigger. So until you begin to understand, for example, what the word "light" means in that play, you can't actually play the scene. So I do a great deal of research, for example with *Ghosts*, on Norway; I did a lot of medical research; I like to know as much as I can about the playwright. My dream is to have the playwright in rehearsal with me. Then you don't have to spend three hours wondering what did he mean when he wrote this, what did she mean when she wrote that. You just say to them, "What did you mean when you wrote that?" If I could have, I would have had Ibsen with me.'

Intuitive responses, clarifying that which is dark and mysterious, exploring the sub-textual meaning of lines – all are valid approaches or partial approaches to the play in the planning stages. Before my first meeting with Annie Castledine, I saw her production of *Marching for Fausa* by playwright, Biyi Bandele, and was fascinated by her ability, as a white Englishwoman, to penetrate so completely the politicised world and culture of black Nigeria. 'I'd done a lot of research, of course, a lot of talking to Nigerians, a lot of looking at videos, a lot of going to the African Centre, a lot of talking to the playwright who was there all the time in rehearsal, a lot of work with the musical director, a superb Nigerian musician, very rigorous, and very politicised. I wouldn't have let a moment pass if it hadn't been something he approved of. And that's fine, that's great. You surround yourself with colleagues who are very, very rigorous, which I find exciting.'

In direct opposition to those who approach their work intuitively or through sensory stimulation, are those women who rely on a disciplined and rigorous technique of analysis like Di Trevis, who says, 'I read the play a lot. I think lots of directors don't actually, and I think it's vital. I have a whole set of processes that I subject the play to. I open a log on the play and that involves buying a very thick book that I write in. And I do very detailed analyses of the text, of all the characters, of all the scenes, of all the settings, of movement of time, of the movement of weather, of the movement of day and night – all these kinds of details in the play. I read and make notes for many days: I do not read passively but actively with a pencil and a notebook. I research the author's life and times. I read around the subject; I place the play in its historical perspective and chart the events of the times in which it is set, the music, art, and literature of that time. I make detailed columns for each character, writing down by hand everything that the character says about himself, everything that is said about him. I analyse time, place, weather, geographical references. For a language play, I look up nearly every word in the dictionary. I use the dictionary a lot. (I'm talking about classical works on the whole; I do an enormous amount of work on a classical text.) I do not let a single reference in the text pass without thoroughly researching it. (I think Katie Mitchell who was my assistant at Stratford uses a lot of this.) I make plans of houses and gardens and apartments, of streets, of rooms, of districts – not designs, just how it must be to make the text truthful: what the world of the play is. I analyse the language a particular character uses. I note repetitions of phrases, words, questions. I make notes on eating, drinking, clothes. This works whether it's Webster or Pinter. I do a lot of preparation. I work quite a lot in the model box. I don't work in it . . . I mean I don't plan moves or anything. I've never blocked a play in my whole life, and I don't know how it gets on the stage quite. But I do play in the model box, and I notice my daughter does the same thing in her doll house. It's exactly the same. She plays in her doll house and I play in the model box. When I built her doll house, I realised that the doll house was really very much like my job. She dreams in it, and I dream in it too – and construct. But I don't plan the play, I just dream there.'

None of the directors has a more meticulous and exacting pre-rehearsal process than Katie Mitchell. She begins by reading the play probably twenty-five to thirty times. 'I will then look at the historical, social, political, and economic context in which the play was written and is taking place. I will try to find out as much about the author as possible. I will look at paintings of the period, the sculpture of the period, the architecture of the period in which the play is set. In the case of a classical drama, I will look up the etymological root of every word because words can change meanings over long periods of time. In the case of a translated play like Ibsen's *Ghosts*, I would be working with a literal translation and the translation of the play which we will be using in the production so that I'm constantly in touch – as much as one possibly can be in another language – with the exact intentions of the author.'

Another major aspect of Mitchell's preparation is the research trip which she takes with her designer, Vicki Mortimer. For example, *Rutherford and Son*, written and set in Newcastle-upon-Tyne in 1912 and centring on the glass making there, required a trip to the North-East to explore the natural environment – the moorlands – and the industrial environment. Photographs are taken and all of this research is then offered to the actors during the rehearsal process. An extended trip was undertaken in preparation for *The Dybbuk* by Solomon Anski, a play set in a Hasidic community in the Ukraine in the early part of the twentieth century. 'We did a huge amount of research in this country, meeting members of the Jewish community, Rabbis, and practitioners in Yiddish theatre, talking to them about customs, rituals, and lifestyles. We also read a huge amount of literature about Hasidism, and then we went to the Ukraine. Before the First World War, Anski, an ethnologist, had travelled around the Ukraine collecting stories, songs, and ritual artefacts from the Jewish community. It was during this period, and later when he was working for the Red Cross in the First World War, that he had written the play. The play was very much influenced by the Ukraine, its people and its landscape. The journeys he made were well documented, and so we decided to visit the country and retrace his steps. It was an extraordinary and moving experience, taking us from Lvov in the west right across to Sumy in the far east. And the trip directly influenced the design, the lighting, the mood and feel of the production. Also, while there, we met several members of the Jewish community who had survived the Second World War and talked with them about their pre-war experiences. We returned with about ten tapes of stories and songs, recorded live, and reams of slides. This whole research process took about five months to complete.'

Julia Bardsley has found her own unique method of dealing with the script before the rehearsals start. 'I do a score of the whole piece. I find it very difficult to read a play on the page, to find the whole shape of it. I do a score in order to see how the piece moves visually, so I'm not flipping through pages; then I can see the whole piece as a shape. I can see where I think scenes could be placed simultaneously or where something needs to be emphasised with a movement, or where I can just forget about text and realise the scene with a purely visual sequence. It's so I can start plotting it and orchestrating it. It's just about seeing the structure because I like to see the shape of things, like to have a visual sense of things. It's a very useful reference. What I don't tend to do at that stage is go into any nitty gritty of the text but try to get an overall feel about the piece: What sort of qualities am I going to explore with it? What sort of world operates within? What's the feeling of the world? But the detail of the text, sentence by sentence, the specific meaning, I'm not interested in at that stage. That can happen with the actors when you start working things with them.'

While several of the directors claim to be wary of the exacting pre-planning demanded of a tight rehearsal schedule and large cast sizes and further claim not to plan a concept, it is not unusual for some of the women directors to use a particular play as a vehicle for a journey or exploration that they wish to pursue. Lynne Parker says, for example, 'I certainly think that the writer is where it all starts, that there wouldn't be a theatre without writers. We have a literary tradition in Ireland, and I'm very interested in preserving that. The visual and the musical are important, but it's the words that really matter. And I have total respect for writers, having worked so closely with them. I know I can't do that, and I have great admiration for anybody who can. But I would be very unhappy and sad if the show didn't have something of my personality in it, and it's bound to have just a little style in presentation and something of my trademark upon it.' Concerning a production of Brendan Kennelly's adaptation of Euripides' *The Trojan Women* at the Abbey, Parker speaks of the very contemporary value she finds in the classic Greek play. 'It's really about women, the way they are demeaned and ridiculed by pornography, and how woman emerges from a situation where she is going to be used in this way as an object and takes control of her life. It seems very clear to me that that's what the play deals with. The play is over 2000 years old but if you look at Yugoslavia at the moment, it's exactly the same situation. I feel very happy and pleased to be a woman in western Europe in the second half of this century; I couldn't have a better break really, and yet so little has changed for so many women.'

Annie Castledine, too, likes to put her very personal stamp on a production. No matter how well she knows her play, she'll probably 'throw it all up anyway' so she doesn't plan in huge detail. 'I know I want to play with it. I need to explore an idea whether it's suitable to the text or not. I could be quite outrageous on that level. I *think* it's suitable but if it isn't, it won't be. So it's where you push yourself as a practitioner, as an artist, both through text and the work you're doing. I'm going to do this now because it's what I want and need to play with. All right, so I'm going to explore it in public, and if it fails, I'm going to fall and I'm going to hurt myself, but that's too bad. It doesn't bother me at all. I think sometimes I ought to be a little bit more judicious about falling down so often, but at other times it doesn't matter. It seems to me to be the right thing to do.'

However long they might debate these questions – fidelity to the text or freedom to use that text to explore an idea or contemporary theme, the need to prepare in detail or to remain loose and flexible – all of the directors agree on one principle: not to block the production in advance. Each of the women believes that the dynamic of finding the physical action through the rehearsal process is far more interesting, creative, and productive than moving figures around a model box or charting the movement patterns by diagram on ground plans. A few of the women used to block in advance; most never did; all agree that it is time consuming, tedious, and a virtually worthless task.

Although the topic of the dramaturg entered into the discussions, few of the women have the luxury of working with a dramaturg as is done in Europe and is now being emulated in the United States. Phyllida Lloyd explains, 'The dramaturg is viewed with some suspicion in this country. I'm not sure why. On my production of *The Way of the World* at the National Theatre I had a dramaturg, but I wasn't allowed to credit him as such. I put it down to economics; that is, that they enjoy high status in Europe and expect to be paid accordingly. The present economic climate makes everyone afraid of more demands on an already bursting budget.'

Jenny Killick often enjoys acting as her own dramaturg and communicating with the playwright without restricting or limiting. 'I might say "OK, this show's not quite there". I might take the script and talk it through and describe to the writer how it will be. It's a great focuser of the mind. The writer says, "No, we can't have that," or "Oh, yeah, that's good." Actually dramaturgy is very easy in those terms: "OK, the lights go

down, what are we going to see? What are we going to hear?"
It's imagining it all in advance, knowing what's not right, and
then making adjustments. The writer can get very lost or get
totally wrapped up in the fiction and the word and forget about
the public exposure, the public nature of the play. And I can be
wicked and push things to an extreme or act like a cold draft;
what have we got to show? what have we got to communicate?
what are people going to come and see? That's all it is really,
and everything follows from there. In essence you're just a
sounding board.'

As a part of their dramaturgical skills, the British director is
often called upon to work very closely with an adapter or
translator. Phyllida Lloyd shared her experiences working on
her 1992–93 RSC production of Ostrovsky's *Artists and
Admirers*. 'A new translation hadn't been done in this country
[England] for the last twenty or thirty years. We had an
American translation that was very woolly. But we used that in
deciding whether or not we were going to do the play. We
then commissioned a literal translation from which our adapter,
Kevin Elyot, worked. He's not a Russian scholar, and he was
working from that already second generation text. But he's an
actor and a playwright, and I was particularly keen to get
somebody who had an understanding of what actors needed.
We gave the actors a huge amount of voice in the translation.
We spent the first three weeks of rehearsal at the table; we were
then able to go away and do another draft.'

When directing Ibsen's *Rosmersholm*, Annie Castledine
worked so closely with a translator that she knew the play
intimately by the time rehearsals began. 'The preparation for
that production actually involved making a fresh translation, and
so, therefore, I sat with a Norwegian scholar and went through
every word of the Norwegian in the making of that fresh
translation. So, of course, when I went into rehearsals I knew
the text verbatim, like a score. I think that's essential with a
wonderfully complicated classic.'

A number of the directors emphasise the importance of
casting. Garry Hynes, in elucidating her pre-rehearsal process,

notes how much she learns in the casting process. 'I do all the natural things: involvement in the casting, discussions with the writer if the writer is alive or if the writer is present and involved, choice of designer, discussions with the designer; and it would be a constant process of talking and in the time that you're talking about casting possibilities, you are in fact finding out something more about the play.'

That grand old director of the British theatre, Sir Tyrone Guthrie, used to say that casting is ninety per cent of the director's job. Annie Castledine concurs, 'Absolutely. Peter Hall would say the same. The wise old men of our theatre knew about that. They knew about it absolutely. I have yet to learn about it. And I've made very silly choices for very silly reasons.'

Thought, exploration, collaboration, experimentation, time, trusting one's intuition – all are part of the director's pre-planning that either launches or sinks the vital rehearsal process. Lynne Parker sums it all up with humour and common sense. 'I think in terms of preparation – this sounds really ridiculous – clear the mind as much as possible, get a lot of sleep, be as healthy as possible, and in really good form so that you are going in there to have fun. And mentally and physically nimble enough to cope with all the situations that arise. And what I hope to evolve towards is a situation where I cast and structure the company so well that they can feed themselves. Ultimately I would like to do a production where I didn't say a single word to the actors from start to finish except for compiling them and letting them run with it.'

Whether the directors work intuitively or analytically, whether they impose a concept or regard the text as sacred, whether they make a detailed score or leave the detail to the inspiration of the rehearsal room, invariably the women added one final thought about the pre-rehearsal process: the need to learn to trust your initial thoughts, impulses, and feelings about the play. Too often, the directors believe, a woman can be consumed by self-doubt or can easily be dissuaded from what she knows in her gut is the right response.

PART II

THE PROCESS
and
PRODUCTION

CHAPTER 4

Pursuing a mutual objective

How does the director move from that which exists on the printed page or in the mind's eye to that which is a living entity on the stage? What is the rehearsal process like? It was interesting to me that none of the directors like to have visitors in their rehearsal rooms. They consider it not only a very private time but also a time when actors are often vulnerable and emotionally fragile. In Kenneth Rea's inquiry into the training of directors, *A Better Direction*, Deborah Warner recalls that as an aspiring potential director 'I wrote endless letters to Peter Brook to see if I could come and watch his rehearsals, and he very sensibly wrote back and said, "No you can't because you'd be bored," which is absolutely true. And I don't let people watch mine, and I'm always feeling guilty about that.'

So the major way we can approach the director's methodology is to listen to her talk about that process and about recent work – the production – that embodies those working methods. Although I invariably asked a very direct question such as, 'Could you tell me about your rehearsal process?' very few of the directors could do that. They would start with the very best of intentions, usually after a deep sigh and a muttered, 'What *do* I do?' under the breath. We would usually get as far as whether or not the play was read by the actors and whether or not the director actually blocked the action; then suddenly, any kind of clear progression disintegrated. If one were a very traditional director, one might say something like this: First we read and discuss, then we block, work, polish, run, then we tech and dress, then we preview and open. That *is* a process but it really doesn't explain or reveal much. So in the following discussions of process, while there may not be a consistent, systematic scheme, there are certainly great gems of wisdom and insights into, if not blueprints of, how the women directors tackle the rehearsal process. We must remember at all times that this is a highly creative and individualistic process, making an almost impossible demand on the director: to articulate that delicate process in a simple or logical progression.

Heretofore, the organisational pattern has been topical – various kinds of training, different methods of approaching designers, varieties of techniques in approaching the script – but now the pattern changes as I explore the craft of each director as she presented it to me. I considered attempting to group the directors as to the innovators, the experimenters, the classicists, the traditionalists, or the feminists. But such categories seemed somehow insufficient and diminished the scope and range of the directors' perspectives. Also, a number of the directors defy easy classification. A director like Annie Castledine, for example, moves gracefully from student to professional work, from workshop to formal production, from regional work to London, from new play to classic, from stage to television. Moreover, methods or approaches depend on the play, the people, the experience of the director, the objectives. So I decided to group the directors into three categories: those who are artistic directors of theatres, and those who work primarily as freelance directors, and those whose theatre work has taken them into new areas of exploration and creativity. I hope that the less structured presentation in these three chapters will allow the reader glimpses into the humanity of the individual women as well as procedures with which each of them takes her production from page to stage. The first group, whose working methods we are examining, are those associated primarily with a particular theatre: Garry Hynes at Druid Theatre Company in Galway, Ireland, Nancy Meckler at Shared Experience Theatre, Katie Mitchell at The Other Place, and Lynne Parker at Rough Magic.

GARRY HYNES met me in her office at the Abbey Theatre

towards the end of her tenure there. There was no doubt that Hynes was under tremendous stress as artistic director of Ireland's major national theatre. 'There are huge pressures', she said, 'and obviously the thing that suffers most is your own work because, in terms of priorities, that has to come second to the running of the theatre.'

Yet the strain of her dual position launched Hynes immediately into a discussion of her process. 'I think what attracted me to theatre in the first place and why I continued to do it at university was because I enjoyed so much – and still do – the sense of being involved with a group of people in pursuing a mutual objective. It seems this is the essence of theatre. This process is at the root of directing a play but it's also at the root of running a theatre. I enjoy the process of building something, of a group of people sharing the same set of understandings about something and pursuing the same objective, and I find that is satisfied in me by running a theatre. However, there is a very great difference between being artistic director of a company like Druid Theatre Company and being artistic director of a national institution such as the Abbey. And there is no question of the fact that there have been times for me when the strain of the process of running a theatre is just something that I feel, "No, I don't want this." '

Hynes was equally articulate about the fact that there clearly is a rehearsal process. 'For instance, every time a play is read for the first time by the actors who are playing the roles, or indeed if the play is read by anybody, my sense of the play comes forward all the time. However much work I will have done, when I hear the actors come at it, something else happens. And that starts the process. Then it is really a sense of mutually exploring text. That is what we're about more than anything else . . . and I suppose inspiring ourselves. An actor inspires me as a director, and I hope that, as a director, I inspire an actor. I say, "Yes, perhaps it's about this" and the other person would say, "No, I don't think so, but I think it's this . . ." It really *is* a process, that's how I would characterise it. And it's best when it is *most* a process because it is organic to circumstances. I mean for me what crucially is the production is this time and place, these people, now. If I do this play in four weeks' time, it's even different than if I do it now. It is about that chemistry of these people, in this place and time, doing this. And out of that should grow something which is obviously about the play but also obviously about them too. You know, there is nothing more interesting than a person; and there is nothing more unique than people. The more the process is about the people who are creating it, the more exciting it becomes. It's the transforming quality of the individual and the material which to me is the most extraordinary thing about the theatre.'

Hynes likes to spend the first several days of rehearsal reading and exploring the text. She does not, however, like to have the actors sitting. 'To me basically it seems much more interesting to be standing in a circle reading a play than sitting down reading a play. It's not a literary process, so the sooner it can become three-dimensional the better.' Improvisation is not a part of Hynes's exploration, nor does she work with a choreographer. 'The types of language plays I do don't have the need for a choreographer.' Hynes usually stages her own fights and employs a fight choreographer only in the case of sword fights or when it's necessary to insure safety.

'I've always thought', Hynes explains, 'directing was common sense. I thought, well, this is terribly simple. Anyone can do it. What is it more than making this play live on stage? Taking this book and making it live up there on stage. To me it's like breathing in a sense. And I think when one begins to examine it, it's a bit like looking down from the high wire; that is, it isn't necessarily a constructive part of the process. So my sense of myself as a director is very much about what happens, what the relationship is with the actors and designers, and it's about that thing of beauty which does not belong to any one of us. It's about that thing we create. Details are terribly important. Yet I think sometimes I can lose sight of the overall objective of a production because I get so interested in making something wonderful that I don't stand back sufficiently enough. Passion is really important. But you can't be passionate unless you really

know the text, unless it means so...
wonderful thing about the process is that yo...
time; you learn from day to day, exploring a ...
worlds.'

Several years later, Hynes had returned to Druid a...
busily implementing her initiative of new plays and directing
Martin McDonagh trilogy as a joint production of Druid and
the Royal Court. Hynes is able to take McDonagh's quirky,
sometimes violent characters and imbue them with humour,
whimsy, tenderness, and passion. While one may be appalled at
some of the actions of the plays – a woman who scalds her
demanding mother with hot oil, a grave-digger and his assistant
who amuse themselves by demolishing skulls and bones with a
mallet on the parlour table, and a man who has cut off the ears
of his brother's beloved dog – Hynes manages to make the
perpetrators of these deeds somehow touching, human, believable, and universal. Without sacrificing the poetry and the lusty
Irish speech, Hynes makes the plays seem almost naturalistic. At
other times they achieve mythic, ritualistic dimension and
depth.

One could characterise Hynes's direction as taut, rhythmical,
precise, gutsy, and full of surprises. Above all she achieves a
remarkable sense of ensemble. It is evident that her actors
respect one another and that they work together comfortably
and skilfully. Hynes works in a culture she understands
completely and with a great sense of truth. There is no attempt
to hide ugliness. These rural Irish characters are drunken,
blasphemous, cruel, ridiculous, guilt ridden, and fabricators of
lies. The hand of a gifted director moulds what could be
disjointed, repulsive, and horrifying into a theatrically eclectic
whole in which humanity and compassion triumph.

NANCY MECKLER has been Artistic Director of Shared
Experience Theatre since 1988 and speaks of the differences
between freelance directing and directing for her own company. While her work is more conventional when directing in
an ad hoc situation, Meckler says, 'When I'm working for

what sort of a rehearsal
seven weeks' rehearsal.'
...ion of *War and Peace*, co-
...any had only nine weeks.
two rooms, and we almost

...ed Experience had a core of
she indicated that there is a
have returned more than once.
...and who've been through the
pro...   to the ones who haven't done it
before.' If act...   ...rstand where the process is going,
it can be very reassur...g to have actors around who have
experienced it and understand it.

Meckler explains, 'I spend the first days trying to free things
up, playing games being one method. Also simple physical
exercises which necessitate people having to touch each other.
Physical contact creates an easy familiarity and requires a certain
trust and giving-over of the self to another person. These games
and exercises do speed up the process of getting actors to
interact well together. I would also do exercises which get a
group working as a unit and try to get across the idea that you
can be connected with someone without simply copying each
other; a movement that counterpoints the other person's
movement can also link you with that person. Games that
develop group dynamics help people learn to pick up impulses
from one another and how to go with what other people are
giving out.' Besides games, Meckler emphasises improvisation –
improvising around the text, character improvisation that helps
an actor understand the character's main obsession, situations in
our lives that help us to understand what is happening in the
piece. For example, in *Anna Karenina*, the actors playing Anna
and Vronsky needed to get in touch with the elevated social
position held by Anna and her husband and the consequential
real threat that their affair posed. They created a parallel
contemporary improvisation. 'And it made it clearer to the

actors that it wasn't just about an affair, it was about an affair between two people whose lives were very much on show.'

Meckler believes in a very open rehearsal process. 'I think it's important to impart what you think the piece is about, what your basic theme is. So, in rehearsal, I would talk to the actors about what that is and then provide improvisations to help them to understand the basic themes or experiences that inform the piece. For example, when we were doing *Anna Karenina*, we talked about a theme we extracted from the book: It's about living one's life in relation to one's mortality. So we did various exercises that made everybody consider that instead of sitting down and having lots of chats. There are two main characters in *Anna Karenina*, and they both have a very different attitude towards mortality. We decided we would improvise Anna's and Levin's dream; the actors could do anything at all in the dream. Anything could happen. It was interesting how many images of birth and death came up in those dreams.' Playwright/adapter, Helen Edmundson, watched the dream improvisations and incorporated many of the images into the play itself.

After these improvisations, Meckler says, 'I would be open to anything they [the actors] might offer. Often actors bring something which deepens the interpretation. I invite people to talk quite a bit in the beginning because I feel they need to and want to and will feel frustrated unless they get a chance to. But I prefer not to talk. As quickly as possible I try to do things, and if someone has a point to make, well, let's think of a way we can actually do it and then see whether or not it makes sense. I try to cast actors who are going to be open to my techniques of working, and I'll listen to anyone at any time: Anything anybody wants to do they can show me or they can try. I like to take my ideas off of things that happen in rehearsal. Very often it's something they do that they don't even realise they're doing and I say, "Oh, you did this and this and this, and it gave me an idea for that." For me it's always about it being a collaboration, and the really theatrical ideas coming right off the floor.'

Besides the openness of her rehearsal process, Meckler believes that her work has a very strong visual sense and that it is highly emotional both for the actor and the audience. 'And recently with Shared Experience, I have looked for material that has allowed me to get into expressionism where the actors are physically expressing their inner lives. I'm fascinated by that, and it's the sort of thing one can't do so much when one works as a freelance director with very short rehearsal periods. But with Shared Experience obviously I can spend time on these things and train people, have more time for exercises, and choose material which will allow for that.'

I asked Meckler to discuss her directorial process in relation to a specific production, *War and Peace*. 'The decision to adapt *War and Peace* came out of a brain-storming session. These choices are usually a gut feeling in the pit of your stomach. I actually feel a physical excitement at the idea of doing a piece but I can't usually justify it intellectually. Later, once I'm working on it, then I realise, "Ah, now I know why I wanted to do this."'

Leo Tolstoy's masterpiece was a commissioned work, adapted for Shared Experience by Helen Edmundson, who has also adapted *The Mill on the Floss* and *Anna Karenina*. 'They're very unusual adaptations', according to Meckler, 'because they're almost complete when we go into rehearsal. I think she's rare in the sense that she can picture the action, and she has a lot of very strong visual ideas, but also she will write something knowing we'll be able to find a way to abstract it physically.' Besides her desire to do new works, Meckler feels there are few existing plays that lend themselves to the expressionistic way of working that she relishes. 'I think the Greek tragedies lend themselves, and I think somebody like Molière lends himself because he was interested in these kinds of primal urges that obsess people. There aren't that many plays that ask for that kind of expressionism. In order to define expressionism – because people tend to think it's going to be a bit like Edvard Munch – I would say it's about making visual those things that are usually hidden. So we're talking about things that can be in a character's imagination or things which he or she might hide from other people. You can find ways on stage to physicalise what is really only being thought or felt.'

I asked Meckler to offer examples of both the physicality and the expressionism that inform *War and Peace*. She chose two. 'There is a scene in *War and Peace* that was written as a traditional firing squad, which is an image we all know and understand: we know the form of it, and what it would look like if it were done on film.' Rather than create a literal firing squad on stage, Meckler states, 'I would be interested in trying to physicalise the underneath, trying to find a physical expression of the horror of the firing squad from the point of view of the people who are firing and from the point of view of the people who are being shot at.' Meckler would divide the actors into groups and let them explore the image, or they might explore it in a naturalistic manner and then discuss the scene's meaning. 'For Tolstoy', Meckler believes, 'participation in a firing squad is hugely dehumanising. Can you actually ask someone, in the name of whatever political idea, to stand in a line and shoot another person? The people who fire often seem unfeeling whereas Tolstoy's view is that they are very distressed. So that became the challenge: to present a firing squad; but the physicality should somehow express the inner life of the soldiers. One of the solutions that came up was that the guard doing the blindfolding would actually hold the person who was about to be shot, stand next to him, so that victim and soldier were both looking towards the gun, but the guns were the audience. In this way you got a real sense of the horror of the person who was holding the victim. So it became a metaphorical or inner image of what it would be like to participate in a firing squad.

'In the battle scenes, we wanted to be true to Tolstoy and express the horror of it. He describes the battle scene as something beautiful, which gradually deteriorates into chaos. We had both men and women playing soldiers. In trying to express the horror of being on a battlefield rather than create a realistic representation, we tried to create the chaos and fear and blood without rifles. The actors had white silk scarves that they had used previously in social scenes. We found they could be stretched out as though they were instruments to threaten with, they could be snapped, they could be held across the chest to represent a standard. Later they were replaced by red scarves which were held to parts of the body as if they were wounds. I think something like that can be more distressing than pretending somebody's actually been shot on stage. It allows the audience to create the real battlefield in its mind.'

It is perhaps this exploration of the physical and internal that made Meckler's move into film so graceful even without any film training. 'My son gave me a book for Christmas before I was about to make *Sister My Sister*. It was called *A Beginner's Handbook to Film Directing*,' she laughs. 'I tried to read it but I didn't get very far.' Although Meckler has enjoyed her foray into film, she says she would not like to do it exclusively. 'The time you actually spend directing actors is quite minimal.'

In some ways *War and Peace*, which Meckler regards as quite filmic, reflected her sojourn into the new medium. 'I think *War and Peace* fits together like a film on the stage because I had just been editing a film and had enjoyed the idea that you can come into a scene at any moment and that you can leave something before the audience gets too familiar with it, or you can offer surprises by starting something later than you thought you were going to start it. So *War and Peace* has this enormous fluidity, one scene cutting across the other. I think the film work has influenced the stage and probably vice versa.

'People often ask "How did you find the switch, going from theatre to film?" As a theatre director I've always been fascinated with the idea that the frame can tell a story: that the placement on stage, where characters are in relation to each other, and in relation to the furniture and the architecture should be part of the story telling. In the same way sometimes when you look at a painting you can sense the relationships between the figures. I've always been interested in trying to make that clear so that the production is telling as much of the story visually as it is verbally. In fact, I'm probably more interested in making the visual work than I am in making the words work, and so film was like a great gift. Suddenly you can look at things from different angles, or you can cut in close, or move further away. And if you say to the designer, "This table has to represent this, or this room has to reverberate with this," in the film world people take that seriously and get excited about the fact that you care about the colour of the flowers or the length of the tablecloth. I feel everything in the frame should be helping to tell the story, that nothing should be there just in order to create a background.

'*Sister My Sister* is about two maids who spend a lot of time in the kitchen. Realistically the kitchen would be full of all sorts of cooking equipment, but I wanted the kitchen to be almost a prison with a sense of desolation. So we took out all the props and made it very spare, more spare than a kitchen would be, so that you might get a complete frame with only the actress and a scrubbing brush behind her on the window sill. But because that scrubbing brush is the only object in the picture, it becomes something that actually adds to her emotional state. The scrubbing brush actually plays a part. I am fascinated by that and always have been.' Her more recent film, *Alive and Kicking*, is a relationship film in which one of the characters is HIV positive. 'It's about a dancer, and I love that world. I took dancing lessons as a child and wanted to be a dancer for many years, and I had a chance to put that world on film.'

In spite of her successful film work, Meckler is still very much a person of the theatre. She explains with an example from *Anna Karenina*. At a certain point, Anna becomes addicted to morphine as an escape from how unbelievably complicated and painful her life has become. 'Together with the actress and our movement person, we created a movement sequence which was repeated every time Anna took morphine. For me what's exciting is that Tolstoy could write at length about why Anna took morphine, what it meant to her, what she'd lost in her life, and what she was longing for, and we could express so much of that in one movement pattern. That seems to me to be a totally theatrical solution. It wouldn't work on film. It's something that needs to happen live.' Carrying this idea a step further, Meckler believes that a director can work with actors to a point where even in stillness the body can be incredibly expressive: just sitting in a chair, relating to a chair, the body contacting the chair. 'I find it very exciting that you can actually know someone's in distress by the way he or she is sitting in a chair – not through signals – but through something much more central.' We often believe it's the words that tell us what a person is feeling or thinking, when in fact, Meckler tells us, these messages are conveyed through what we see and not through the words we hear.

I asked Nancy Meckler what she thought people might say about her work that distinguishes her from other directors. She pondered, 'I wonder what they would say?' Then she added, 'Here at Shared Experience we're often asked to describe our work so we can help those who sell our shows. People tell me that seeing my productions is an emotional experience, something that's felt and that you think about later. It isn't a cerebral experience; it's an emotional experience first and foremost. That doesn't mean that it doesn't engage your intellect because there's often a strong intellectual line to what we are doing. But the actual experience for the audience is something they feel. I think that's a great compliment.'

Meckler summarises her very clear and succinct rehearsal process, saying, 'I want there to be as much freedom as possible, but I also make it clear that in the end I will make the choices. My work tends to be rather elegant. I love line and direction. Once I've got the raw material of what something is going to be, I find myself wanting to give it form, form which reflects the content, not form which is just elegant in itself.

'I want people to feel free to try anything, to be as creative as possible. I'm attracted to scripts which deal with universal themes, plays about the meaning of life and the ambivalence of being human and the complexity of human nature. I'm keen to understand what drives a character. If you can define that "want", then everything should fit into that, and even a seemingly two-dimensional character becomes human. I'm not particularly attracted to scripts which are trying to recreate the problems of modern life or political problems that are facing us at the moment. I'm attracted to large universal themes.'

When I asked her to name her strength as a director, Meckler responded, 'I'm good at finding emotionally truthful actors to begin with, people who can really engage an audience's emotions although I find casting excruciatingly difficult, and I'm always full of self-doubt when I'm doing it. I have a strong visual sense and my productions are physically potent: the use of space and light and colour. I think I can nurture actors, but also challenge them, and give them courage to go beyond themselves.'

KATIE MITCHELL's production of Gorki's *The Last Ones* was previewing in the Abbey's Peacock Theatre while I was in Dublin interviewing Garry Hynes and Lynne Parker. I saw the production and recognised Katie Mitchell at the back of the theatre; but, understanding the pressures and tensions of previews, I made no attempt to speak to her that night. Besides, we had tentatively scheduled a meeting time for early March. March came, and she was off in Norway, preparing herself for directing Ibsen's *Ghosts* at the RSC. Finally we planned a meeting at Stratford, but Jane Lapotaire had been struck with a virus that not only took her out of the Kenneth Branagh *Hamlet* but forced the postponement of the first *Ghosts* rehearsals and hence Mitchell's arrival in Stratford. I arrived at the stage door for our appointment only to find a note of apology and explanation. But I had run out of time, and it appeared that Katie Mitchell – a young, intelligent, visible, and very successful director – would not be a part of this study. Fortunately, she consented to respond to written questions via cassette tape, resulting in comments that are very focused, articulate, and concise. Mitchell, an Associate Director of the Royal Shakespeare Company, is now Artistic Director of The Other Place in Stratford-upon-Avon where her productions of *Creation* and *Passion* were successfully mounted in 1997.

Speaking of her directorial process, she says, 'In general I tend to rehearse for six weeks. For the first one to two weeks, I create a situation where none of the actors read or act their own parts.' Mitchell learned this technique while working with Deborah Warner at the RSC. 'They don't read the part they're cast in until the last reading. So they've explored and experienced the play from a variety of viewpoints. This technique prevents the terrible nerves of the first readings, prevents the actors from worrying about their performances prematurely, and focuses on the group effort. During this time we, as a group, research the political, social, and economic context in which the play is set. We do movement work daily, and that movement work will be specifically designed to the needs of the world or the environment that we are creating. In many cases we'll do singing work – music that's going to be integrated into the performance. A cappella singing is also a very good way of bringing a group of people together. We will read the play probably daily during those one or two weeks, and also we will go through the play, as a group, word by word so that everyone understands everything in the play. We will do work on character. Each actor will go through the play and write down everything that his or her character says about his or her character and everything that other people in the play say about his or her character. Then as a group we will discuss each character in turn, looking at the function of the character in the play and also looking for the differences between the characters in the play. Where possible I would take the actors on a research trip. Sadly, in the case of something like *The Dybbuk*, set in the Ukraine, it didn't prove financially possible to take the actors to the Ukraine, but if I had my way they would have come with us on our research trip. In cases like that, we would return from our trip with slides, recordings from people we'd met, both of songs and stories, and even recordings of bird songs so that we give the actors an audio-visual representation of the experience that we had. After all, the research is primarily for their benefit.

'After this first one and one-half to two weeks, we read the play with everyone reading their own parts. Then we divide the play up into scenes and we rehearse, the aim of the rehearsals being to try the scene every which way, constantly looking for different ways, different choices, for each scene. Towards the end of the fifth week, we'll run the play to see what we have, to give the actors the opportunity to see their journey through the play, and to give me an opportunity to see the structure and the rhythm of the piece. And the last week, the sixth week, will be about making sense of the characters' journey through the play.'

Mitchell uses a great deal of improvisation and game playing both in the early stages of rehearsal and during the later stages of scene work. Status games are frequently used. 'If one feels the relationships are unclear in a scene, it can often help the actors to try out different status relationships on a scale from one to ten. You give each of the actors numbers between one and ten, and they have to act that status accordingly. It can be a very simple way of isolating where the relationship is inaccurate in what the actors are doing in the scene.' She finds physical exercises particularly helpful in sixteenth-century British texts. 'Simply running around the room and shouting can often liberate the material; or whispering at high speed; or in the case of metered verse, literally doing the text *just* obeying the meter can liberate meaning and so help the actor with the thoughts.'

Like so many of the directors, Mitchell sees her role primarily as that of a facilitator. 'I would hope that my role is to enable the actors to release the play. And I try to listen and to help them see as many different ways of doing each scene as possible – so they really feel they have tested all the different options. I try to create a rehearsal environment which is not hierarchical but rather is democratic, which is the hard way. It would be easy just to boss them around and to tell them where to stand and how to say the lines, just give line readings. But I don't think that yields the most thrilling work. Ultimately it's a democratic situation where everyone can say whatever they feel about what they are doing; anyone can propose a different way of looking at a scene, and it will be immediately and practically done. So first of all, I must throw open as many choices and respond to all the choices and propositions that the actors throw at me; later I must help them collate, choose what is right for them, focus what they are doing. Ultimately I think it's wiser to listen more than it is to speak as a director.'

LYNNE PARKER is the last of the women directly associated with a specific theatre. She is Artistic Director of Dublin's Rough Magic, which was established in 1984. It is interesting that two of the women who started off sharing leadership positions with men have subsequently relinquished that authority: Annabel Arden at Complicite, Julia Bardsley at both the Leicester Haymarket and the Young Vic; whereas Lynne Parker, who shared the directorship of Rough Magic with Declan Hughes, has become sole Artistic Director and since 1990 has been directing the work of her colleague who is now Artist-in-Residence. Parker has directed five of Hughes's plays.

'I won't say it's all been fun,' Parker muses, 'I mean you have to be prepared to put in five to seven years of total grasping. You're not earning any money, and you're not receiving any plaudits. There was a period right in the middle, say five or six years into the company, when we really didn't think we were going to survive. But we have, and we've learned a lesson about what we put ourselves through in the first years. I think that made us a stronger organisation. Every first day of rehearsal, I feel like a complete novice, and I've been at it, what, fifteen years? I don't think that's going to change although I'm on about my fiftieth show.'

At her first rehearsal, Parker rejects the idea of the director's speech about plans and objectives. 'I stopped doing that years ago because you always end up contradicting yourself.' Like so many of the women directors, Parker likes to begin by playing a lot, talking about the text, encouraging thoughts from her actors, and struggling through some degree of rough blocking. 'The actors are always very awkward: they can't move, they can't talk, and they feel very self-conscious. So the first week is about trying to get them to feel easy about what they are doing. I'm eager to get anything going, even if it's horrifically wrong, just so you have something to depart from. Do anything. Encourage the actors to kick back at you and say, "That's an appalling idea . . . why are we doing it?" Keep questioning. The whole way our company works demands input. It's not an option; it's absolutely vital.'

Responding to my questions about the use of improvisation, Parker answered, 'I'm not keen on it to be quite honest, and I don't feel completely comfortable using it. You really have to take each moment as it comes. I will know by looking at something whether or not its wrong. I may not know what's wrong, but I have to use my intuition which guides me as to the next step. Sometimes actors may be running a scene, and you simply don't know what you're going to say to them when they finish. You just have to hover on the brink until the next idea comes. With experience I'm confident enough now to allow myself to hover, to go for the idea that comes to me. It may be the wrong idea, and when I see it I'll know that, and the actors know I know, and they trust me. That's really all I can say about the day to day process.'

Flexibility is the key to Parker's directorial process, knowing how to spot what's useful and to scrap what isn't. 'You've got to be able to change, and the actors have got to be able to go with you. Also you've got to know how far to push them. There are times when you might want to move on to something else, and you know they need time to assimilate what they've done. You really have to be sensitive to what the actors need. Sometimes I will actually stop rehearsal short and say, "Look, I don't know why but this just isn't working, and you're going to have to let me think about it for a bit, and I promise I'll come in tomorrow with a fresh approach." There's no point in me pretending that something is working when it isn't.'

Collaboration is another key to Parker's work. She believes actors are both bright and intuitive. 'They know what to do. They love that . . . when you say to them, I want you to try to find some solution to that. Here are the problems. Now go on and deal with them. You'll find it so much more useful than if you sit there hammering at them that it's got to be this way or that way, do this way, do that way, over-working them and making them think they've got no creative sense. You may not arrive at what you thought you wanted, but it's quite often a lot more appropriate.'

When I asked Parker whether or not she divided her play into units and objectives, she answered that she wouldn't know how to do that. You have to know how a play is structured', she said, 'and what effect that has on an audience. That's all. And you have to keep asking those questions: "What am I getting from this performance picture that I see before me? What information am I getting?" And I don't care how an actor gets that information; they can do exercises until they are blue in the face; or they can just come in, learn the lines, stand there, and not even think about it. That's not my concern; my concern is what information gets over. If it's fake I don't care; if they're pretending I don't care. (I think you can always tell when it's fake; maybe with really brilliant actors you can't.) It's not for me to judge the right or wrong of their technique. If it works, it works. That's all I'm interested in.'

Like a number of the directors, Parker will not permit smoking in the rehearsal room and does not welcome visitors. 'It's a very naked situation. People have asked me if they can come in and watch a bit of rehearsal. They say, "You won't notice me." But I do notice them and so do the actors.' Parker drew an interesting analogy. She said no one comes into the writer's study and stares over his or her shoulder while the writing process is going on. 'That study is the writer's place; the rehearsal room is our place.'

Although the process is very important to Parker, she maintains that she is always working towards a product. 'If the process starts dominating, then what's it for? I mean you're putting on these things for people to see. The idea is to communicate something to an audience. If you're not doing that, then what's the point? It's always got to be about the finished product. There are many ways of getting there, and you've got to be able to satisfy the actors along the way, or you won't get to the product. But it's always for the audience, and I am the audience's representative in that rehearsal room. If it's not clear to me, if I'm confused by it, then what about them?

Actually I would like to detach myself in the late stage of the rehearsal process, go away, let the actors work by themselves, then come back in and watch what they are doing. Then it may be clearer to me where there are gaping holes in comprehension. You've got to explain yourself. The audience has got to feel that you knew what you were doing.'

In her very candid manner, Parker concludes, 'I think I'm slightly addicted to this process because a lot of the time I hate it. I hate being in the rehearsal room. It drives me crazy. I'm frustrated, bored, raging. But I keep doing it. It seems finally to give me some sort of delight. And I'll tell you what that delight is. It's not when the production has opened. I hate seeing the show then. The part of the whole process which gives me the most pleasure, and in our company is the most hurried, is the technical rehearsal. Once the performances are in place and the play has a shape, I love playing. I think I'm a complete child at heart. I like having a big toy box at my disposal: the theatre, the lights, the sound, the music, the actors, the costumes. I love playing with them, making pictures, establishing the rhythm of the production. Fine tuning. Getting everything slick. Powerful and confident.'

In summarising her abilities as a director, Parker says, 'I'm inclined to be a little disorganised and sometimes avoid the ordinary things I should take care of. Worse than that, I'm probably too willing to let people run with an idea that I know is not going to work because I don't want to have to break it to them that they're barking up the wrong tree. Sometimes I just don't push people hard enough. Actors are mischievous; sometimes they'll tell you they can't do something when I know they can. On the other hand I've got a lot of imagination, a very good sense of humour, and I am acutely aware of the kinds of vibrations that are generated between people. I've got good instincts.'

These, then, are the women who are associated with specific theatres, who balance administrative duties with directorial ones. Although several of them feel the weight of their heavy responsibilities and dual roles, they truly enjoy running a theatre and value not only the control that their position of authority offers them but also the freedom to choose their plays, their actors, and their colleagues. In spite of this power, they unanimously spurn the concept of director as authority figure and cherish a process of collaboration, communication, and mutual trust.

CHAPTER 5

Rehearsals reveal the play

Phyllida Lloyd says that if she were ever confronted with running her own theatre, she would run screaming in the other direction. The following group of women would probably agree with Lloyd and have shunned – or abandoned – the administrative burden of artistic directorship in order to gain or maintain their status as freelance practitioners. It is interesting that several of these women have been artistic directors. Annie Castledine was Artistic Director of the Derby Playhouse from 1987 to 1990, Brigid Larmour held that position at the Contact Theatre in Manchester from 1990 to 1994, and Sue Sutton Mayo was Resident Director at the Library Theatre in Manchester from 1991 to 1993.

These are the directors who now, whenever a job is finished, join the ranks of the unemployed until the next job materialises. By and large they direct a wide range of productions: television, educational drama, and opera among them. Often they travel more; from regional theatre to London to the Continent or the United States. They are enterprising, resourceful, and resilient.

ANNIE CASTLEDINE's production of *Marching for Fausa* was in preview when I saw it, the night before I was scheduled to meet with the director. I remember looking around the theatre, wondering which one she was. My quest was not difficult. In the back row sat a large woman with a seriousness, intensity, and focus that were unmistakable. We did not meet the next day; Castledine was swamped. But she invited me to Totnes in south Devon where she was directing Sheila Yeger's *Variations* at the Dartington College of the Arts. So, weeks later,

81

we had our first conversation in front of a roaring fire in a comfortable old inn for several hours.

Castledine was very articulate about her rehearsal process. She likes to spend one day sitting around a table, reading and talking about the script. The second and third days are often spent dealing with archival material; for example, Castledine was preparing for her second production of *From the Mississippi Delta* by Endesha Ida Mae Holland, having directed the first English production of the play at the Young Vic in 1989. 'Even though the performers are black, they're not American black, and I'm not taking for granted that they know the history of the civil rights movement. I've got a colleague who is an archivist at the British Film Institute, and every bit of wonderful material that takes us through to the heart of this particular period will be a part of those two days. And music will be a part of those two days. Also the nurturing of the performer is crucially important. That will always be a feature of the early part of the rehearsals.'

From the outset of the rehearsal process, Castledine demands that the whole energy be very positive. 'There will be a row if it isn't!' she warns. She does a lot of exercises on that positive energy, the philosophy of and reasons for the work. Especially when working with younger and less experienced actors, Castledine stresses interdependence, the sense of ensemble, the importance of the quality of life of all the participants, their responsibility towards their fellow actors. 'Sometimes there are performers of middle age who have reached a certain level of expertise and don't want to endure the rigours of ensemble and will do so only if you can point out that it's hugely desirable.'

Playing is important to Castledine, and she has developed a unique approach to involve all of her actors all of the time. 'I like the actors to look at all the other roles. Not just their own. I work ensemble, totally ensemble, whatever the play. So all the performers are at all rehearsals all the time. It doesn't matter who the performers are. They have to agree to this before we engage them. They are all totally involved all the time because they are playing all the time. They're either supporting the work that's going on on the floor or they are in fact pursuing that [theatrical moment] in twos. I will probably divide the company up and say, "Let's look at this moment. Let's *all* look at it. *You* look at this moment, *you* look at this moment, and then we'll see the result of our imaginative endeavours." Let's take a stage direction in *Variations*: she puts her hand in the chocolate and smears his mouth with chocolate. I divide the company into twos and ask them to play that and interpret it, and then we'll share the result of that. So we're always playing with the text. Then we say, "That's a brilliant idea; that's a lovely idea. Do you want to use that?" I'll leave the directing of that moment to another day because we've already explored that moment. So, I'll go on and work on another bit of the text and let those ideas about that moment of the text wash around a little. I won't use it or destroy it or comment on it. Sometimes an actor who is not playing the role has played that moment, and it's absolute perfection. So the actor playing the role has to take that on board really. He or she can either use it or not use it or be inspired by it. But it gives you a wonderful conversation, we're all talking together, and there is tremendous generosity within a company. If there is temperament, then it's absolutely shared and open. We did have a little bit of temperament in *Marching for Fausa*. An actor could not find the dynamics of a particular piece of text at all, and everybody did play with that moment. There was a certain objective – not just to reproduce the text – so it was an improvisation, too. I wanted to take this to an absolute extreme. It yielded some very interesting work, and from one particular pair, inspirational work. The actor playing the role knew that particular work he'd seen was absolutely spot on but hadn't got, at that moment, the generosity of spirit either to say so or to absorb it for himself. It took a long time before he was able to do that.' Castledine concludes that actively playing with the moment is much better than talk. She says, 'I don't like a lot of talking in rehearsal; I like a lot of doing.'

In her rehearsal process, Castledine maintains that she likes huge precision. 'There's a lot of work on playing, a lot of work on exploring, a lot of free-range work, but when it comes down to it, I very much favour the presentational style of performing.

Therefore there will be an enormous amount of play on absolute precision of intentions, huge awareness of audience, consciousness of every single moment; the intention of every single moment. I'll throw up the scene in every which way. A scene will be explored in a huge number of ways depending on the complexity of the scene and whether or not it can stand that. And it depends on how long a rehearsal period. I like to rehearse a production as though it were a workshop. I'm asking for precision all the time but I never want anything to be totally settled.' An actor must be precise, Castledine believes, must make a decision and play that decision even though the next day a different choice can be made. 'So that will be the kind of work that's being done, but always leaving a huge area of possibility within those strict parameters. And always asking everybody to be involved, and always really having a workshop on the text as opposed to "We are going into a production".'

Annie Castledine is confident about what she likes but also is aware 'that there might be something I *really* like just around the corner but don't know about yet. I want to find that, so there is continuous surprise and excitement. I'm driven to do it, and I don't want to be doing anything else, and I want to do it continuously. I love, love working with performers. It's constant experiment and adventure, a quest for seeking to understand what it is that actually makes performance and process come together in that glorious moment when the sublimity is created in the theatre. Can the charisma of the performer be enhanced? Yes, it can. Can it be found if it's not there, can it be made? No, I don't think it can be.' Enhancing that charisma is what Castledine believes the rehearsal process is partly about, helping the performer reach heights he or she did not know could be achieved. Castledine likes rehearsals that are multi-faceted. There will be music, singing, a lot of physical work, a great deal of exploration. She is seeking – whether in music, dance, or singing – to create an imaginative response to the text, to free the imagination of the actor from the literal to the creative imagination. When I asked her to develop this idea, Castledine explained that if you look at a window frame and conclude that it should have glass in it, that's literal imagination. If you conclude that a play written in 1886 must be costumed in the period clothes of 1886, that's literal imagination. 'It is that ordinariness that I think is a curse, and the inability to see that time can be transcended. All performers must have the ability to see that someone like Ibsen is not limited by time or by ideas that may have occurred in a certain way at a certain time.'

Perhaps above all Annie Castledine brings an avowed passion to her work that she hopes will be transferred to her actors. She expects, even demands, their best work and highest level of commitment to the project. She likes going to the edge with a production and is not afraid of failure. Summarising her approach, Castledine says, 'I'm always working on texts that either I've been involved in the creation of or texts which are incredibly familiar to me because they are a part of my blood stream, and I've always wanted to work with them. Idea is important, what the play says, what you think the play says, what you'd like the play to say. The nurture that the text might be offering is incredibly important. The physical life of the play is hugely important. I'll always do the physical things; it will always be an adventurous physical production whatever the text. There will always be music. There will always be certain basic design elements.'

Castledine is unique in emphasising the importance of an assistant director to her workshop-like process. She continuously asks an assistant director to comment, to work with and in front of her, to be a part of the decision making, to develop his or her own relationship with the performers. 'When you leave the production, which as a freelance director you do, they [the assistant directors] have a wonderful and real involvement – not a cosmetic involvement – with the performers and the production.' In this way, Castledine believes, the assistant director becomes a respected person and also one who is being nurtured and trained. 'I find that working with young assistant directors is rewarding and invigorating. It gives me another responsibility. They are also in receipt of an oral tradition, and they become a part of your family. They continue to keep in contact with you; they invite you to their work, they take your ideas and then go further with them because they're so energetic and bushy-tailed. I love that. And they get you complimentary tickets to things they've done elsewhere! And the thing is, they're having a wonderful time, that's what!' And, oh, the good fortune for a young assistant director to work with a creative, passionate dynamo like Annie Castledine. Riding home on the tube after seeing *Marching for Fausa*, we met one of the actresses in that production. I asked her about Annie Castledine. She beamed, 'A great lady. A brilliant director.'

Annie Castledine chose to expand her discussion of process and production by selecting Marguerite Duras's *India Song*, which she co-directed with Annabel Arden at Theatr Clwyd. 'It was a moment where the process and the consummation of that process actually fused and celebrated one another. When I told Helena Kaut-Howson that I wanted to do *India Song*, she rang back and said, "You can't do that; it's impossible; it will fail."' But in spite of the odds, Howson allowed Castledine and Arden to proceed.

'The text of the two-hour piece is, of course, a physical text. There is a verbal text, a very complicated verbal text, but it is off stage, so there is no live sound to be heard on stage except for the sobs of the Vice-Consul of Lahore. Duras is exploring the space in front of the audience as an echo chamber: an echo chamber of events and situations which happen outside, an echo chamber as a space people pass through. So it's extremely problematic in the sense that no one has ever been there before, untrodden snow. And Annabel and I wanted to go there, wanted to see whether we could create and make it work or not. Therefore a physical language had to be found for the beats. We worked through an enormous amount of improvisation and physical work. It wasn't dance; nor did it have anything to do with any aspect of contemporary dance or ballet or tap. We were finding a way that could make natural movements formal, heightened, and fascinating. And through working with the performers, we found that vocabulary.'

When I asked Castledine to offer an example she said, 'The

moment when the Vice-Consul of Lahore explores the bicycle of Anne-Marie Stretter. Duras asks him to caress the bicycle. *How* is he to caress the bicycle? We worked as an ensemble and the whole company explored every problem through improvisation and exercises. So with bicycles all over the rehearsal room, how was this bicycle to be made love to? One actor, Robert Pickavance, worked on his own, unobserved for quite a long time, until I became riveted by what he was doing. In obeisance, he was minutely exploring it [the bicycle] without touching it, caressing every part of it without making any kind of physical contact. His spatial and physical relationship to the bicycle suggested images of a lover. The rehearsal was halted, and everyone looked at the actor while he worked. That exploration formed the centrepiece and point of reference for the physical style of the production.

'Lilo Baur played Anne-Marie Stretter. She's a famous Theatre de Complicite actress. Duras says that the character stands underneath the fan, lifts her arms to the fan, and then the arms suddenly drop; the heat is so intense. How do you explore the journey, the path, and then the collapse of those arms? It's not the same as the bicycle moment because there's nothing to caress. There was a tension in the reaching of the body and then a kind of heightened naturalism in the absolute slowness of the movement. Every part of that movement was so effortful, demanded so much energy in the overwhelming heat. The courage to explore that and complete it and sustain the image was unbelievable.

'There is a slow walk of the young attaché, Anne-Marie Stretter, and the ambassador in the garden of the French Embassy in Calcutta just after the rains have stopped, and there's that moment of refreshment before the heat settles in again. All the physical conditions within which people's bodies were moving had to be suggested by that movement, yet there had to be a degree of stylisation, such as everyone starting on the same foot. So there were choreographic concerns coupled with natural, realistic concerns. It was the figure of a dance, and yet they were not dancing. It was just fascinating experimental work. The translator, Barbara Bray, came to see it and felt it was definitive. The reviewers said they'd never seen anything like it. People came from London. Yet it was marginalised by the fact that it was performed at Clwyd, out of reach. All attempts for Annabel and me to explore it further have come to nothing. It's a great pity. The National Theatre commissioned it twenty years ago, and I really wanted the National Theatre to allow us to develop it.' Castledine was clearly feeling the hurt of this rejection of what she regards as 'a most sublime process and highly successful production'.

BRIGID LARMOUR, although now associated primarily with the National Theatre's Shakespeare Unplugged was, at the time of our first meeting, Artistic Director of the Contact Theatre in Manchester; a middle-scale repertory theatre that tries to balance new plays and classics, plays by women and by men, in almost equal numbers. Larmour confessed she started in theatre because of her immense love of Shakespeare. 'I think it's the most fantastic writing, and when you perform it properly it's like being a medium to some sort of other spirit. There is an extraordinary charge in the language that, when properly performed, is the most exciting thing I've ever experienced in theatre – and that doesn't mean cerebral and detached. On the contrary it's very visceral, very emotional. I learned a great deal about that from Cicely Berry, who is head of voice at the Royal Shakespeare Company, and Patsy Rodenburg, who is head of voice at the Royal National Theatre. I also learned a lot from Terry Hands, whom I assisted for three years at the RSC. He's capable of absolute brilliance in mise-en-scène in terms of the distribution of people on the stage, the rhythm of a production, the use of lighting, of music, and of design. I have a totally different approach to actors, which is much more open and collaborative, but I think I have taken on board a great deal of what I learned from him about mise-en-scène. These are the two things that started off being important to me: really detailed, accurate, emotional text work and a great interest in mise-en-scène, design, spectacle, rhythm, lighting, and sound. Then in recent years I have added an interest in choreography and in developing the physical side of theatre.'

While she begins her process with careful text work, Larmour does not use Stanislavsky's vocabulary of super-objective, objective, and action. She explains that she has never found that language helpful but instead finds it rather clinical and irritating. She prefers to study the imagery, the poetry, and the rhythms of the piece. Working at Juilliard several years ago, Larmour found the students reluctant to play a scene spontaneously without first agreeing on intentions and objectives. 'That way', Larmour explains, 'you have no accident, no chance, no invention, no spontaneity. It's a very good system and a lot of the best directors I know use it, but it doesn't work for me. I'd much rather have an actor try something, and the other actor try something completely off the wall in response, that will open up an area of meaning in the play that you would not have known existed if you sat down with your Cambridge degree and worked it out. So mostly I will use that kind of vocabulary by saying, "Your intention isn't clear there. What are you playing?" I don't want to know *in advance* what the actor is playing or I can't tell if it's being actually done.'

Besides careful text work, Larmour is profoundly interested in dramaturgical work on new scripts, 'trying to help the play become its best self. I'm not interested in trying to rewrite people's plays or trying to make them into something else, but if I do a new play it's because I see something there that the writer is trying to do. I do a lot of working with the writer, creating workshops to try and develop a script to its best potential both before and during rehearsals. During rehearsals of the first production of a play, you have an overriding duty to the play, to serve it, and make it live as the writer has written it. But when you do a play that's been done 200 times, you can do what you like because it has an independent existence. So there's a process of midwifery: going through line by line with the writer, saying, "That bit doesn't work; the rhythm's funny here, or what do you mean by that?" ' Larmour does not, however, like to have the playwright at all rehearsals because he or she needs a bit of distance from the script at certain times.

Trying to articulate the actual rehearsal process, Larmour states, 'Everything starts with the text, a lot of reading of the text, a lot of discussion of the text, and a lot of questioning of the text. If there is choreography, the first week of rehearsals involves building the physical language of the group. With a new play, you're testing the text and putting it through its paces, where it works, where you understand it, where you don't understand it. You try to find out who the characters are. They may not be there yet from an acting point of view.

'In a classic play or verse text, I am doing a great deal of work on rhythm, meter, use of consonants, use of vowels. What exactly does that word mean? What are you thinking about when you say this word? It's no use having an image and not knowing what it means. That is completely dead. All those kinds of text things: they tell you about character, they tell you about emotions. They are the map of the play and until you have a grip and the actors have a grip on the text and know what it means, and what it feels like to say it, and how to say it, how to achieve saying it technically, you can't rehearse. It's a waste of time. And most of the bad Shakespeare acting that you see is the result of people not really knowing what they're saying; they're one step behind the language. Whereas when people pull the language into themselves, then they can fly and they can do extraordinary things.

'So I'll start in a very conventional way by presenting a model and explaining how we came to the model and what I want to concentrate on in the production. I have a sort of a blueprint of the production in my head. Let's suppose it's a blueprint of an apartment. I know that there will be a kitchen and a bathroom and that the living room will have warm colours. But where the chairs go in the living room can be discovered in rehearsal, and actually if somebody comes up with an idea which means moving the bathroom, then I'll just have to rejiggle the architecture of the place. In some scenes I will know that I want to do this last speech of Faustus's on a twenty-foot ladder, and I want Lucifer coming down and stopping Faustus from coming up. In other scenes we can place the action anywhere we want it. I don't have it all planned out, and I don't know how a scene's going to work until we try it, and it reveals its meaning; because its meaning is three-dimensional and emotional and rhythmic and not just verbal.' Essentially, Larmour tries to give a coherent framework within which her actors can work. That framework can be changed and redrafted. 'It's try and see,' she adds.

Brigid Larmour does not use improvisation. 'The text is the text, and the text is what we're here to do.' Sometimes Larmour improvises the moment before a scene happens as a means of clarifying that scene for the actors, and she likes any scene to have an improvisational quality as though anything might suddenly happen. 'But', she says, 'I've never found any value at all in improvising words in a classic text because the words are the architecture of the play.' She has used improvisation with new plays in order to reveal dimensions of the characters. 'I will sometimes give one person a direction that takes the scene in a particular direction; or I'll give an objective to one performer and allow the other performer to respond to that.'

Commitment to text, technical mastery of text, emotional openness, truth, and physical flexibility – these are the directorial elements that are important to Larmour. Her greatest commitment, she believes, is to the emotional truth of a production. 'I think the thing I say most is, "I don't believe you," or "What's that you said? What did you mean?" '

Larmour concludes, 'I've got a good analytical intelligence; I've got an emotional affinity with certain kinds of writing; I have a very good eye for design and stagecraft. I'm a good craftsperson. I can make good pieces of theatre. And I know how to marry my head and my heart. I respect other people, and I enjoy working with other people, and I think I can bring out the best in people because I value them without giving up my own power.'

My most recent discussion with Larmour centred almost exclusively on Shakespeare Unplugged. 'It started off', Larmour states, 'as a really incredibly unglamorous, very low-budget, tiny-cast, theatre-in-education project: six actors in a van going around to schools, workshop in the morning, performance in the afternoon. "This is lunatic!" I thought. The idea of chopping a Shakespeare play down to an hour and a half seemed like an absolute sacrilege. Yet I thought this was the most tremendous opportunity to make theatre in a different way because you had this community of people for a whole day, and one of the things I go on about is that if we are going to compete with cinema and television we have to celebrate and exploit the fact that we bring people together in a room as a community, and the experience sometimes has a sense of communion. So I thought, "Which Shakespeare play would I like to do with six actors?" I always have a few bubbling along at the top of the list, and some that come and go. Could I find a play that I was interested in that didn't rely on more than six protagonists or where I could see the doubling working? And I realised, of course, that in *Henry V* frequently there are many characters on stage but very often only a few of them are carrying the story. Then, of course, I remembered all the wonderful stuff about the Globe "This wooden O", "Think, when we talk of horses, that you see them/Printing their proud hoofs i' th' receiving earth", "Piece out our imperfections with your thoughts". And I thought, "This is like a manifesto for non-naturalistic theatre, isn't it?" We could do it with six actors plus a hundred others in the audience. So I thought, "Let's evolve a kind of promenade where the audience is in the world of the play." So, of course, the audience is Henry's army. We structured it so that each actor had a company of people, and each actor shared a relationship with that group, which in turn felt it had an investment in the play.'

In the morning the workshops, which are run by Larmour's colleague, Richard Hahlo, looked at language, structure, story, and characters but also imaginatively explored what it might be like to be involved in a war, what it might be like to sit on the night before battle wondering whether you were going to survive it. The workshop groups were also taught simple instructions like 'Make camp', which meant sit on the floor, and other signals to sit, kneel, or move to one end or the other of the room. 'So whenever we wanted to change the acting area, the actors would shout one of these commands. So you could suddenly find the whole audience backed up against one wall, and then Henry rushes through carrying a ladder and says, "Once more unto the breach . . ." to them and looks up at the French king, who is standing on a vaulting horse, like in a gym, at the other end of the hall. Always this relationship with the audience was part of the story. One of the most powerful moments occurred when the audience sat scattered on the floor for Act IV, scene I where the soldiers talk about "all those legs, arms and heads chopped off in a battle" the night before Agincourt. These actors were sitting among the audience. When Henry comes to them for "The little touch of Harry in the night", the audience had the excitement of the king coming to them, talking to them, and being among them. It gives the audience a very direct involvement in the story and a sense that their participation is the essential part of the event.'

In a similar way, in *The Tempest* the audience was the island, so Ariel commanded the audience to move in certain places. Stones were placed throughout the audience, so that when Antonio, Sebastian, and Alonso are lost, they tried to step from stone to stone through the audience. 'Then at a certain point we were reshuffling where the island was, and we did a game with the audience where they moved the stones around and some of the "bad" characters didn't know what was happening. They couldn't understand how these things were moving through the air. The audience was collaborating with Ariel in making a world in which people could go on a spiritual journey – or not as the character chooses.' In another instance in the masque scene, which became a kind of carnival, suddenly the audience danced and sang, 'Honour, riches, marriage-blessing'. Although they had learned the song in the morning workshop, they did not know until the performance how it would be used.

Larmour's adaptation is done in advance, although it invari-ably changes through the course of the four-week rehearsal period. 'You have to find things out through the process. You find things out from the actors about what works and what doesn't work. Also at the end of each day of rehearsal, the company talks about how events from that rehearsal might be used in the workshop process. Again in rehearsal it's text, text, text. It's a question of how you release yourself into what's there and how you release what's there by playing with it yourself. Patsy Rodenburg has done voice work on all of these projects, and I find her brilliant at helping people release their vocal and emotional power.

'We also read the play a lot in the beginning and I try to give the actors some idea of the crazy process they're in for doing Shakespeare Unplugged, a feeling for the production we're trying to create, and an idea of the parameters, so they know that within that structure anything is possible. It's all about them being absolutely on the language and absolutely free with it. We do exercises on text, and we do exercises to do with instinctual connection between the actors. When we come to play with scenes, I'm not interested in it being done right; I'm interested in the words being inhabited. One of the exercises I use is based on an exercise that Monika Pagneux uses, a very simple exercise involving a bamboo garden cane and keeping a connection between two actors through this stick. It's a playful, instinctive connection rather than a cerebral connection. I use it to free up the actors' relationship with the text and with each other. By the time we've got the text free in people's mouths and bodies, we play the scenes using sticks. It's incredibly liberating because you're always connected, and if you're not connected the other actor knows, if the stick drops.

'Very often at the early stage of rehearsal we'll play a scene a few times. I'll push it in one direction and then I'll push it in another. Then I'll say, "Well, it's not quite this and it's not quite that, but there were flashes of something here" and then I'll leave it to marinate for a bit because people need just to allow things to go deeper. The real trick, I think, with Shakespeare text is getting it to the point where the actor has taken it into his or her blood stream and understands all the things about rhythm, rhyme, alliteration, how it feels physically in the mouth, what's making the character say that. I'm not at all interested in sub-text. It's all in the text.'

Larmour continues, 'I had a very telling moment in one of my rehearsal periods. There was an academic sitting in part of the time – someone who was writing an accompanying document – and we were having a conversation, and one of the actors, very nervous about Shakespeare, thought he didn't understand it, thought that he couldn't do it. Wonderful actor. He said, "I don't know what this line means." I said, "What do you think it means?" He answered, "Well, I'm not sure but . . ." Suddenly this academic said, "Well, it's the Elizabethan conceit of the corruption of the rose, isn't it? Blah, blah, blah, blah, blah." And I said, "Yes, thank you." This was a very unhelpful intervention. It prevented the actor from being able, with my help, to work out the sense for himself and to "own" the meaning. It reinforced his feeling that other (highly educated, middle-class) people knew better than he did. It was infuriating, however well intentioned.'

Certainly the promenade style is not the only way Larmour plans to work, nor does she feel it would be effective for every Shakespeare play. 'I've been evolving not just a style of production but a style of what the performance is, a form of performance. It's incredibly personal. It's openness and emotional honesty and moral complexity that I'm looking for, the evolving nature of the performance, the idea that it is not fixed. Sometimes you hear a sentence spoken by an actor, and is it a line from T.S. Eliot? "Anatomised like a butterfly." Something that's dead and pinned down, so you can see its wings; but it's a dead sentence, not a living sentence.'

Henry V was strictly a school project, but with *The Tempest* and *Twelfth Night* a mixture of theatres, schools and community venues were played with audiences ranging in age from four to eighty. *Twelfth Night* came into the Cottesloe and toured out of Lincoln Center in New York in 1998. In our conversation, Larmour's pleasure in working with Shakespeare Unplugged was unmistakable. She has clearly found a venue and a method of working that challenges her, excites her passion and her intellect, and inspires her as a director. I hope she will write her book about the project; it is a programme that theatres all over the world might emulate.

PHYLLIDA LLOYD holds a very special place among the women represented here simply because she was the first to respond to my request for an interview and the first director with whom I met. I found Lloyd not only highly intelligent but also wonderfully articulate. Much of that meeting set the tone for all of the interviews to come and helped shape the questions I asked all of the others.

Much of Lloyd's discussion of her process revolved around Ostrovsky's *Artists and Admirers* which played in the RSC Pit in the 1993 season and around her 1992 Royal Court production of John Guare's *Six Degrees of Separation* starring Stockard Channing. Before commenting on the two productions, however, Lloyd outlined her basic approach. 'There is a pattern but it is always adapted to the circumstances. I try to base the shape of the rehearsal on the demands of the play and potential of the actors: how much process older actors participate in, for example. It might waste time and confidence to insist that a seventy-five-year-old actor improvise when he's never done so in his life; but that's not a reason not to ask other members of a company to do so. Part of the process is to release and inspire the individual, another part to unify the company.'

Because the company was working both with a translation and an adaptation of that translation, Lloyd did a huge amount of improvisation on *Artists and Admirers*. 'It was the first time I had committed to it thoroughly. The actors had been working together for a couple of years before the production and were trusting enough of each other truly to exploit the exercises. The play was set in the theatre and about a group of actors who had known each other for many years. We wanted to generate a great background of shared experience and domestic ritual which I felt working directly from the text might not release.'

Lloyd commented on the history of Ostrovsky productions in

England, many of which have demanded an expressionistic style of presentation: 'white-faced make-up, leaning at forty-five degree angles, characters who are either brutal, horrifying specimens or angels'. Lloyd believes, however, that Ostrovsky's later work, of which *Artists and Admirers* is an example, has become more 'complex, multi-layered, more Chekhovian, more ambiguous, richer, allowing all the characters to be at once both ridiculous and delightful. I felt that it demanded quite a light touch, and I felt that had we heightened the characterisations in a more commedia dell'arte sense, we might have destroyed the fabric of it. But sometimes in rehearsal we did think, gosh, should they be leaning at forty-five degree angles?'

The early stages of the rehearsal process were difficult, primarily because the actors had accepted the assignment on trust, before the adaptation was finalised. 'They were part of this very searching period where we were all trying to refine the text. And that was a tricky time where actors were fighting for more of a voice for their characters.' Lloyd says she did not assume an aggressive role, which would have been out of character, in the lively dialogue between adapter and actors. Ultimately it was about trust among the actors and their willingness to lay themselves on the line. 'We were doing work on the translation for the first three weeks, and then for two weeks we improvised, played games, did exercises trying to create the relationships. By now, of course, we were very familiar with the text even though we'd never rehearsed it. We did quite a lot of Stanislavsky "actioning" of the scenes, breaking into units and giving them titles, finding objectives. I see all that as one way of coming to some sort of shared understanding of what the structure of the piece is.'

These things, Lloyd explains, were used selectively for particular actors or pairs of actors. On the whole the young actors who had learned how to score their roles as a part of their training were more receptive than those who had been trained in the 1950s, and Lloyd had to be both sensitive and humble about these text demands on older actors. In fact, humility is a key factor in Phyllida Lloyd's process. Like so many of the directors, she emphasises a collaborative process and a willing-ness to admit you've made a mistake. 'You come into the rehearsal room having a clear idea about something you want to try, you try it, and then face the actors, allowing the possibility that you've made a mistake. "That was a dreadful idea; I don't know why I came in with it. Now let's do what you suggested which sounds much more interesting." And as soon as they've heard that you are prepared to acknowledge that you're fallible, then it seems a huge amount of ground has been covered. The way has been paved for a real workshop.'

Besides her work on *Artists and Admirers*, I asked Lloyd about her critically acclaimed work on *Six Degrees of Separation*. 'I wasn't quite sure what I was going to be able to bring to it,' she began. 'I was excited by the form of it, slightly alienated by the content, excited by the potentially bare stage. I responded warmly to John Guare's sense of humour and his sense of theatre.' Lloyd flew to New York where Guare interviewed her and approved her as the Royal Court's choice as director. 'I was trying to cast the leading role in London. I couldn't find the right person to do it. The people I wanted to do it were not available or didn't want to do it, and the people who were available and wanted to do it, I was worried weren't up to it. So I decided to ask Stockard Channing whether she was interested in coming over to do it again.

'I felt it was crucial to make subtle shifts of emphasis in order to make the play work for an English audience. I didn't want them to dismiss the characters' behaviour as self-indulgent or sentimental – a "we'd never behave like that" attitude. Of course, it was very challenging to work with someone who had played the part for two years and believed passionately in the play and production. I had to create a situation in which to open new doors seemed worthwhile and exciting. If I wanted a new way it really had to be a better way. We had many battles but ended up respecting each other a great deal. I'm sure we will work together again.'

This brief narrative about *Six Degrees if Separation* tells us something about Phyllida Lloyd as a director: her perseverance, her taste, her calm, her steadfastness, her respect for her fellow workers, her instincts as a director, and her ability to work with dignity in all situations.

SUE SUTTON MAYO, whom I met in her office at the Library Theatre, Manchester, before a matinée performance of her production of Ibsen's *Ghosts*, is unique among the women directors. Mayo was at the time a resident rather than an artistic director, that position being held by Chris Honer, who invited Mayo to direct three plays a year and become part of the management team. 'He's totally supportive of me and of my work and has shown absolute faith and trust in everything I've done. We have a card on our wall here which we both read occasionally when we're feeling down. It says:

> No matter.
> Try again.
> Fail again.
> Fail better.

It's Brecht, of course. That's our philosophy: to try, to fail abysmally is better than not to have tried.' Although she is now a freelance director, Mayo confesses that, prior to her engagement at the Library Theatre, she was not very good on the freelance circuit. 'I'm not terribly good at selling myself. People think of me as being quite a bold sort, but actually I'm quite a hothouse flower, and I need a lot of nurturing and support. I think I always felt I would do my best work in a company where I could forge relationships with people.'

While Mayo admits to tremendous respect for actors, she has an equal respect for the technical elements of theatre. 'It seems to me that all of us are as important as everybody else. If the cleaner doesn't turn up to clean the auditorium, then I can't let the audience in; if I can't let the audience in, there's no point in the actors getting up on stage. So everybody has a responsibility; if you give somebody responsibility, you have to give them rights. Therefore I feel that everybody has the right to comment on the way a company's going or to offer ideas on programming. I mean the box office can tell me more about the way a show is being received by the audience than I can ever know. The house manager tells me what people are saying or what the feel of the house is. For example, she once said, "You've got no music at the interval; I feel it's dipping and it's harder for the company to pull the audience back in the second act." I said, "I think you're absolutely right." We put music in, and she reported a real difference in the way the audience returned to the house for the second half.'

As a part of this collaborative process, Mayo dreams of working with a team of collaborators. Just as she sees things in directorial terms, she feels the potential of having people who filter musically, or who filter through movement, or who filter through text with writers would be phenomenal. For example, she worked with choreographer Fran Jaynes, who had attended all rehearsals of a production of *A Christmas Carol*. Mayo would block, get feedback from actors, and ask James to respond. The choreographer came up with extraordinary images and things to try.

When I asked Mayo if such collaboration, in which someone else shaped and enriched her basic work, ever made her feel vulnerable or threatened, she responded, 'Not at all. I have two rules in my rehearsal room. One of them is that you dump your ego at the door. The other one is that you don't smoke. Apart from being offensive to other people, smoking is a kind of sitting-back-and-putting-your-feet-up energy. If you have to do that, or you want to read a newspaper, go do it, and I'll wait until you're ready to come back. But we are working in the rehearsal room, everybody's working, and even if you are just sitting waiting to go on, then the energy coming from you is either positive or negative. Negative energy sucks out; positive energy recharges, refuels, enlivens, enriches, energises. So I won't have people smoking in the room because it makes everything horrible and is a metaphor for people not concentrating and not working.

Most of the time, I've only got three weeks to get a show on,

Sarah Pia Anderson. Photograph © Fatimah Namdar.

Helen Mirren with members of the cast of 'Inner Circles', an episode of *Prime Suspect*, directed by Sarah Pia Anderson. Photograph courtesy of Granada Television.

Sarah Pia Anderson's Royal National Theatre production of Ibsen's *Rosmersholm* with Roger Lloyd Pack and Suzanne Bertish. Photograph © John Haynes.

Annabel Arden. Photograph © Joâo Quintino.

Kathryn Hunter, featured in Annabel Arden's production of Dürrenmatt's *The Visit* for Theatre de Complicite. Photograph © Red Saunders.

Annabel Arden's production of *The Return of Ulysses* for Opera North. Photograph © Bill Cooper.

Julia Bardsley as the Witches in her own production of *Macbeth* for Leicester Haymarket Theatre. Photograph © Stephen Vaughan.

Anastasia Hille as Thérèse in *Thérèse Raquin*, adapted and directed by Julia Bardsley for Leicester Haymarket Theatre. Photograph © Stephen Vaughan.

Franz Xaver Kroetz's *Dead Soil*, directed by Julia Bardsley for Leicester Haymarket Theatre. Photograph © Stephen Vaughan.

Annie Castledine. Photograph © James Manfull.

Rosemary Harris (left) as Martha, and Elizabeth Sprigg (right) as Abby, in *Arsenic and Old Lace*, directed by Annie Castledine for Chichester Festival Theatre. Photograph © Simon Annand.

haron Maughan and Peter IcEnery in Ibsen's *A Doll's ouse*, directed by Annie astledine for Chichester estival Theatre. Photograph John Timbers.

Garry Hynes. Photograph © Amelia Stein.

Right, Tom Murphy's *Famine*, directed by
Garry Hynes for the Abbey Theatre.
Photograph © Tom Lawrence.

Below, Sean McGinley and Marie Mullen in
Garry Hynes's production of *Conversations
on a Homecoming* by Tom Murphy.
Photograph © Tom Lawrence.

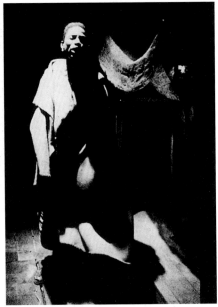

Above left, Jenny Killick. Photograph © Sean Hudson.

Above, Decima Francis in Amy Hardie's *Noah's Wife*, directed for the Traverse Theatre by Jenny Killick. Photograph © Sean Hudson.

Left, Hilary McLean in Simon Donald's *Prickly Heat*, directed for the Traverse Theatre by Jenny Killick. Photograph © Sean Hudson.

Brigid Larmour. Photograph © James Manfull.

Left, Virginia Radcliffe as Prospero in Brigid Larmou production of *The Tempest* for Shakespeare Unplugged, Royal National Theatre. Photograph © Hugo Glendinning.

Above, David Rubin (left) and Mark Lacey (right) in Brigid Larmour's *Twelfth Night* for Shakespeare Unplugged, Royal National Theatre. Photograph © Allan Titmuss.

Phyllida Lloyd. Photograph © Henrietta Butler.

Right, Henry Goodman as Freud in Terry Johnson's *Hysteria*, directed by Phyllida Lloyd at the Royal Court Theatre. Photograph © Richard Mildenhall.

Clair Benedict as Medea in Euripides' tragedy, directed by Phyllida Lloyd for the Manchester Royal Exchange Theatre. Photograph © Stephen Vaughan.

Sue Sutton Mayo. Photograph © Ed Mayo.

Below, Neil Bartlett's translation of Molière's *School for Wives*, directed by Sue Sutton Mayo for the Library Theatre, Manchester. Photograph © Ian Tilton.

Left, Collette Stevenson in Arthur Miller's *Two-Way Mirror*, directed by Sue Sutton Mayo for the Library Theatre, Manchester. Photograph © Ian Tilton.

Nancy Meckler directing *Anna Karenina*, with actress Teresa Banham. Photograph © John Haynes.

The original cast of Shared Experience's *Anna Karenina*, directed by Nancy Meckler. Photograph © Paul Carter.

Tilly Blackwood and Teddy Kempner in the Shared Experience production of *Trilby and Svengali*, directed by Nancy Meckler. Photograph © Henrietta Butler.

Katie Mitchell. Photograph ©
Hugo Glendinning.

Saskia Reeves and Michael Maloney
in Thomas Heywood's *A Woman
Killed With Kindness*, directed by
Katie Mitchell for the RSC at The
Pit. Photograph © Richard Smith.

Below, John Normington as
Engstrand in Katie Mitchell's
production of Ibsen's *Ghosts* for
The Other Place. Photograph ©
Ivan Kyncl.

Lynne Parker. Photograph © Amelia Stein.

Below, Eleanor Methven (left) and Carol Scanlan (right) in *Pentecost* by Stewart Parker, directed by Lynne Parker for Rough Magic. Photograph © Amelia Stein.

Below, Barbara Brennan as Lady Wishfort in Lynne Parker's Rough Magic production of *The Way of The World* by William Congreve. Photograph © Amelia Stein.

Di Trevis. Photograph © Clive Barda.

A scene from the Royal National Theatre production of *The Resistible Rise of Arturo Ui* by Bertolt Brecht, translated by Ranjit Bolt, directed in the Olivier by Di Trevis. Photograph © Clive Barda.

Lilo Baur and Robert Pickavance in *India Song,* co-directed by Annabel Arden and Annie Castledine for Theatr Clwyd. Photograph © Phil Cutts.

and if I have to spend the first week contending with egos, it's wasted time. I say this wholeheartedly because I have found that for me personally, dumping my ego in the bin at the door is the only way I can work. If I were concerned all the time about what people are thinking of me, whether or not they think I'm a good director. Often I walk away from the room thinking, "Oh, they think I'm crap." But what I've become very good at is being able to see where something is my fault and where it isn't. I don't mean I'm interested in putting the fault on somebody else but rather I'm interested in taking on board only those things which I think I was wrong to do. You see, what I want is people who wish to come into a room and just do their best all the time. If they're not doing their best, it's a terrible, terrible crime against our work. If I can honestly say at the end of a day, "I did my best," even if it was the worst day you can imagine, I still feel OK.'

Mayo confesses that it is frighteningly easy for her to say that she has made a mistake or that she doesn't have all the answers and tells a delightful anecdote to illustrate her point. During rehearsals for *A Christmas Carol*, Mayo had tried, over a period of a week, three or four approaches to a scene that wasn't working. Finally she was forced to confess to her cast that not only were all attempts futile but that she was out of ideas. 'Now it was quite difficult to say that because the director's supposed to have ideas. They were angry, not with me, not with each other, not with themselves, but with the situation. We knew we were a good company, we knew we could make good theatre. Why couldn't we make this work? I went home and cried. I felt like I'd let them all down.'

Next morning there was a huge box of doughnuts on the table, someone brought flowers, another actor complimented Mayo on her attire. The company assembled and the director confessed that she still had no solution. ' "Has anybody, *anybody* got anything they could suggest?" ' And, indeed, one actor offered a solution which, once presented, seemed perfectly obvious. And everyone said, ' "That's it; that's brilliant!" ' And at the end of the hour we had it.' Mayo and I discussed the possibility in such a case of getting too much input. 'I'm quite good at filtering ideas. They know where they are with me.'

In responding to queries about her working methods, Mayo observes that some directors are very rigid and say, 'Here is your rehearsal schedule for the next three weeks, and you know on day one where you are going to be on day twenty. I'm not like that. Other directors go in and have no idea where they are going and allow it to drift. And I'm not like that. I think I fall somewhere in between; that is to say, they will know at least a day in advance what we're doing and who is called. I will never allow an actor to be called and then sit around doing nothing. People's time is precious. All time in the rehearsal room is precious. I want them in top form; I don't want them having spent three hours in the green room twiddling their fingers. So it's a headache because scheduling *is* a headache. But I force myself to do it, and I do it with some degree of success. If I know I'm going to keep an actor waiting – because it happens – sometimes you hit a problem or you hit a wonderful moment and you don't want to let it go, you want to solidify it while you've got it. I make sure the actors know what's going on and I give them the choice of going away and coming back later or coming into the rehearsal room and seeing why we've kept them waiting. I mean communication is what it's all about, isn't it? And if people know what's going on, you don't get problems.'

Speaking specifically of what she does in the rehearsal room, Mayo admits to having no method, no system. She doesn't pre-block (she says she wouldn't know how), doesn't often play games, doesn't work on status exercises, rarely improvises, and doesn't routinely break her script into units. 'I will do it [a breakdown] to unlock a passage if I'm having trouble with it, but if I did it for a whole play, I think I would just get bored.' What then does Sue Sutton Mayo do or not do as she practises her craft?

She drew a delightful analogy to illustrate her approach to rehearsals. 'You call a plumber, and you say, "There's something wrong with the tap on my bath." Now he doesn't know what's wrong with the tap on your bath, but he has a rough idea. Still he has to bring with him a whole bag of tools because he's not quite sure what the job is going to entail. He plunks his bag down, and he looks at your tap. Now it might be that out of that huge bag of tools, he only uses two for that particular problem, but he's got the bag with him, right? That's how I feel when I go into rehearsal. I feel like I've got a bag of tools. I feel like I've got improvisation, I feel like I could divide the play into units, I feel like I could talk in terms of objective and super-objective, I feel like I could physicalise. I take them all with me. Now depending on the situation, the play, the actors, the particular moment we're working on, I might need *that* tool. So I'll use it. I don't need the rest, so what's the point of getting them out of the bag?'

In summarising her approach, Mayo says, 'I like to be very open, to work in a very collaborative way, and to have a very free atmosphere in the rehearsal room. By free I mean egoless – where people feel free to attempt things, to try things, to share things, to make fools of themselves.'

DI TREVIS has responded twice to my requests for interviews. Our first conversation was in one of the guest directors' offices at the Royal National Theatre. She was in the midst of casting understudies for her production of John Osborne's *Inadmissible Evidence* and had only a limited amount of time to spend with me. As a result the interview was highly concentrated and focused. The following discussion incorporates both her early and more recent comments.

'Process depends enormously on the project in hand, and I think as I grow older I'm more inclined to respond intuitively and make fewer rules for myself. You can do nothing to enhance your talent or your sheer flair on your feet in the rehearsal process. No one can learn how to make a good rehearsal atmosphere or predict how an actor will make a breakthrough. It's frightening, but this is a given: talent. But Brecht said, "Work makes you confident." And so I always prepare thoroughly those things that can be prepared.'

In her concise analysis of her process, Trevis confirms that she respects the actor's craft and personal approach to the work. 'I don't work with actors who like a very conventional way of working. If I suspect an actor's work method is going to give me problems, then it's no good, because he couldn't work or she couldn't work properly and neither could I.' Given that she has assembled the right group, Trevis says, 'With a group of actors and theatre artists gathered together in a room, I think I'm able to build an atmosphere in which they feel able to create. And I think I can push them to do rather more interesting things than they're often called upon to do. I think that directing is a very interesting mixture of the passive and the active, and they have to be properly balanced in a personality . . . there's this sort of passive, intuitive, sensuous quality that one has to have. But one also has to be able simply to organise and get everything together in a very practical way. It has been said that there's a balance there that could be characterised as masculine and feminine. Whether that's the balance I have found in myself, I don't know; but I *do* have an organising skill and I *do* have the ability to give it up, to sit and listen and sense and feel. I also think there's a sort of indefinable element in directing which is an instinct, a taste, a feel for psychological truth, and you've either got it or you haven't. And I always know when people have got it, and I knew I'd got it myself. It sounds very arrogant, doesn't it? But there you are, that's my experience. It doesn't mean that it translates itself into marvellous work necessarily because I've had as many failures as successes. I feel it's very mixed, the results of the work, but the raw ingredients are those, I think.'

In relation to her day to day rehearsal process, Trevis says that her husband, Dominic Muldowney, who was Musical Director of the Royal National Theatre, used to come into her rehearsals after several weeks and say with a very pale face, 'When are you going to start rehearsing?' Because Trevis believes in a large amount of physical exploration of the period in which the play takes place, she places the actual constructing of the play for the stage quite late in her rehearsal process. 'I invariably work with a movement person. I often start with a dance of the period, though it rarely appears in the play itself.' With *Elgar's Rondo*, for example, Trevis taught the turkey trot, the military two-step and other dances of the period. 'I never do a play without the actors being able to dance the dances of that period. It's my one way to get the actors working together, to get them to inhabit their period clothes instead of using the body language of people who are used to wearing blue jeans. I consider it of vital importance that the actors have the use from the beginning of really good props and clothes, especially shoes. So I do a lot of very basic physical work which I hope the audience is not conscious of, that they don't come and say, "Oh, a lot of movement work's gone on here." But somehow it gives texture and makes it feel right.'

Trevis frequently uses period photographs and strongly believes in non-verbal improvisation, often creating scenes previous to those in the play. 'I do a lot of work on all kinds of moments behind the text, events referred to before the action began.' For *Revenger's Tragedy* she explored not only the dances of the period but exercises about being in court. During rehearsals for Lorca's *Yerma*, she worked on heat, walking in the heat, travelling in the heat, looking after babies in the heat, preparing food in the heat. Trevis also worked extensively with the women: what they did in the house, how they did the washing, how they filled their daily lives. While words were not used, large amounts of stage props were: the women constructed their houses and their village; they served meals, prayed at the shrine, went to confession. 'It's a sensuous approach to character really. If a character has a job or a skill, the actor has to learn it or at least have a good physical sensation of what it might be. For instance, in *Arturo Ui*, all the hoods wore and handled their guns all the time. They were taught how to protect Ui by a professional bodyguard, and [Antony] Sher never walked onto the set without his gang fanning out before him into the room, all ready at a moment's provocation to fire. I even set up attacks on him to test them. Then slowly I start to bring those exercises towards the text. I hardly ever discuss the play theoretically; I hate to talk about it. I only like acting or exercises or movement. I don't give wonderful, inspirational talks around the model box on the first day. I've never done them, because I don't know how to do the play. That's what we have rehearsal for, to discover how to do the play.'

It will be remembered that Trevis fills a large notebook with her analysis prior to beginning rehearsals. This book gives Trevis the thorough preparation and confidence that she needs as she begins the rehearsal process. 'I show this book to no one, and I often don't open it once rehearsals begin. But the information sinks into the subconscious and helps me as I work on my feet in the rehearsal room. I don't really make plans any more, the text work usually gives me a notion of what areas I should begin exploring. I work entirely on my feet, listening and looking. I listen, listen, listen.' Again, Trevis says, 'I hate talking and I look at the text only when the actors are not working in the space. I believe that acting is sensual. It is about being in the space, about experience. It is not theoretical.'

Other directors, like John Dexter, Trevis says, used to block a play within two days, utilise the actor in the stage space immediately, with the ground plan of the set drawn up on the floor. Certainly Trevis's actors are made aware that their exploration relates specifically to the text they are performing; for instance, when Trevis directed Brecht's *The Mother*, her cast spent two days learning to assemble, dismantle, and hide a printing press (quietly and at high speed) and to print in secret. 'A good prop can massively inform an actor's whole performance. It [the printing press] was their essential prop: the whole work of the group, the hierarchy, the relationships, their marvellous choral singing stemmed from these early improvisations. Printing was their work; that's what we started from. They could sense straight away that this was about constructing the whole world of this young revolutionary group, and therefore, they could see immediately that – although they weren't doing the text – by the time it came to our doing it, I didn't have to block the scenes because they knew exactly the atmosphere of how to do it. I was delighted to learn years later that Brecht had a similar conviction about this and based hours of work on it. Ignorant people often deride this kind of approach as a kind of obsessive "method". It is not. It stems merely from an understanding of what acting requires. And I just had to make sure that once they were put in the space that my designer and I had devised that it worked theatrically.' This process leads Di Trevis to what she wants most in her actors: that they be truthful, that they convey meaning, that they provoke audiences to thought, and that they never, never be boring.

These, then, are some of the rehearsal techniques of those women who move from theatre to theatre and job to job. There is tremendous energy demanded by the constant moving, the constant adjustment to new circumstances, new people, and new environments. So many of the directors maintain that they dislike too much talk at rehearsals and consistently emphasise the collaborative process. They have little opportunity to build an ensemble and sometimes have little say in the project they will undertake. Yet it is interesting to me that whether they are working in a school situation, a regional environment, or a major subsidised theatre in London, they embrace each job as seriously and passionately as the next.

CHAPTER 6

Suddenly the wind's blowing
in a different direction

The final four women whose processes and productions we examine – Sarah Pia Anderson, Annabel Arden, Julia Bardsley, and Jenny Killick – are those whose most recent work has taken them in new directions. There is no suggestion here that their current labours are any less important than their previous theatre work. These four women are truly women of the theatre. Two of them, Jenny Killick and Julia Bardsley, have been artistic directors of theatres: Killick of the Traverse, Edinburgh, where her commitment was primarily to new works, and Bardsley Co-Artistic Director of both the Leicester Haymarket and the Young Vic. Similarly, Annabel Arden was co-founder/director of Theatre de Complicite, where she still acts and teaches. But these are the women whose most recent work has taken them into new avenues of creativity: Killick and Anderson into television and film; Bardsley into visual arts and film; and Arden into the world of opera. Each finds challenges, vitality, and excitement in these new directions.

SARAH PIA ANDERSON's involvement with film led her to begin the discussion of her process by comparing stage work with television. 'With the schedules we have to work to, you don't have time [in TV] organically to discover anything. Although I always do try to make space for that [discovery], I think any decent director does, but you do have to pre-form an awful lot of the staging. Whereas in theatre the staging is allowed to evolve, you arrive at the staging. In film really the actors have to be blocked fairly quickly; otherwise you don't have a scene to shoot. In film things are broken down into moments, into shots and takes; it's intense focus on detail. If you look at it there's probably the same amount of time actually spent but in a different way. A lot of the theatrical rehearsal process is really about actors learning their lines and their moves and actually arriving at something that's believable and that fundamentally they can reproduce every night, whereas in film they don't have to reproduce it longer than the take lasts. It's not like arriving at a performance that has to take responsibility for renewing itself every night. In some ways in the theatre the actor is much more in control; I think maybe film is more of a director's medium.' Both film and theatre have to do with dramatic action, Anderson concludes, and because of her theatre training she is very comfortable working with actors and thinks of them always as collaborators. Some directors for the media don't think it's necessary to guide the actors but are more focused on the technical aspects of the craft.

Anderson thoroughly enjoys her work in film and television, believing that it exists on 'the cutting edge, dealing with life as it is now'. She enjoys the bigger audience, the contemporary technology and issues of film and television. 'I can tell a story in a different way with a camera. You are working in and with a very different kind of space.' Theatre, Anderson continues, frequently takes place inside a building whereas film moves, the camera reveals, the artefacts move around the world. Because theatre is expensive and is confined to a specific building, it cannot command the huge audience that television and film generate. Economics are very difficult in the theatre just now. As expenses rise, live theatre is being forced to become safer and safer. Yet this is not to say that one form is better than the other, Anderson maintains; she merely feels fortunate to be able to practise both. Theatre is the root. We've simply invented these new technologies, and they take us into a different area. 'It is all part of what it means to be human.'

On the practical side, Anderson believes that one can earn a decent living in film and television, something not always possible in the theatre. Working as a freelance theatre director for twenty years did not, even in the best of times, offer

Anderson the financial security that the media allow. Yet it was not for financial gain that she worked but rather for personal fulfilment. 'My talents are being asked for in different areas. I feel equally wedded to film and theatre. I find it very satisfying to be allowed to work in both.' Sometimes Anderson thinks she should specialise, that she should force herself to concentrate on film or on television or on the theatre. 'I'm bravely going on trying to do it all. I don't want to close off any part of my existence.'

Turning from a consideration of her film directing to that for the theatre, Anderson is drawn to plays that are not immediately comprehensible and that she can bring into the light. She likes to sit her cast down, go through the play, and make sure that everybody understands what's happening, what they are saying, and why they are saying it. Anderson clarifies that she's 'trying to encourage people to look deeper, further, and perhaps trying to open out the actor's first choice or first impression'. Anderson would try to explain why she had arrived at certain choices and decisions with the designers. 'I wouldn't dwell on these things and try not to indulge myself in terms of talking about them. And then after that . . . straight off with a new play you've got the writer there who hears it for the first time, wants to make changes, people have got things they want to discuss. So you arrive at a consensus of the text. Then I would start to block it on the replica of the set marked out on the floor and sort of stumble around really until we get to the truth of each scene. I try to arrive at a cohesive sort of rough shape relatively quickly and then go back to the beginning again and start to refine that. I think I'm probably what is described as a minimalist by nature. I don't like excess; I like to get to the intrinsic action in something. That doesn't mean I don't like people moving around a lot, but there's no point in moving for the sake of moving if they're already focused in a way that they can be seen or heard.

'So the gestures and the movements of the play are as much to do with inner meaning as the language and the visual elements. I'm not necessarily interested in naturalistic gestures, although that would depend on the play. I mean you ignore Ibsen's stage directions at your peril because they are about the inner action of the play. However, not every dramatist is as deep as Ibsen. Some of them can be ignored, and different choices can create a similar effect or something better. But when Ibsen says she goes to sit on the sofa, there's a reason. If you look at the pattern on the stage, she's either moved towards someone or away from someone ... those stage directions cannot be ignored if you want a deeper understanding of the play. Film scripts are full of action because films are more about movement, less about what people say. The meaning is conveyed as much by what somebody does as by what he or she says.'

There was a time in her career when Anderson was involved with improvised drama, when she was rebelling against the use of words and the study of drama as a literary form. 'I don't do it any more but a long time ago it was a way of creating a character without a text by basing the character on somebody the actor knew but altering some circumstantial factors so that hopefully the actor created fictional characters and made plays ... put them together. It taught me about actors really, how they work. What seemed to me to be so exciting about theatre then was the mysterious, that which couldn't be analysed simply, that was, I suppose, more like what Artaud described as a sort of drum beat. It was a sensual thing, a spiritual and a pagan thing. It was because of Dionysus, really, that I think I fell in love with theatre. Improvisation unlocked. Work with improvisation and actors unlocked something that language doesn't do. Now I suppose I'm less interested in how actors achieve performances of truth than I used to be and more interested in interpretation, text, story telling, imagery; other elements of the theatre.'

Clarity, a kind of strength which is graceful, power – all are things Sarah Pia Anderson strives for in her direction. An actor working for her described her as 'a very gentle giant'. Anderson herself feels that she becomes intensely focused on the fictional world she is seeking to elucidate. She also believes that one of her directorial strengths is an ability to work well with actors. 'I can encourage actors to give performances that they would not normally give under different circumstances.' She tries to do this by 'placing them in positions where they have to take responsibility for their performances and responsibility for each other'. When I asked Anderson to develop this concept, she explained, 'I think it's really just as simple as instead of telling actors what to do, you encourage them to discover and make their own choices within a certain environment. It's like nurturing. I'm not a particularly autocratic director. I can resolve conflict, I can be a channel, I can bring people together, I can bring the elements of the production together, I can make it appear whole. I can integrate these elements which are sometimes quite disparate and bring them and hold them together in a sort of tension.'

Yet Anderson confesses she has to guard against certain areas of production being indulged too much, whether it's the actors, the designer, the musicians, or the composer. 'In the end I'm good at bringing them all together; when it doesn't work it's because I haven't put limits on how far an individual can go. But I've got better at actually going with my first instincts and saying, "It's terrific but perhaps it's too much; let's see," instead of feeling nervous about saying no. I always find it difficult to say no.'

The difficulty at saying 'no' also applies to just how many jobs Anderson is able to manage at one time. While her teaching at the University of California, Davis, fulfils a different part of herself than directing, there are times when she feels she is trying to juggle two full-time careers: her university teaching, in which she spends two academic quarters in residence, and her professional film and television directing in Los Angeles and England. Teaching, she believes, allows her to distil and synthesise her own philosophy of directing. 'It allows me to analyse more what I do.'

The program at the University of California, Davis, where Anderson, Killick, and Trevis have taught is both interesting and unique, and perhaps a model that other universities might emulate. The program, funded jointly by Davis and Granada Television in Britain, began approximately fifteen years ago when the theatre faculty at Davis agreed that one of its positions would be awarded each academic quarter to a British director. The directors selected for the position of Granada Artist-in-Residence are screened by a committee of eminent theatre professionals in Great Britain to assure the highest degree of professionalism, experience, and craft. While it is an honour for a director to hold the position, it also serves the students, allowing them to relate closely to working professionals and to understand something of the craft and discipline required. After twice holding the Granada post, Anderson was invited to join the faculty as a tenured professor in Davis's Department of Dramatic Art for a part of each academic year.

As a part of her teaching, Anderson directs one play a year and has chosen three productions; *The Three Sisters* by Anton Chekhov, *The Rover* by Aphra Behn, and *In Extremis* by Howard Brenton as examples. *The Three Sisters* was a very comfortable experience but one that appealed to Anderson's interest in 'the paradoxical nature of humanity. It explores the human heart.' The students loved the process of performing the play or, as Anderson expresses it, 'experiencing the text'. Reading Chekhov is rarely a meaningful or moving assignment for young students; but involving them in all the intricacies, foibles, pain, love, joy, and despair of Chekhov's very human characters through performance was powerfully meaningful for these young people and gave them a rich understanding and appreciation of the Russian master. One student was so inspired by doing Chekhov and found it so satisfying that he chose *Ivanov* for his directing project and Anderson says, 'handled it splendidly'. This student went on to post-graduate study at Juilliard. Such experiences are the satisfying rewards of teaching.

In the winter of 1996, Anderson directed Aphra Behn's Restoration comedy, *The Rover*. After centuries of neglect, Behn's work – and the work of other Restoration and eighteenth-century women writers – has recently found both an audience and critical acclaim. The British director, John Barton, for example, did a successful production with Jeremy Irons and Sinéad Cusack at the RSC's Swan Theatre in 1986. Anderson felt inspired to explore Behn's masterpiece in an academic setting. How would it be to explore a woman's work written in an era so dominated by the male comedy-of-manners playwrights? How would it be to explore the work with students in an academic setting? How would young actors handle the Restoration style? How would American audiences respond to Behn's work? Instead of simply moving from production to production as one might do in the professional theatre world, Anderson had time to explore the period, the manners, the style; in short to delve deeply into 'what one can do with one's work' given time and space and freedom to explore. Basing her concept on the idea within the play of masquerade and carnival, Anderson found working on *The Rover* a rewarding, alternative experience. The Restoration was a time when the actors themselves were the stars of the theatre, had followings, were on display, and developed a sparkling repartee and rapport with their audiences. Anderson was particularly delighted with how well these presentational aspects of performance were suited to the students' instincts and how well it was received by the audience.

More recently writer Howard Brenton visited the University of California at Davis as a Granada Artist-in-Residence so that a distinguished English playwright could work in tandem with Anderson on the development of a new script. Brenton's epic, *In Extremis*, written at Davis, deals with the medieval love story of Abelard and Heloise and the conflicts with church ideology that their union provoked. It was a fascinating process in which Brenton wrote by day and the students rehearsed that material the same evening. The students were thus able to experience something very like the day to day professional process of developing, rehearsing and presenting a new script. Such experiences with talented, responsive, and committed students is a rewarding and vital part of Anderson's work. She feels free to try new and different approaches and ideas, and she believes the program challenges students to a very high level of professionalism.

Beside her directing opportunities and responsibilities at Davis, Anderson teaches directing, where there are two undergraduate courses: a beginning and a more advanced class. In the elementary class, her main objective involves familiarising the students with a process of text analysis, for which she selects a text from American realism that is straightforward and accessible. She doesn't want to use a complex text because the point is to understand the process of analysis rather than the difficulties of analysing a particular play. 'I divide them into groups and they work in these rotating groups throughout the ten-week quarter. They prepare ten-minute scenes in which they have the opportunity to play the role of director, stage manager, and actor at different times.' Anderson also generates class discussions, shows video tapes of directors talking about their work, and gives demonstrations to the class of her own approach.

In the second quarter, for which the first course is a prerequisite, Anderson allows the students to select their own directing projects, again concentrating on ten-minute scenes. Choosing their own projects allows the students to express both individuality and the work about which they feel passionate. 'You have to feel connected to something you have chosen.' Both Anderson and the other students offer criticism at certain points in the work, and ultimately these projects are performed for anyone who wants to come and experience them.

There is an old adage about those who teach and those who do. Anderson exemplifies the best of both worlds as she simultaneously teaches and directs professionally. In California, where film and television are centred, Anderson, as a successful working film and television director, provides a vital and strong role model for students learning their craft. Sarah Pia Anderson has come to the realisation that 'I'm content with what I do. It comes naturally to me. Why would you be perverse enough to do it otherwise? We tend to think that the director is one thing, that the role can be defined. We think the director is someone who knows, who is giving directions, taking charge. The irony is that as an artist you have to have faith, you cannot be all knowing. It is not all ego and taking control. You have to serve as well as lead.'

ANNABEL ARDEN and I first met at the Playhouse, Oxford, where she was acting in Theatre de Complicite's production of *The Street of Crocodiles*, directed by her colleague, Simon McBurney, and based on the stories of Bruno Schulz. We talked in the auditorium with the set in front of us, and Arden frequently used examples from Complicite's work. Our discussion dealt primarily with her 1992 Complicite production of Shakespeare's *The Winter's Tale*, co-directed with Annie Castledine. Two years later, the two women also co-directed Marguerite Duras's *India Song* for Theatr Clwyd.

When I asked Arden about the difficulties of co-directing, she responded, 'The point is that if the material is really right for two co-directors they tend not to disagree. Obviously, if you do disagree, you try to keep it out of the rehearsal room.' Arden and Castledine work together in an atmosphere of mutual trust. Such collaboration is not unusual, Arden believes, because there is often a duality in theatre work: actor and director, director and choreographer, director and conductor. If you worry about confusing the actors, Arden says, you are assuming that actors wander around in a terrible state of darkness. 'They know what has to be achieved. They need to be watched, they need to be guided, they need someone who does not forget a single thing they do. One of my jobs is to be able to remember everything I have seen and to be able to say, "Last time you did this there. It was very nice. You've lost that little punctuation mark." And the actor says, "Yeah, yeah, I forgot." That's an enormous part of my work.'

In sharing her experience of co-directing *The Winter's Tale*, Arden began with a brief history of Theatre de Complicite. Complicite began with a group of four people who created texts and theatre pieces and has grown to a group of twenty: ten actors, a technical team of five, and an administrative staff of five. Because of this development, the position of director has become increasingly important. The Lecoq training of both McBurney and Arden, however, is principally concerned with the performer as author of his or her own creation; hence the first five or six Complicite shows, while perhaps inspired by literature, were devised from nothing. 'When you devise as a group, a lot of the dynamic is to do with each actor taking absolute responsibility for the creation, being able to stand back and watch the others, being able to fit in and access one's own work without losing the actor imagination or the actor inspiration. There is not this artificial distinction between actor and director which I do believe is an artificial one. Olivier was an actor/director. One does direct oneself, and any decent actor will tell you that mostly actors do direct themselves, especially if the director has neither time nor understanding to do so.'

So a major objective, Arden maintains, is to create a fertile working environment. 'If people work in the right environment, they work well.' By a working environment, Arden undoubtedly means creating an environment or atmosphere which is conducive to creative collaboration. However, it ultimately became necessary for the group to have a director: one person responsible for the vision, the unity, and the shape of the work. 'One of the reasons is that the productions grew in complexity, technically they became longer, the ideas became more complex, there were more actors, and someone was needed to organise it all. I mean great hunks of directing is organising. Also, our visions began to diverge. [*Crocodiles*] is very much something that comes out of Simon's head, and I support it, I defend it, I'm part of it, but I didn't direct it. *The Winter's Tale* is something that I absolutely insisted on doing because I wanted to do Shakespeare, and I wanted to do it with this company. It was our first try, and there were great flaws in it. But it was a hugely creative working partnership between myself and Annie, and it was great between us two and Simon because he played Leontes and therefore was a major collaborator in the process.' *The Winter's Tale* was for Arden a huge undertaking: a vast canvas, rich poetry, extraordinary physical work for which the group had only eight weeks to prepare and eight actors who doubled or tripled in roles. 'We worked it on the principle of a spiral because of the cyclical nature of the play.' In other words, taking the concept of the cycle of the seasons, the winter symbolising death, and the cycle of life, Hermione being reborn, Arden chose to reinforce this idea by working in circular rather than linear patterns and shapes.

In speaking specifically about her approach to her work, Arden says, 'I think we are unique in that we have a discipline – a discipline over many years – a discipline which I can quantify, a series of exercises, a method if you like, which is about the articulation of gesture so that it becomes very rich and very full of meaning, and it is as important as the spoken word. I think the audience has to have an absolutely physical experience. In order for that to happen, so must the actor. And I think in England we're just coming out of a period of complete gentlemanisation, and most of the work that goes on is incredibly tedious – I'm not afraid to say it. Olivier was hugely physical, and at the time people thought he was over the top. Anyway, that's what I'm interested in.

'We begin the day with an hour or two of physical work which is both designed to train and open the body, but also we explore movements which are essential to the interpretation of the piece. All of the exercises we do are designed to promote an interrelationship with the play, a huge awareness, so that one can improvise as eight or ten people, which is very difficult. Now you might just want to connect, or you might – as we often did in *The Winter's Tale* – work on the forms of folk dances because we needed them in the Bohemian scenes, or we might work on enormous movements of violence, and we did an enormous amount of running and circling because for some reason or other it seemed to help going into scenes. We want to work physically first and foremost, and then we try to set up improvisations essentially on the themes of the play.

'The process depends very much on what we are doing. If we are doing a text, it is fundamental that the actors understand that text.' Arden employs a technique whereby each of the actors must literally stand up and tell the story of the play in five to fifteen minutes or as the character. 'There are hundreds of ways of telling a story. The actors thought they were prepared, yet they could not tell the story of the play.' When I asked Arden why she considered this so important, she answered, 'Because if you don't understand what you're performing in its overall sweep, you can never really articulate its meaning as a member of an ensemble. OK, with *The Winter's Tale*, if you as an actor don't feel and understand what the storm's place is in the whole poetic structure and how it's going to affect the audience, then at that moment when the storm happens, you cut off as an actor and the storm is done by effects. But our storm was done by everyone. They had an enormous piece of cloth and they created the storm, and they also knew what the sound effect was and that it was created out of mixtures of Tchaikovsky and Shostakovich and other sound effects, and wind. They had to work very hard to create the storm because they'd all just been in the great trial scene, and then they ripped down the whole fabric of the set which became the sea, so they're all wafting great pieces of cloth like mad (bloody hard physical work), somebody's doing the little boat out of the top, somebody else is changing into the bear, and the others are changing like mad underneath the cloth to become shepherds. The rest of the cast is changing into sheep, storm music is ranting away, they've got to listen like mad to make sure they know where the actor who's playing Antigonus is as he crosses this landscape, and they calm it down, and they are responsible for the beauty of the storm calming. They can see the light changing. They articulate the play.

'We are different, I think, from other companies in that it's important that the actor is not just a character. The actor is an actor. So I could play the whole of *The Winter's Tale* for you on my own. And I think that's how it should be. Because the stories that mean most to us are the stories that we can tell. And part of the difficulty with modern culture is that nobody can tell a very good story any more. Who can tell you the story of President Kennedy? Suppose as an American you had to explain to someone living in India who Kennedy was. What do you say? Well, it's difficult because it's all been taken away from us by a hundred billion re-creations in the media. Can you tell the story of Jesus Christ? Or your own parents? No is the answer; most people can't do this. Or if they can it's very broken and very unpossessed. Generally you find that people who come from cultures where talk is still appreciated and human contact is ritualised can do this. And I think that's why I'm still passionately committed to this form of theatre. Because essentially theatre is about telling a story in public using all the means at your disposal to enliven it. How do you make the material of Shakespeare become that possessed by each actor on the stage?' Arden goes on to praise Kenneth Branagh's portrayal of Hamlet as an instance when an actor does possess a role and really reaches out and talks to the audience.

'There are', Arden maintains, 'so many processes that you have to accomplish to realise the production of a complex classic text like *The Winter's Tale*. We read it and we read it and we read it and we analysed it. We talked it through as most actors do. Continuously. We tried to break it down into units the way some directors do. We also tried to make it clear. I tried to make the meaning of each scene clear through its language. It's very important that the language that is used in reference to women in the first three acts becomes continuously more and more abusive, that the words become ugly, so that must be reflected in how the scene is played. And it must be heard by everybody.'

Arden believes that what she wanted to say with *The Winter's Tale* evolved through the rehearsal process. 'I knew basically that I had to achieve an ending with the great reconciliation and the rebirth and the reconstruction of a man through the power of a woman. That was always clear to me, but I didn't quite know how to do it. We were always trying to make it work. Also it was an exercise in the integration of our physicality with a very poetic text. It's very difficult to find the places where the action would tell the story because in a sense the story is told by people speaking. But that's just the beginning of my research on classic texts. For example, we tried to understand the movement of each scene, the shifts in energy, the points of tension, the action – all of which I think is fundamental. Shakespeare is almost director-proof because there are always lines that say, "Do not approach; stay back; draw the curtain." The action is all there; it's very clear. But actors are very personal and want to get carried away in their own personal response to certain aspects of the poetry. But that kind of work is irrelevant until the story and the dramatic action are there for everyone on stage. It doesn't matter what your inner psychological responses are; that is, you can't just do it inside yourself and hope it will communicate. We need to see physical evidence. It's a question of physicalising things and making action very clear. Film is very clear in terms of action. Often there's not a word spoken but we understand. So it's very important that the audience is satisfied on that level, that they're not just relying on the spoken word.

'We develop new processes to do this all the time. Some of the scenes are difficult to play because they are so intense and really shocking, like the last scene when the statue comes to life. We had the most glorious rehearsal in which we decided we just had to do it. We turned off most of the lights, and we had Hermione, the statue, on a ladder, and we played the wonderful mazurka from *Eugene Onegin* very loudly. Polina ran in front and she took the others to the part of the castle where the statue was. They ran and they ran and they ran until they were really exhausted, and they laughed as they ran. They ran in circles, they ran like horses, they overtook each other, they held onto each other, they held hands, they pulled each other, and they laughed. Suddenly they stopped running; they were there with this shrouded statue, and they played the scene. There was something about that movement that allowed them to believe in the situation they were in. It was real in the most tangible way. Leontes [Simon McBurney] delivered that line, "O, she's warm!" like a howl. It was true. His words actually brought her to life because that is the meaning of the scene: Hermione can't move as a statue until his heart is reawakened to the truth of what he's done, who she is, the fact that he really wants her to live again. It is a miracle, a miracle of love. People just rely on

Shakespeare's exquisite writing to do that. But you can't rely on it, you have to do it. She has to awaken his faith. That's what I have found so fascinating about the theatre: you have to do it. You can't cheat. Well, you can because you have to rehearse and work it out. But every night you have to do it.

'The last thing about our process is that it is never finished. We rehearse all the time that we perform, and we change things because we discover things. You're not supposed to get it all right in four or six or eight weeks. This is why we do physical work for two hours every morning, so that when we say, "All this is going to change," the actors can handle it. They don't have a private, sacrosanct area of the play which, if you touch it, will destroy them. We have a technique which we share as a cast which enables us to get through that hard part for the benefit of the story as a whole.'

The night of that first meeting, I saw *The Street of Crocodiles* performed by the ten performers of the Complicite Company. It was one of the most compelling and haunting evenings I have ever spent in the theatre. All that Arden had told me about the physicality, the importance of gesture, the psychological truth, the ensemble work were poignantly evidenced in that moving performance.

Many of the ideas Arden developed working with Complicite informed her work with Duras's *India Song*. It is perhaps interesting that both Arden and Castledine regard this shared experience as a major directorial event in their careers. 'Duras is a very experimental writer,' Arden says. 'We had to find the experimental form that would go along with what she's doing.' There were two monumental challenges: first, that the characters are in a state of listening to their own voices, and second, that Duras wants to discover the palpable physical reality, non-naturalistic, that would accompany that listening. The characters don't speak from the stage, Arden explains. 'There are various ways of doing this: you could have a whole second cast with microphones in the wings or you could do it as we did with the recorded voices of the actors. The actors memorised their words, but when we actually recorded it, they used their pages.

We always said that if we had done a longer run and had had more money, we would have [periodically] re-recorded the play. After a few performances, they started listening to themselves and they realised, "Oh, no! I would do that differently now." It grows. Duras does say it should be the voice of the person that you see. The characters are both listening to themselves and doing at the same time.

'The quality of movement couldn't just be naturalism; yet if you are too stylised or are too much into dance it becomes annoyingly aesthetic. You've got to take the essential movements of what a person is saying or thinking and translate that into a form that has got to be recognised. The movement has to have a peculiar intensity such as you can achieve in cinema or do achieve in your dreams. The way people move in a dream is quite normal by the standards of the dream. And we had to develop a language that was a lot to do with touch. We worked an enormous amount with sensations: touching the furniture, touching each other, touching the air. We had to remember that it was stifling hot, and a lot of it happens at night. We had dust and water and flame on stage. So it was to do with physical being really emanating from the text.'

Like Castledine, Arden discussed the movement of actor, Robert Pickavance, who, as the Vice-Consul of Lahore, made love to Anne-Marie Stretter's bicycle. 'He spent hours in the rehearsal room figuring it out . . . the way he looked at it, the way he walked towards it, the way he extended a hand, the way his hands move all over it without ever touching it. Duras is a very erotic writer.

'At some point we found we actually had to improvise the party that is going on most of the second act. We found that we had to improvise being hot, being in the residence late at night. We played a lot of music; actually, Duras specifies all the music. We had to learn to foxtrot and to waltz and to tango and to rumba – all dances which are specified in the text. The whole thing was like a dance really but it came from a realistic situation. I think the actors got more and more into it as they understood the rhythms of the text, the music of the text. We also played all kinds of other sounds: rain and street beggars.

'We were lucky enough to be working with a woman who is a French/Vietnamese actress, Helene Pataro and with Lilo Baur, who is Swiss. These were people I had worked with at Complicite, so it was a very interesting cross-over production. We explored everything together. A difficult thing was coming to grips with the intensity of meaning in the text; being able to speak it was the most difficult actually because you have to be able to perform a kind of interior dance and project that with frightening accuracy into the rhythm and sonority and punctuation of the text.'

India Song provided a kind of transition for Annabel Arden between her work with Complicite and her new venture into the world of opera. 'It's funny because I went to the opera a great deal as a child, but I never thought of directing it, and I was asked to direct *The Magic Flute* at Opera North in Leeds where they sing everything in English. I insisted that every word be intelligible. I can't stand it when opera is so badly articulated. The whole point of opera is the marriage of words and music. Perhaps that's not so true in the nineteenth-century repertoire. But if you're dealing with the earlier repertoire, which by and large I was, then it is true. I suddenly found that there's this relationship between text, music, and movement which I understand.'

Arden likes the fact that opera is not naturalistic and that it offers her enormous freedom to explore both the poetry and the theatricality of the work. 'These are fun dramas,' she says. 'The singers were delighted that I wanted to make *Flute* fun and funny. And the singers felt very supported by me. I made them tell the story. That was probably the most important part of the process because the classic opera singer says, "Well, there's Act I and Act II, and near the end of Act II there's my aria. Then there's the interval. Then there's Act III, and I have my death. That's the story." ' Adding to this thought, Arden says, 'There's this thing called "the production". And what's so funny about singers is that they think the production is something separate from them. They think it's sets, costumes, and an idea. My part, as the director, is to say to them, "You are the production. Yes, we can make you look beautiful. Yes, I pay a lot of attention to lighting, always. Yes, your costumes will be wonderful. But it's *you*; there is no idea. There is story and there is you. Now do you know the story?"'

Arden believes implicitly in the interrelationship of singing, acting, and movement. When she first introduced movement, the singers '. . . resisted like crazy. But if you stick to it, they love it because they sing better as a result of it. They are transformed, they work to the space. It's a small world,' Arden smiles, 'all singers talk to each other, so they say, "Oh, yeah, are we going to do all that physical stuff you do?" because they've heard it will be beneficial. I like their attitude because they're into anything that will make them a better performer. And their world is so hard. Actors just don't know. The margin for error is zero. They have to do all the work that an actor does, but within a given tempo.

'Another thing I've learned from singers is that you have to be very direct. They're not interested in pussyfooting around their emotions and their sensibilities and their understanding of character. They want to know louder, slower, faster, softer, what do you mean? They're not trained to explore. It cut out a lot of crap in me. There's no problem saying to an opera singer, "I don't believe you." You'd get shot if you said that to an actor, but the singer will say, "Well, why? what? what shall I do then?" When singers are good, they are very good actors. They have to be because they are dealing with emotion at such a pitch. I have such boundless respect for opera singers. They have unbelievable discipline. They all know they're in competition with one another, yet they like being an ensemble. They crave that; they also respect success.'

Arden loves the work when a bond of trust is forged between her and the singers. 'They're suspicious people. They have to work in such silly circumstances. They get flown in and out for three days, and the director says this, that, and the other. And they have to look out for themselves. If they lie on the cold floor and take off their shoes and they get a cold the next day, it's not the director's fault; it's the singer's fault. It's the singers that the management will get pissed off with.'

I asked Arden about singers getting too emotionally involved in their roles, and she responded, 'Singers do sometimes get over emotional and the singing goes to pot. The secret there is casting. Also, you need to get them to a point where they break down in rehearsal very early. What I've noticed about singers is that they don't really understand that rehearsal isn't just vaguely doing it. They've all been bullied by their coaches not to oversing in rehearsal, so they don't actually perform until it's too late. When they really perform and become moved, they don't have time to get over that phase before they have an audience. They need to have the shock of performance in rehearsal and then spend time getting over it so they can sing the music without being carried away. Most singers will resist like mad because they work in a culture where they're supposed to save everything up for the first night. It's as if they could have only one orgasm!'

While *The Magic Flute* launched Arden's opera directing career, her production of *The Return of Ulysses* (*Il Ritorno d'Ulisse in Patria*) by Monteverdi seemed to her to be a fulfilment of the potential of musical drama. 'I've been very inspired by reading the writings of a German, Walter Felsenstein, at the Berliner Komische Oper in the forties and fifties, and he writes brilliantly about the singing actor or the acting singer.' Arden believes that Felsenstein's approach emphasises the humanity of opera as did Peter Brook's production of *Carmen*. The early operas, Arden feels, are wonderful for the singer. The singer leads and, with the continuo of lute, harp, and harpsichord, does not compete with the heavy orchestrations of the late nineteenth and early twentieth centuries. Given the huge sound potential of Wagner and Strauss, there is a temptation to mike the voice. 'This is not good,' Arden says. 'It cannot help us with our understanding of what it is to be human. And that is still the job of the music theatre.'

Arden's conductor for the Monteverdi was Harry Bicket,

who attended every rehearsal and who even got down on the floor and did the movement exercises with the singers. 'They [conductors] like playing, but it has to be musical. They think musically. And one of the things they often don't understand is that the musical beat is one kind of beat, and the physical beat – the way dancers beat – is different. They should, because it is in fact that combination that makes live music live. Some conductors, like Bicket, get it because they understand how they themselves move. After all,' Arden maintains, 'conductors move, they really move. They have to be performers too.'

In *The Return of Ulysses* Arden made the singers speak it like a play from memory. At first they couldn't remember the words unless they were singing them. 'But', Arden claims, 'they got good at it. "Oh," they said, "this feels like we might be doing Shakespeare or something." 'Yes,' Arden agrees, 'it's very like that!'

So enthused is she about the potential acting power of opera singers that Arden hopes to be more directly involved with that training. 'When you're dealing with young singers you have to remember that they have so little experience compared to actors. They sing relatively infrequently. How many shows will you have for an opera? Very few compared to an actor. They have no idea of doing a twelve-week run with eight shows a week. I always think it would do the singers no end of good to do a one-act play or a scene every day at the festivals like Glyndebourne, Wexford, and Glimmerglass. They could do a Chekhov or a Beaumarchais – things that are relevant to their repertoire. They're terrified when you suggest it, but in fact they love it.'

Just as she is concerned about the training of young artists, Arden is interested in what a director needs for the opera stage. 'I think one of the secrets to being an opera director is understanding what they are actually doing when they sing. You have to know something about singing, and you have to be able to read music. There are a lot of directors who don't seem to need to, but, to me, the joy is directing note by note. I'm taking lessons in all the things I ought to know: harmony, the relationship of one key to another, the historical development of music. I'm also doing an interesting thing called Opera Lab organised by a woman named Susan Benn who runs Performing Arts Labs. I work with five new composers, five librettists, and two singers. My job is to create five short stageworthy pieces in ten days. Very exciting!'

Arden concludes, 'To do it well is so interesting, and you have to be such a technician. You have to understand form and structure in music – and big sets. How do big sets work? Do you want them? If you don't have one, what do you do? Then you get into acoustics.' Also it is useful, Arden feels, for the director to speak languages (Arden knows French, German, and some Italian besides her native English). In some ways, Arden feels that her years with Complicite trained and prepared her for this new endeavour. 'You see, what I've found in opera is this very intimate relationship between the movement and the text, and it is essentially a musical relationship.'

JULIA BARDSLEY elucidated her process primarily through examples from two productions, *Blood Wedding* and *Macbeth*, and her recent film, *Snow*. She has always had a profound regard for working with text. 'All of the work that I'd done before had been text based. What I like about Lorca is the very heightened poetic language that is so appropriate to the theatre. Lorca's imagery is brilliant. Also the whole Spanish quality – the strength of it, the passion – is inherently theatrical, which I really like. There's one level of reality, and then there's another level, another world. That has always interested me, that spiritual world, the supernatural, other-worldly elements. The first half [of *Blood Wedding*] is very much rooted in reality and then the second half is in the forest with the personification of moon and death. I wasn't interested in trying to be Spanish; that doesn't work for me. I tried to abstract the qualities that I thought were what Spanishness is about: a certain concentration, a certain awareness, a sense of themselves in space somehow. I worked with a choreographer as well, and we had a chorus of thirty who became the public. I set it in an ambiguous arena, a place of ritual, and the chorus was on the stands watching the action at all times. And the action took place in this intimate circle of sand, so you were constantly aware of the violence and death and honour which is very concentrated with the matador, the bull, and their relationship to the audience.

'To get an authentic voice, rather than trying to make the actors speak or sing in a Spanish style, I went to Seville and found a *cante hondo* singer, Matilde Romero. It was difficult finding somebody who was willing to come over and work with the production . . . those English people trying to do Lorca! But she was great. She was like a spirit, and in between the scenes she sang traditional songs. That was the only music. It was very stark, unaccompanied. I just wanted that lone voice. So it became the soul for the play. She knew the play well and brought over a number of songs that her mother had passed down to her. She actually sang the lullaby that Lorca had based his lullaby on. So for that scene we had an abstract movement sequence performed by the chorus; the actresses speaking the text in English; and the singer singing the lullaby in Spanish. It was very layered and concentrated. Some found it confusing, but I said, "Rather than specifically knowing what every word, every line, and every meaning is, I want you to get a feel of it, to experience it in another way." It was interesting.'

Bardsley was also willing to share a number of ideas concerning *Macbeth*. She confessed, 'I'd never seen a production of *Macbeth*. This was the first Shakespeare I'd ever done. I didn't have the weight, the baggage, of how so-and-so did it in 1960 or this interpretation or that interpretation. I saw it as a piece of text that I was putting on the stage with my group of performers and my creative team, and we came to it with surprise and without all that weight of history and superstition.'

Speaking at the time she was just beginning the rehearsal process, Bardsley said, 'With *Macbeth* I don't really know half of what it is I'm looking for, hoping that through the rehearsal we'll find exciting things to pursue. Hopefully all the people I've chosen – and I try to choose very carefully – are willing to go down that road with me. It's very difficult if you've got disruptive people in the rehearsal room; it's very difficult if you've got people struggling against what it is you're trying to do. That's often the case if you have a large cast. With *Macbeth* I've deliberately cut it down to eight people. Some of the characters have been amalgamated and some have been cut. For example, Angus, Lennox, and Ross, some servants, some nobles and kinsmen are consolidated into Ross, who is in all places at all times. Everybody's on stage all the time, so we can do away with formal entrances and exits. The events that are reported are unnecessary because we see them happening. The letter might be delivered, for example, in a slightly different way. It might actually be written up by Macbeth on a wall as it's happening in the scene, and Lady Macbeth might read it off the wall. But it's something we [the audience] might read also, so she wouldn't have to read all of it.' Ultimately she hoped to convey a sense that her actors were trying to do this production of *Macbeth* with all of these forces conspiring against them: lighting, sound, all the theatrical trappings actually being difficulties for them to have to overcome. The characters would seem to be in quicksand, not knowing what was coming next. 'If we ever get half of what we're trying to do, it will be a very good exercise for everyone involved.'

In another context but certainly applicable to the preceding comments, Bardsley stated that she hoped academics would not come to the production and attack her for her cuts, rearrangements, and liberties. She would ask, 'Why can't you just respond to it as a theatrical experience? Why can't you just shed the cerebral barriers and try to respond to this as a piece of theatre on an intuitive level? I think people come expecting to see something and when they don't get what they expect to see, they sit there seething rather than saying, "OK, it isn't what I wanted, but let's see what it is." You give them something, and they can't somehow receive it for what it is. Instead they project what they want it to be and are, of course, left disappointed or angry.'

Besides her comments on the two productions, *Blood Wedding* and *Macbeth*, Bardsley spoke of several vital elements in her rehearsal process. One of these is the performer, Rory Edwards, who appeared in all of Bardsley's productions at Leicester. 'It's a situation where I don't want to be in the rehearsal room without him. He's incredibly intelligent about what he does and is able to translate that into actuality. I think he's got a quality of concentration which is really electric for an audience.' Bardsley and Edwards share mutual respect, commitment to their projects, and shared trust. 'We talk a lot about what's possible to achieve, how we ought to push things, and what it means to perform. We have constant dialogue; we take ideals and try to make them into reality.'

Extending her respect for Rory Edwards to all of her actors, Bardsley states, 'I care about the performers in the pieces that I do. While from the outside it might look as though my interests are with the look, the technology, or the feel of the piece, I fundamentally care very much that the performers are never lost on stage, that they know what they're doing, that they've been helped to support and care for one another. Then the work can be pushed into more dangerous territories because you've got support in the rehearsal room. On the other hand I'm increasingly impatient and intolerant of certain types of performers. There are fewer and fewer people I want to spend time with in rehearsal.'

Just as Bardsley explained that before rehearsals begin she likes to get a feel of the world she and the actors will be inhabiting, she does not like to analyse the text, word by word and sentence by sentence, until the rehearsal process begins. Nor does Bardsley like to sit at a table for a week or two analysing the script with her actors. Instead she chooses to put the work on its feet immediately. 'I don't do a read-through sitting down on chairs. I usually put a load of things in the space, the actors have their scripts, and they can move and sit wherever they want. I like them to get the idea of themselves and each other in space. I don't analyse text at all in an intellectual way. It sounds perverse, but my theory is that it doesn't matter how much history you know about the characters, how much academic knowledge you have about the play or the situation.

No amount of knowledge will help an actor get up on stage and perform the piece of work. Physically they've got to get up and do this, and if it's locked in their heads, there's no way it's going to be able to live.' While Bardsley believes that knowledge is important, she believes it must be released through psychological and physical work.

When I pressed Bardsley for an example, she said that physical work is a good way to find out about the actors' instincts and to help them learn and understand the text without them knowing they're doing it. She might say to two actors working on a scene, 'Go through this block of text, go through line by line or sentence by sentence and then develop a movement sequence which encompasses the sensation and qualities of that line.' In developing these so-called 'psychological movement sequences', Bardsley acknowledges her debt to Michael Chekhov, whose books, including *To the Actor*, she says, are her bible and whose emphasis on 'psychological gesture' informs her work.

Psychological gestures are, to Bardsley, beautiful and poetic even when they're ugly. 'And the language with which he [Chekhov] describes it [his work] has a real spirit and a real truth and a real honesty about it. It's not dry and cerebral. He's really trying to address the intangible components of theatre which I don't think we do enough of. Theatre and art are about dealing with intangibles, about exploring those intangible planes. He's trying to make that concrete, physical, to find ways to harness the intangibles.'

Besides her exploration of Michael Chekhov's techniques, Bardsley uses a lot of ensemble work, believing that 'a group of people work as a group of people and not just as individuals. So I use a lot of ensemble exercises, not dressed up as games, but more integral to the whole rehearsal process, making them relevant to the thing we're doing at the time.' In other words, Bardsley adapts specific exercises to suit her current project.

Another point concerning Bardsley's process is her concern about when she must let the production go. She constantly reworks scenes through previews and makes changes until press night. 'I have a strange relationship with shows. I find it difficult to go back and watch them without making comments which might be disruptive to the actors, to how they are making it live. The performers have to go out and do it, and they have to find their own way in the end. The work has its own life in a sense.' Bardsley confesses that she is almost always disappointed in the end product, never quite reaching her vision of the piece. 'Maybe', she muses, 'it's bad to want too much.'

Since 1994 Bardsley has been concentrating her artistic talents on visual arts and film. In 1997 she was awarded a Wingate Scholarship to develop her research in the area of Artificial Memory Theatres. 'When I stopped doing theatre after the Young Vic, what I really wanted to do was try to understand what was good about the theatre to me and what was not good. I started reading about the ancient art of memory, particularly the work of Frances Yates, in which she talks about the origins and development of memory systems. I want to make theatre but I need to reformat it; I need to find a configuration. It seemed to me that these memory systems were a possible way forward: to appropriate these ideas and develop a form in which key ideas could operate.

'Part of the problem with theatre is that it isn't a big enough frame, in a sense, to contain everything I want it to contain. It works in a linear way – you've got two hours and you start at the beginning and go through until the end – but when you're researching, there's so much material that is interesting which somehow you can't include in that vessel which is the theatre. I wanted to find something where you could have all those things happening simultaneously, where you have the line of a story or a play or a novel or a poem but also critiques, references to past productions. You could go off on tangents that your mind has picked up on, distilling the ideas into images and placing them in space.'

Bardsley sees her new work as a possible fusion of visual art, film, theatre, location, and objects. 'The idea of the performer probably isn't going to be a part of it. I think it might be performerless, unless I place myself within it as some sort of curator or narrator or tour guide. The film that I'm making, *Snow*, doesn't have a performer. There is a narrator, a voice-over, but there's nobody in it. It's all about white and light. I've never made a film before, so I wanted to take myself through all the technical processes so I understood from beginning to end how film was constructed and physically how you made it. I wanted to concentrate on what film was about: basically motion and light. And this story, 'Snow', by Ted Hughes seemed to me to be a good vehicle to explore the bare essentials of film. The story is about a man who finds himself in a blizzard. You don't know how he got there; he doesn't know how he got there. It might not be a real blizzard, it might be inside his mind. The visuals are minimal and quite abstract: playing with visual perception, blurring, distorted focus, mirage, and hallucination. But it's not illustrating the story in a linear way.' In trying to understand her work, I asked Bardsley if her film depicted the kind of raw images you might experience if you closed your eyes and listened to the story. She responded, 'Exactly, because that's what it could be – that the narrator has gone through some sort of sensory deprivation, or he's at the rapid eye movement phase of sleep, or he's at the point of dying. It could be any of these things, but it's trying to make thoughts visual.'

Bardsley has also applied her scoring technique to film. She spread a long, horizontal sheet of paper on the table before me. It was filled with visual images, one after the other, and carefully pencilled notes. 'See,' she said, as she talked me through the images of *Snow*. 'It's like a composer's score with notation: rapid eye movement stage of sleep, paradoxical sleep, persistence of vision, panic, pulse, breath. This bit is very closely cut. Here it moves to an idea of amnesia with this section totally white. Here is where text begins. Here we're moving into a section which is TV snow where images infiltrate. Memory section here; blue is the only colour. Very minimal.'

Perhaps it is performance art; perhaps Bardsley is truly breaking new theatrical ground. She reflects on the recent years of her career, saying, 'I had started to get bored with the theatre and my own work within it, so I said, "That's it; I'm going to stop." I won't say never again but for the time being I want to put theatre aside and clear my mind. You have to ask yourself: what is it you really want to do, are you really pursuing the course you want to be involved in, or are you just doing a job, the next gig? That's not what I wanted. It wasn't a heroic move; it was the only thing to do. And in a way I'm very grateful that the situation developed as it did because it has pushed me into new territories, which I am finding truly stimulating.'

JENNY KILLICK's career is one of the most unusual and eclectic among the women. She is currently not directing, although she dreams someday of directing a feature film. Also, of all the women, her life is the most divided as she struggles to raise her two young sons and to pursue her present career. 'I was beginning to feel a definite conflict between directing and kids. I decided it was impractical being away from home on location, so I looked around, and was offered work developing drama for the BBC which I've been doing pretty consistently since 1995, getting my own series to develop these strands of short films called *Brief Encounters*, specifically designed to bring on new writers, new directors, and new producers.'

Discussion of Killick's process encompasses three areas: her five years as Artistic Director at the Traverse Theatre (where she became the first woman to hold that position and youngest artistic director in Great Britain), her reflections on the acting process through her teaching, and the application of her theatre knowledge to television. At the time of our first meeting Killick was preparing to spend a term teaching and directing at the University of California at Davis, offering a course to design students, directing for television, writing a film script – all the while balancing the responsibilities of motherhood. She says, 'I want everything. Who doesn't want everything?'

Killick's passion at the Traverse was commissioning and directing new plays, and she loves the dialogue and debate with a new playwright. 'You can't do that with Shakespeare!' she laughs. Although the thought would terrify most directors, Killick believes that she does her best work when there are no bounds, no limits, and no framework. A director has to be irresponsible, she maintains. 'While I was running the theatre [the Traverse], I was losing my sense of irresponsibility as a director. I think to direct well you have to be totally irresponsible: you can't worry – or care – about going over budget, you can't worry about selling tickets. These two things, directing plays and selling tickets, are incompatible if you want to break ground. I suppose deep down that's why I stopped running a theatre. I felt that I was being compromised by my responsibility to the people I employed.'

Besides her commitment to new scripts and her desire for artistic freedom, Killick likes to work with the best actors she can find. 'There are those who need to be told what to do and those who don't need to be told. I tend to work better with people who don't need to be told what to do. To work with the very best actors is ideal; then the collaboration is genuine. Going to rehearsals is brilliant: you set off not knowing what is going to happen but the actors are so inspired it just feeds on itself.'

Killick also prefers theatre that is highly theatrical to that which is realistic. She tells of sitting in a black box in Edinburgh watching something that wasn't very good and suddenly being inspired to strip away all the black paint and restore the space. The Traverse staff rallied with blow torches and scrapers and disclosed a magical space: an eighteenth-century Edinburgh loft with Georgian windows running down either side. 'We just did plays in that space. And if the board had let me I would have got rid of the seats as well and let the audience find its own informal way of being in that space.' Killick used to dream of a foyer full of old furniture, which audience members would carry into the performance area and randomly claim their own space and location. The actors would have a repertoire of approximately four plays which they would choose after observing and getting a sense of the particular audience. 'I didn't like the fact that everything was organised prior to the audience coming in. I wanted to let it just grow out of the informality of an attic.'

Moving from rumination to fact, Killick explains her basic

rehearsal process. 'The first week is generally given over to the writer, whoever he or she is, to talk to us, and to answer the actors' questions about the play. Now you may have a writer who is shy or tongue-tied, which would make the first week very different. The early process also depends on the style of the writing. For instance with John Clifford's *Losing Venice*, it was required that the company form itself into an ensemble who were very playful and light with each other, so I played a lot of games to bind them together.'

All games must be competitive with Killick. One of her favourites demands that an actor fantasise richly, setting the scene in a fictive place and describing it. 'It's such fun to do,' Killick says, 'because they get carried away and make little movies.' The actor then selects two or three players to create the scene. 'So I'm getting the actors to direct as well as act and to think creatively about the work. It releases atmosphere and mood. It liberates the imagination. But I'm always utilising the script. I don't improvise away from the script. Sometimes I get them all to play other parts, which is particularly helpful if you have an actor who doesn't want to be stretched. Girls can play boys; it releases all sorts of insights for the actor. So I think my rehearsal process is about getting the company to play together, understand each other's roles, and think about the whole play rather than just their own parts.'

Like so many of the directors, Jenny Killick likes to avoid too much theoretical talk on her part. 'Actors should be moving and doing and talking and playing.' Also, not only does she not pre-block but she literally avoids blocking at all. 'I find scenes have a natural shape if the actors are inside them. If it's working, the actors are usually in the right place.' Killick likes run-throughs after which not only the actors discuss their experiences but also Killick, as the only one who wasn't performing, communicates the sensations she received. With these run-throughs Killick believes that the sweep of the piece becomes apparent to everyone involved in the process. 'If we're going to communi-cate a piece of theatre, everybody needs to have the whole in their heads, even though they are just a part. Brecht said the play has to encompass everybody.'

Killick confesses a love-hate relationship with technical rehearsals. 'I love the practicality of putting shows on. I like it all coming together. It's a mighty headache though. Sometimes it's murder and you just want to die. You're in the theatre until two o'clock in the morning and you're still on the first cue. It's dreadful. But when it all starts to come together – the music, the design, the acting – it's very good. I'd love to find a way not to lose touch with the actors when I become totally bombarded with the technical demands of putting the play up. After the final run in the rehearsal room, which is a magical time, the actors are abandoned in the tech. So they just want to fart and be naughty. And you're sitting out there having to do the lighting. There's about a week of dislocation and disorientation, and then slowly through previews you all come back together again. I have a fantasy about building a theatre with the rehearsal room on a lift and you'd just slot it in for the audience. There would be no tech! Seriously, I enjoy the plastic nature of the theatre. But during tech I think, why did I embark on this lunatic project! Next time no music, no lights, no set!'

In summarising her approach to stage work, Killick says, 'I like to think that I am a good observer, that I have a good ear and eye; an ear for the music of the play and an eye for the composition. I can tell actors what I see and what I hear. They can ask me, "Is it right? Is it good?" And I can go, "Yeah, well maybe this would be better." That's the most important thing: being alive to ideas and being able to communicate effectively.'

Killick's process of working with actors was explored further in the classroom at the University of California, Davis, where Killick taught a course in acting, which she titled 'Comparative Text'. 'I did *The Rivals* and *A Doll's House*, comparing and contrasting the very different acting approaches required by each. You have to be almost a totally different person to act in both. So we started with *The Rivals* as comedy, doing character sketches to stimulate the imagination. They had to find from any source – magazines, books, photographs – the image of who their character was going to be, the physical presence, the thought process. They had to present these to the rest of the group, to entertain the group. It was a very competitive performing environment: they had to be good; they had to get our attention; they had to make us laugh; they had to make us sit up and watch them; they had to fight for their own space. All the parts written for *The Rivals* have a hugely inflated sense of themselves. How do you get those egos going?' At first Killick found the young actors very cerebral. She had to stop them from analysing and get them doing; fighting for attention in that jungle of egos.

'Then we switched to *A Doll's House*; no showing off here! Such a totally different approach – in terms of psychology, in terms of layering, in terms of what you reveal when, what you withhold. Ibsen is like a sleuth in the way he writes his plays. It's not like putting it out there, grabbing attention, and go, go, go. So I worked through with the actors on how they control what they reveal. You need your objective when you go in, and you need to know when you've achieved it. In *A Doll's House* they had to get out fine pencils, sharpen them, and plot their journey through the play. What I often feel is that actors like to get an approach and apply it to whatever material they're involved in. This is always something I would try to dismantle because the chameleon quality of performing is so essential as is the translucent quality that you need. I know this much more from film acting now; but when you move into the theatre, I think your approach has to change depending on what text you are doing, what space you are in, all the material circumstances confronting you. How can you know your approach until you're in those circumstances?'

This comment lead Killick to a discussion of film acting. 'If a young actor has the right face and the right bearing, he or she can get cast in television very quickly. They can get an agent, and make money, and have a career. Whereas acting in the theatre is a different thing. It's not necessary that you are a person; you can be many different people. You have to be able to speak and have a tangible stage presence. I think telly is voracious in its need for talent, and its ability to pay well, and employ large groups.' Actually finding people who can act for the stage, Killick believes, is becoming more and more difficult. 'While there is a generation of incredibly experienced performers, there are those younger television actors who are totally dependent on their directors to teach them to act.'

Continuing her reflections on her work in television, Killick says, 'I went off and trained and got bitten. As soon as I got put behind the camera, I felt like I was coming home, which is strange because I spent my whole time at the Traverse being absolutely anti-television and saying that the theatre should be a place of non-realism and of experiment and of live performance. So with the move to television I was surprised how taken by it I was.' Killick perceives a direct link between the work she did at the Traverse commissioning new scripts and this new phase of her career. The films she develops are shot on 35mm film, and they are designed to provide a bridge between student work in film schools and professional film production. 'It is their moment where they can demonstrate to the industry their skills and their talents.'

Killick describes the process of her television producing in the following way. 'The film maker submits a script, and I commission the film on the basis of that script. Then there's a period of script development. We organise the material together. It's exactly the same process as working with a writer on a new script, except that you're preparing it for a different medium. So instead of thinking about a play in live performance and what's going to happen when the audience turns up, you're preparing a linear narrative for the screen. You're simply saying, "We go into the cinema and what do we see? How do the pictures flow together?" Then I help them with casting and crewing. I introduce them to new people that they might not have heard of. It's rather like producing at the Traverse. Then we work through and help them in the cutting, the editing, and getting the work into the cinema before it goes on TV. Very interesting and enjoyable.' Killick concludes, 'I'm more involved in real things than I've ever been. Normally I'm involved in fiction, make-believe. Now I'm more involved day to day. I'm learning all the time about film because I am saturated in the process of moving from script to screen. What are the casualties as you make this move? Where do you start your screenplay? What is actually achievable? And if television is anything at all, it's entirely contemporary. It's out there!'

These then are the rehearsal processes or techniques of thirteen extraordinary women directors. Not one of them offers a blueprint for rehearsing a play; how dreary it would be if they did! Exploration, experimentation, improvisation, play, searching for truth, new directions – all are a part of their quests. All of them agree that what you do in rehearsal depends on the play, the people, the time allotment, and the circumstances. None of them dictates or sees her role as associated, in any way, with power, authority, or control. All of the women are so very candid about what they do, so very willing to share, so positive and humble about their working methods.

PART III

THE PASSION

CHAPTER 7

Theatre has ever been in crisis

Director Deborah Warner once said that maybe the theatre has ever been in crisis and that we are naive to think that those great eras of theatre – Greek, Elizabethan, the Independent Theatre Movement of the late nineteenth century, for example – were free of problems and financial hardships. However the British theatre, which seemed to the rest of the world a very model of what government subsidy can offer – low ticket prices, encouragement of new playwrights, commissions for new works, freedom from box office control and financial limitations, grants for companies and schools all over Great Britain, help for small experimental and fringe groups, bursaries for young directors – has eroded and weakened. Americans in particular, who have planned trips around the bounty of the British theatre, shake their heads and say, 'It's getting expensive; it doesn't seem as daring or exciting as it used to be; it was a disappointing season.'

The women directors, similarly, respond to these difficulties. But always with hard times in the theatre, so aptly referred to as 'the fabulous invalid', most of us cherish the belief that something wonderful and innovative is just around the corner. Even in arduous times Phyllida Lloyd praises subsidy, believing that a play like Ostrovsky's *Artists and Admirers* performed by the RSC at the Barbican's Pit, is too rarefied and special ever to achieve any kind of commercial life. 'That group of actors', she maintains, 'had worked together for two years and offered a director a wonderful level of mutual trust – a richness of imagination and preparedness to explore as an ensemble. The RSC remains a unique enclave in this respect.'

Julia Bardsley, on the other hand, is critical of the limitations of subsidy as it exists today. 'In Britain today we have established theatres, places like the National, the RSC, and regional theatres, that are doing a particular sort of conventional work. We have some "receiving houses" (like ICA and Tramway) who are booking experimental work. What we don't have is a building that is actually creating subsidised experimental work. There's a gap here that needs to be filled.' There isn't any true support, Bardsley feels, for establishing companies that are devoted to making interesting and challenging work. 'The trouble in England is that there's no recognition that investment in process is necessary for the future health of the arts. There's no investment in process at all. It's just results. You've got to get it out as quickly as possible. I'm amazed that people produce anything of any worth at all. Against all odds people do.'

Both Annie Castledine and Katie Mitchell express the same concept in a highly different way. Castledine says, 'We don't honour our practitioners in this country very much. We're a bit rude actually, and we take things for granted. I think we're a bit afraid of being pretentious, which is fine, but we're awfully stiff-upper-lip about artists' work. We have this rude and rather crude, philistine attitude towards what is *work* and what is *not* work. We tend not to give the arts practitioner pride of place.' Mitchell expresses her feelings even more directly when she says, 'It would be truly fantastic if the government in Great Britain would take the arts seriously. What does that mean? It means pumping money into them and not looking at them as if they were short-term commercial investments.'

While each of them approaches the subject from a different point of view, both Annie Castledine and Julia Bardsley regret that there is not more opportunity for and acceptance of experimentation. 'Being free to experiment', Castledine asserts, 'is not given an enormous amount of room within the theatre world at the moment. Some do have the room, and maybe it has to do with class and privilege and politics. Nothing for us is ever going to be easy in the theatre, and I feel that even more than I did a few years ago. I think the work grows deeper, is more adventurous, is more genuinely questing, and it is very much more difficult to do. Because I don't have wealth or position, I am hugely dependent on the generosity and belief of others. It becomes increasingly difficult to be allowed to work in the way that I would like. I do feel there are some of us, and I count myself one of them, who continue to experiment with form, to push forward and see beyond the last piece of work and want to try to extend our understanding of theatre by seeing what we can accomplish in a theatrical form that may not have been done before or at least in a way for which there are not too many precedents. *Goliath* is an experiment. Can one performer accomplish telling a story of three riots in three council estates? Can she, through her own person, accomplish the telling of these stories? Is it possible to do it, not through linear signposting but through the juxtaposition of testimony from one character and then another character and through placing of the action?'

In many ways Julia Bardsley, likewise, believes that her own work was to an extent compromised at places like the Leicester Haymarket and the Young Vic, that she was never free to be as radical and experimental as she might have wished. Since her background was with the fringe theatre, she says she never decided to work in a regional repertory theatre. 'But the year before I started [at Leicester Haymarket], I had a very bad year working independently, trying to do the kinds of projects I wanted to do. The situation was quite difficult at that moment for independent companies, for people who wanted to make a particular kind of theatre. I thought this job wasn't for me, that it wasn't the sort of system I wanted to work within. But when the Arts Council came back and asked if I would be interested if they made this a *joint* post, it appealed to me because it seemed a more creative prospect.' Bardsley and her fellow Artistic Director at Leicester, Paul Kerryson, were committed to totally different sorts of work. 'Paul's forte is the musical; mine is primarily physical, visual theatre. There was a time when Paul was doing *Hot Stuff*, a compilation of seventies music, on the main stage and I was doing a very obscure piece of work, *Dead*

Soil, by Kroetz in promenade installation style in the studio. That these two pieces were going on within the same building, under the same roof, appealing to a diverse group of people, seemed to me very healthy.'

After Leicester, Bardsley became joint Artistic Director of the Young Vic with Tim Supple. Supple had approached Bardsley about the position while she was still at Leicester. She responded to him, saying, 'We can apply for it but only if we present our ideal vision for the theatre. We had a fantasy about the type of theatre we wanted, and the way we wanted to work. So we put down a very idealistic philosophy about how we might run the theatre. We were very honest about what we saw as the problems of how the Young Vic was being run and what young people's perceptions of it were. We put this to the board, not hiding anything, just saying exactly what we felt in our hearts. And they said "Yes". They gave us the job, and so we assumed that was what they wanted us to do. When we started implementing our ideas, they seemed horrified. I think they probably thought that when we came in and realised the reality of the situation, we'd temper our ideas. Finally, I felt the compromises that were expected were just too great. So after a year I resigned. Now Tim is running the building on his own. It's very successful what he's doing. It isn't what we set out to do, and it isn't what I would have wanted to do in the theatre. It's just the way things are.'

Bardsley dreamed of running a building as creatively as the work that was appearing in it. 'We wanted the philosophy of the building to work in a totally different way, less hierarchical. What I learned at both Leicester and the Young Vic was that the work was the last thing that gets talked about. Everything else takes over: getting consultants in, getting people in business to work out management structures and that sort of thing. That's fine for business and industry, but, to my mind, the way one works and thinks creatively is also a valuable system for organisation and management. I didn't see why that couldn't be applied to the way a building was run administratively or economically. But it seems that economic forces are too strong, and the climate is very wrong ever to attempt having a dialogue about alternative ways of working.'

Under ideal conditions, Bardsley would dream of a year's rehearsal period for productions but admits that she probably wouldn't know how to use the time. 'You get so used to working in such short periods of time. I wouldn't want to have such a rarefied atmosphere that nothing ever got shown. I think that's very unhealthy because the nature of theatre is about the relationship between the audience and the piece of work that you're putting on. That's a very necessary equation. To work with a group of people committed to working in a particular sort of way for a longer period would be brilliant. But that's not the way it operates. I think that the very extreme wave of capitalism that Thatcher was responsible for has been permanently harmful to the arts. It has been incredibly detrimental and disruptive. It made smaller institutions think they had to compete with how the National runs, and they can't and shouldn't want to compete on that level. If you put all your efforts into that, then you haven't any resources left for concentrating on the work. So I think that's been very problematic. It would be great to say, "Well, we're not going to try to compete; we're going to sell our work in a totally different way; we're going to be creative in the way we market it; we're going to be creative in the way we budget it; we're going to be creative in our use of money and space and time, rather than being bureaucratically led by the idea that profit and making money is what it's all about." The trouble is that this whole business mentality has seeped into everyone's consciousness, and the arts feel guilty about the idea of saying, "Look, the arts are subsidised because people feel it's a necessary part of our culture. Its worth lies outside of an economic value system." I don't think that work should be seen as a commodity and part of an industry that operates like manufacturing socks. I think culturally it's incredibly depressing in this country.'

Bardsley is not alone in her criticism. Brigid Larmour concurs: 'I couldn't stay in regional theatre working in those conditions for the rest of my working life. I just couldn't. It's pointless. Five years, great. But it's a factory. There are too many things that one is compromising too much of the time.' One of the pressures that both Bardsley and Larmour responded to in the regional situation was the requirement that they balance artistic and administrative obligations to such a large degree. Larmour recounted her experience at the Contact Theatre, saying, 'I was the joint chief executive of the company, and there was an administrative director who was the other joint chief executive, and she was essentially responsible for the administration of the company, but an emormous amount of administrative stuff naturally fell my way as artistic director. I tried to keep it under control (and I enjoyed the power to determine everything about the company that I did) but I wish I had been staffed to a point where I didn't have to do quite so much administration myself. Because it's always the artistic work that gets squeezed out and never the administration.'

Another major area of concern revolves around Arts Council funding that has been severely curtailed in recent years. Jenny Killick, among others, regrets that the directors' trainee bursaries have been diminished by the Arts Council, the total trainee budget amounting to a scandalous £10,000. Phyllida Lloyd, Annie Castledine, and Jenny Killick all speak glowingly of their apprenticeships as Arts Council trainees. Lloyd made three applications before being accepted as a trainee and praises her experience at the Wolsey Theatre in Ipswich as the beginning of a very lucky roll of work. Killick also says, 'It was great. I had the boldness of youth. This was at a time when the Arts Council of Great Britain and the Arts Council of Scotland were quite serious about training directors, and I was offered a two-year bursary in which the Arts Council would pay my salary for two years to be attached to a theatre. So for my first year at the Traverse, I didn't direct anything. I was just left to watch the actors work or meet writers, talk to writers, begin to orient myself.' Now the Arts Council bursaries are severely curtailed. In his excellent 1989 study, *A Better Direction*, Kenneth Rea writes, 'The Arts Council of Great Britain currently offers no bursaries for trainee directors. It used to have four trainee bursaries each year and two or three associate bursaries. This does leave a serious gap in provision for new directors wishing to enter the profession. The Arts Council needs to consider carefully the long-term consequences of this and to re-examine the whole question of training as a priority among its clients.'

Another area in which the directors are affected by the current austerity is funding in the support of theatres themselves. Sue Sutton Mayo discussed the unique funding situation of the Library Theatre in Manchester and its sister theatre, the Forum in Wythenshawe. Most theatres, Mayo explained, have money that comes from the local city council, some money that comes from the Arts Council of Great Britain, some money that comes from the regional arts board, and, of course, there's private business sponsorship which forms a small part of their income. 'But we the [Library Theatre and the Forum] have no money from anywhere else other than the City Council which decided that they need to save roughly a quarter of a million pounds of our budget, which is just under one and one-half million to run the two theatres in a year. Unfortunately that figure represented the Forum Theatre. Several years ago the Arts Council created Initiative 2000, saying that, leading up to the millennium, they would laud a city each year for its focus on and leadership in a particular art. So in 1993 Birmingham was the City of Music and in 1994 Manchester won the bid as the City of Drama. It's ironic that such an honour was celebrated by the closing of a theatre. It's heartbreaking.'

The fringe theatres have been no less affected by such cut-backs. Julia Bardsley tells about her first successful production, an adaptation of Ian McEwan's short story, *The Cupboard Man*, which, after winning an Edinburgh Festival Fringe First Award, Bardsley took to the Almeida Theatre in Islington. 'The Royal Court had said, "Do you want to do it in the Theatre Upstairs?" and we said, "No, we want to do it in the Almeida." It was a fantastic space, absolutely right for the piece, and we were eager to establish a relationship with the Almeida. In those days, when Pierre Audi was in charge, companies like us had access to those types of places, but over the last seven or eight years those channels have been closing down and the possibilities are being eroded. People have stopped having access to those venues. Either the theatres can't afford the risk or the company can't afford to go into the space. The landscape is changing drastically. When we first started out it was possible for us to do the work we wanted to do. Although everybody was on the dole, we could make theatre, and there were places where it could be shown, but now it's even difficult to do that. It's evidence that we're in a state of petrification now; wanting to make the work but not knowing how or where to move.'

In another context, Bardsley continues, 'I think I'm at a stage where I need feeding, so I'm trying to clarify what it is I want to do, the sort of work I want to explore and how it's possible to do it. It's very distressing because there are so many incredibly creative people out there, but it's very difficult for them to make the work they want to and to concentrate on that fully. With a lot of my peers, it's a constant conversation. How do you support yourself while you're trying to make the work you want to do? Particularly if the work you want to do is in the margins. And in this present climate, it's a conundrum. You feel that people are being stalled; they realise there isn't really any true support for a particular sort of work.'

The plight of the small company is similarly expressed by Jenny Killick, who maintains that in today's depressed financial environment it would be impossible to get a group of quality actors to commit to an extensive project or a long period of time. 'You could do it with students or young people for two or three years before they've become established but for an actor with a mortgage and children, it's very hard now. The times are not right; that's really a dreadful excuse, but it needs to be an organisation that allows actors in and out while certain people remain constant – designers, directors, writers as a kind of bed-rock. These people could be talking and working together and then bringing in actors who would form a company as and when they were free and for as long as they could commit. It's the sort of double bind of having to be pragmatic as opposed to the ideal.'

A number of the women directors are surviving the difficult financial times by augmenting their work with teaching – particularly in the United States. Brigid Larmour has taught at Juilliard in New York and at Southern Methodist University in Texas. Jenny Killick and Di Trevis have taught at the University of California, Davis, and Sarah Pia Anderson holds a tenured position there. Many of the directors have taught in England as well; for example, Annie Castledine periodically teaches and directs at the Dartington College of the Arts. She found her work there on, for example, Sheila Yeger's *Variations* extremely difficult in an academic situation. 'The combination of demands on the students and the disintegration of higher education in this country mean that the underpinnings for the project have been totally inadequate.' Julia Bardsley has also taught at Dartington, at Wimbledon, and at De Montfort University, where she is an external examiner for Master's degree students in the Arts and Humanities.

Some have turned to television. Jenny Killick, Annie Castledine, and Sarah Pia Anderson have been trained by the BBC and find that they enjoy the work immensely. Brigid Larmour has worked with Granada in Manchester. Killick explains her move in terms of her dissatisfaction with the British establishment theatre. Killick explains, 'In my work in the theatre, I'd moved to the position of being interested in new work, in the idea of theatre as a contemporary experience, in a play that's speaking directly on a contemporary level to you now. It may be set historically, but the person who is writing it is alive today, living in the same world and culture as you are. At the time I moved into TV, the theatre was becoming more and more what I call "heritage". It was the peak years of the conservative government, and obviously there had been a trend moving slowly and inexorably in that direction. The whole seventeen years that Thatcher was in power, the word "heritage" was in common usage. So the theatre was about revisiting classics. And so I began to feel a bit disenfranchised really and to wonder – because you want the director to work with the best actors and the best theatres and the best resources

– where all the new material was. I did two new plays at the National, *Shape of the Table* by David Edgar and *At Our Table* by Daniel Mornin. It was near to heaven. I can't tell you what it was like doing those plays in those circumstances when Richard Eyre was Director of the National: the support, the six weeks of rehearsal. But these were very rare moments within the overall structure. Although Richard was very good about new work, increasingly the slots were being taken over by established writers like David Hare, and so I was beginning to feel, am I going to work at the National and nowhere? Everyone was doing Ibsen and Shakespeare; very little commissioning of new work going on. So I swung my eyes towards television. But now', Killick adds, 'we've voted in a Labour government, so the whole thing could turn around. The theatre could open again and be more healthy.'

Brigid Larmour spent some time in television between her period at the Contact Theatre and her more recent stage work. She left the Contact in 1994 when Manchester was named City of Drama. 'I went to Granada TV and I trained as a live studio television director. I ended up directing news and magazine programmes for six months, which was hell really. It was very interesting and terribly good training but as far removed from the qualities of directing drama as you could wish. However, having served my apprenticeship, I was then given a drama, *The Treasure of Zavimbi*, to direct the following year. When I finished my training at Granada, I came to the National and did my first production of *The Tempest* with a woman Prospero which was a significant page in the evolution of my directing of Shakespeare into this thing which I call Shakespeare Unplugged.'

Commenting on her training course and the state of British television when we first spoke together, Sarah Pia Anderson said, 'It was a thirteen-weeks course. There were three women and six men. We were a relatively successful group who went on to work in both television and the theatre. I frankly find British television drama now, on the whole, fairly disappointing. It used to be quite interesting but now, thanks to the new

Broadcasting Bill engineered by Margaret Thatcher, television in this country is going through a sea-change. Some of it will be strengthened no doubt. And yet certain working practices (some of value, some not) will be swept away for ever. It is important to remain positive and strive to maintain standards in the face of an ideology that places profit at the pinnacle of human endeavour. Yet it is also important to stay open to the benefits that change may bring and to stay effective. It is no good hanging on to purity if no one is listening to you. These are the harsh realities of working within our broadcasting system at the moment. Drama isn't being made, or if it is, it's popular entertainment, which is fine. But it's not what it used to be. *The Bill* I like because it's at least attempting to do something that concerns ordinary people and their lives. It's not a soap; it doesn't glamorise the police force nor does it seek to undermine them. It's sort of rough and ready. Given the limitations of anything you can transmit at eight o'clock at night, it's not bad. And it's very, very popular.'

Not only are directors being enticed towards television, even though television is also falling victim to the economic restraints in the nineties, but writers and actors are similarly succumbing to television's lure. Jenny Killick speaks of the days when theatres had monies to commission new works and promising young playwrights. Ultimately Killick commissioned about twenty plays for the Traverse Theatre. Her first was John Clifford's *Losing Venice*, a poetic drama ostensibly about a mad Spanish duke going off to reclaim a small principality somewhere in the Mediterranean and dragging his people into war and carnage. In fact, however, the play, which caught the imagination of audiences all over the world in its two-year tour, was about the British relationship to the Falkland Islands. 'It was very releasing because it said that new writers can be highly theatrical and write with scope and breadth and poetry and imagination. It had come to seem that writers were merely auditioning for television through the theatre.' Indeed, many talented writers worked both in theatre and television, and as Phyllida Lloyd points out, television drama was abundant and healthy. But when commissions for new plays began to be curtailed, the quality of television drama deteriorated as well. There is now much less encouragement of new young talent than there had been in the 1970s and early 1980s.

Both Killick and Larmour feel that television acting has had a detrimental effect on the training of actors. Larmour referred to a *Times* article about the state of classical acting, supporting her contention that there is an ever greater emphasis on naturalistic and television acting in drama schools, a decreasing emphasis on classical plays in the regional theatres for financial reasons, and an inability for actors to get much opportunity to work together in an ensemble situation. 'People aren't in environments where they learn how to inhabit the language, make it their own, and communicate it to an audience. And they're not in a safe environment where they can be very truthful. The model is individualistic. The "successful" young actors are the ones who are going into a movie or into TV. I find when I audition actors for Shakespeare Unplugged, I see hundreds of people and there are two main problems: one is the people who are highly educated and think they know it all and speak it very confidently and clearly but with no personal connection to it; the other the people who have been less highly educated and are afraid of it and feel they don't understand it and can't understand it and never will understand it.' Larmour is talking with staff at the National – Trevor Nunn (Artistic Director), Jenny Harris (Head of Education), and Patsy Rodenburg (Head of Voice) – to see if some of the best actors coming out of drama schools might not be kept together for six to twelve months for training and ensemble work in classical text. Larmour believes such an experience would offer the actors knowledge, confidence, a safe ensemble experience so that 'they can do honest, truthful, spiritually open work. Actors are the invisible redundant in our industry because it's very easy to stop employing them. They can sit at home and not work. Their powerlessness has been intensified. Every time they go in for an audition, they really need to please you. It's very unhealthy because to be able to do what they do, which is extraordinary, they need to feel safe, able to risk, able to fail, able to be stupid and boring and fuck up and not know.'

As new work, on the one hand, and classical training on the other began to diminish, so did a kind of energy and vitality of audiences. They, too, began to want to spend their money on what was safe and reliable. As Julia Bardsley says, theatre must be more than 'just big musicals, money-making ventures, and things that can transfer to the West End. Theatres need to be fed with new ideas, new approaches, new blood. I think it is difficult to sustain momentum and faith in the work you're doing if it isn't being supported by audiences. They come in droves for the big shows but it's very, very difficult to get an audience for straight theatre, for drama, even for well-known classics. It's very hard to get them to come and see the work, especially if it smacks of anything they think they won't enjoy or won't understand. It's quite demoralising for the performers if audiences aren't there. But when you do that sort of [experimental] work, you set yourself up not to have success the way success is normally deemed. Maybe our success is in the controversy we provoke. We had after-show discussions at Leicester that got very heated: "You can't do this with Lorca; you can't do that with so and so." There was actual debate about the theatre – how we treat text; whether or not text should be kept sacrosanct. Fascinating! Maybe that's where the success of the work lies – in making people think, in generating discussion.'

Annabel Arden's perception of audiences is very different to Bardsley's. She says, 'People like opera. It's a myth that it's arty, horrible, and uninteresting. People like it; they go; they find it exciting.' When I asked Arden if she believes young people go to the opera, she responded, 'Everybody is talking about this crisis. I don't know if young people ever really did go. OK, there was a time after the war when a lot of young people did because there was no alternative, no television. If you don't have much money when you're young and there's cinema and there's TV and there's video, it's difficult to get people to go. On the other hand, what's wrong with maturing into theatre?'

Shakespeare is made appealing to adolescents because of school performances, Arden believes, and Complicite's audiences get younger and younger. 'It depends on how you educate people; it depends on how good the work is. What young people respond to is the strength of commitment that they perceive written on the body of the actor, and I think that is also why people like circus and all of those related things, and it's why people like opera. Because there stands a person doing what you can't believe. If you are musically alive and a performance is good, you say, "I don't know how they're doing that!" But there is a lot of dead opera that, no matter how much virtuosity in the voice, it simply doesn't touch you. What directors have to get over to singers is, "Yes, you can do it but you will never really thrill anybody unless you believe what I'm telling you: you're not making my spine tingle. If you are interested I will always tell you, I will never lie, and I won't be personal. On a scale of one to ten, the tingle factor is two!"'

Almost all of the directors believe that the British theatre is not as strong as it was ten or fifteen years ago. When I as an American began to make comparisons between the health of the American theatre and that of the British, Bardsley mused, 'Don't you think that's just sort of nostalgia; that the English theatre is stronger than the American?' When I spoke of tradition, a sense of theatrical climate, the Elizabethan heritage, Bardsley said, 'I think it can also be a negative part of culture. The weight of history can be problematic. I think we should be very critical of that theatrical tradition – even Shakespeare – and not have just a blind reverence for everything.' Bardsley smarted under the hostility and criticism of her *Hamlet*. The attitude seemed to be, 'Well, there's this young upstart who has been very vocal and critical about the theatre establishment, attempting to tackle this play that is the backbone of our cultural heritage, and she ruined it. She's gone a step too far.'

Just as Bardsley suggests self-criticism by theatre practitioners, Brigid Larmour speaks of the need for more informed and responsible theatre critics. Larmour maintains that the problem is not with audiences but with the critics' need for oversimplification and their inability to be alert to ambiguity. 'Audiences watch and listen and respond and notice what's happening. But the critic has to go away and write about a production very fast. So sometimes I think we're expected to make things really grotesquely simplistic. For instance, in my *Measure for Measure* I don't think the critics really saw what I was doing. Because they've seen the play so many times, they sometimes seem to be looking for a heavily signposted interpretation, so they're approaching it thinking, "Well, what's this going to be then? Is the duke good or is the duke bad? Is Isabella good or is Isabella bad?" and neither of these are sensible questions. It's like arguing are humans good or are humans bad? That's not how the play works. The play works by taking you with one of them and then with another of them and constantly contradicting what you *think* you think. And I was annoyed when I got the reviews. Whereas sometimes when I've done things which I consider a bit crass, the critics have really liked them. But it's different for audiences and one of the great virtues of the theatre is that you get a terribly honest response from an audience, especially a young audience. A lot of the classical work I've done has been in theatres with a high proportion of young people in the audience, both in my work at the National and for the Contact. You really know when you're not making a story clear, when you're just being self-indulgent, and when you're not being truthful with those audiences because they'll just switch off or, worse, make a huge noise. So you know whether you're telling the story truthfully, and you have to make it work as if it were for the first time.'

A number of the directors were outspoken in their response to critics, finding that the experience people describe – especially informed theatre people – is very different from what theatre critics choose to say. We might ask, 'Do we really have informed, trained, and responsible critics?' Are they too easily satisfied? Does their brief exposure to a play encourage simplistic responses? Do we have critics or merely reviewers? Who today is provoking the form forward in the same way that a George Bernard Shaw or a Kenneth Tynan did?

Several of the directors questioned whether or not the major institutions like the Royal Shakespeare Theatre are, in fact, living up to their potential in terms of quality of performance and production. Are the productions as strong as they were even five or six years ago? Are such institutions too bureaucratic, too unwieldy? Are the best actors being drawn to and supported by the national theatres? One cannot help but notice how many of the luminaries of the theatre are making films; some are exploring the independent sector; others are seeking fulfilment on the Broadway stage in America or at theatres on the Continent. Several of the directors expressed their belief that while Britain is producing a large amount of theatre, its practitioners are not breaking new ground. As a general rule, the directors express concern about the future of these vast organisations which may not totally be in touch with the essence of theatre; its organic, human, inspired-by-the-moment, small-scale nature. Theatre is about the inspired functioning of an extraordinary tight group and not about domination by powerful, sprawling institutions. Can the way forward come out of such complex organisations? While one must commend the National's support and nurturing of the fringe, it is probably unlikely that a new direction in theatre will come from those megalithic structures. One must remember, however, that it was at the RSC during the 1960s that Peter Brook truly broke new ground with such productions as *Marat/Sade*. Today one can look to the work of a director like Deborah Warner who, with her almost exclusive working relationship with one designer, Hildegard Bechtler; and one actress, Fiona Shaw, has created emotionally charged productions of *Electra*, *The Good Person of Szechwan*, *Hedda Gabler* and *Richard II* in something very like the context of a small and intimate company.

While some of the directors feel that something rash needs to happen to dissipate the complacency of the institutional theatres, others would relish the thought of working regularly at the RSC or the National. We still look to these institutions for standards of excellence and vision for the British theatre. Perhaps the point to be made here, while granting that some of the women were far more political and outspoken than others, is that all of the women directors believe that the British theatre has suffered a decline in, certainly, the last ten years. All of them expressed at least a degree of concern and criticism about the state of their art. Economics, forces of government, Arts Councils cut-backs have in turn affected ticket prices, created box office constraints, and contributed to more conservative theatre philosophies, less innovation and experimentation.

Many of the women spoke of ambivalent feelings about New Labour under the leadership of Tony Blair. Julia Bardsley says, 'It was fantastic the day that all that happened. We were crying with joy after all those years of Conservatism. But I don't think having a Labour government is going to make things any rosier for the arts in the short term. And that's fine. In my opinion, it's more important that the overall tone and philosophical thrust of how the country is run shifts. A genuine change in the general attitude will have a very specific and positive effect on the arts over the next five or ten years, I'm sure.'

Also commenting on the new Labour government, Brigid Larmour says, 'When I was artistic director of a company, people would complain about funding problems, saying, "Let's hope we get a change of government" and I would say, "Yes, let's hope we get a change of government, but they're not going to be able to sort this out. Thatcher has sold the family silver, and we're going to be lucky if we can afford a health service and an education service." So I'm very cautious about funding prospects. But it would be impossible to overstate the transformation in the national mood. There was a feeling that this dark, selfish, shallow time was over and a sense that you could actually be British without being ashamed of it. For the first time since I was nineteen I didn't have to feel alienated from the entire establishment of this country.' But the government might reason that if theatre is able to be one of the great sources of tourism in Great Britain without much support, well and good, so Larmour does not see vast sums of money flowing into the theatres. But, Larmour argues, perhaps change needs to come from within the theatre itself. If the coal mining industry and the print industry, for example, have been forced to reinvent themselves in order to take account of savings that can be made through mechanisation, then we cannot expect the theatre to carry on as it has always been. Ten or fifteen years ago, everyone believed that video would kill the cinema. Now, Larmour maintains, there is an explosion of cinema going with multiplex theatres, 'not like the dreary old musty buildings of the beleaguered regional theatre. So I've always thought there would be some theatres carrying on doing exactly what they are doing and others that would reinvent themselves, which is exactly what is happening at companies like the Birmingham Repertory Theatre.'

Such self-criticism and political criticism, while it may appear negative, is in fact a positive symbol of the women's eternal striving towards excellence. They are not content to accept the present as the best of times, nor are they clinging to a more lucrative past, but as I hope the next two chapters will reveal, they are striving towards the betterment of the status of women, towards fulfilment of their personal aspirations and visions, and towards a greater theatre.

CHAPTER 8

Supporting one another

While I did not set out with the idea that this work would necessarily reflect a feminist point of view, I was nevertheless very interested in the directors' attitudes, beliefs, and concerns regarding feminism. The extremes were complete: from Julia Bardsley who says, 'Not a big discussion; I'm a woman and I'm a director, and it's never been an issue, never been a problem,' to Brigid Larmour or Annie Castledine who are avowed feminists. Yet it was a subject that was thought about in every interview, and as I assembled my notes to write this chapter I was amazed at just how much had been said on the subject of women's issues.

A fundamental question exists: is it as possible for a woman to become a director as it is for a man? One would have to respond that it depends on the woman or the man. One curious dimension of the subject is that we would never dream of discussing a man's work as a *male* director; he has simply earned the title of director. However, until women have also achieved an equality with men in numbers, in status and in acceptance, it remains a topic that must be approached. As Sarah Pia Anderson says, 'It's a sensitive area because there used to be a time when the question would always be, "What is it like to be a woman as opposed to a man directing?" And the whole basis of the interview was about sex rather than about the work. It slightly represses . . .' Nancy Meckler, on the other hand, concludes, 'I don't think it ever really occurred to me that I wasn't going to be a director because I was a woman. I've always just assumed that I could do things which women maybe didn't normally do.'

Responding very thoughtfully to my query about the relationship between male and female directors, Katie Mitchell says, 'If feminism means equality between men and women, equal opportunities for work and life, then I'm a feminist. If it means a separatist movement, which separates itself from men, then I'm not a feminist. In the end I think the work should speak for itself, whether it's made by a man or by a woman. And the audience is the best judge of whether it's effective or not. The gender of the person who made that work shouldn't be an issue. Having said all that, if I were to see a situation in which a woman was being discriminated against as a director or in any other walk of life because of her gender, I would fight tooth and nail to stop that situation occurring or indeed developing.' Mitchell's comment mirrors the responses of all the women who, whether professed feminists or not, are adamant about their desire to help and support one another. To a person they are hopeful about their roles as women directors and encouraged about their abilities to nurture the work of women writers or to emphasise plays with female protagonists. They offer very positive approaches to issues of gender in their professional lives.

Another problem that many of the women referred to is the Oxbridge factor. Julia Bardsley and Annie Castledine mention it as being as much of an impediment (if not more of one) to achievement in directing as gender. Bardsley, for example, says, 'I'm made more aware that my background is one of a polytechnic arts course rather than a Cambridge or Oxford English degree than I am of being a woman. There's an annoying phenomenon of people who studied English literature who feel they know how to direct plays or be involved in theatre. Most of the time I don't think they have any idea or any feel for theatre.'

Castledine supports this concern about class, saying, 'I don't know if I'm an established director or not. Within our theatre, there is an aristocracy and there is the working class. And I definitely belong to the working class. This class system involves inherited wealth, university education, modishness, but it's also to do with trust: the fact that some people can deliver and some people are more suspect.' In *A Better Direction*, Kenneth Rea maintains, however, that the domination of directors from Oxford and Cambridge has diminished in recent years, and that young directors, male and female, are receiving their educations at a variety of colleges and universities.

It is interesting that in, for example, the 1993–94 season at the Royal Shakespeare Company, both in Stratford-upon-Avon and in London, only two women directors were represented: Katie Mitchell doing Ibsen's *Ghosts* and Di Trevis staging David Pownall's *Elgar's Rondo*. In the height of the tourist season, summer of 1997, there were no women at the National and only two at the RSC: Katie Mitchell, and Kathryn Hunter co-directing with Marcello Magni. This is a disappointing change from those days in 1988 and 1989 when there was an increased awareness and a jogging of consciousness that produced four women at the RSC: Deborah Warner, Sarah Pia Anderson, Garry Hynes, and Di Trevis. Half the directors were women. Of those four women who directed for the RSC in the late 1980s, Hynes has resumed her position as Artistic Director of the Druid Theatre Company in Galway; Anderson has directed at the Roundabout in New York and the University of California, Davis, and for television in both America and Britain; Warner has directed operas at Leeds and Glyndebourne and directed internationally in Paris and the Salzburg Festival, and mounted a European and American tour of *The Waste Land*. While Di Trevis still directs regularly at the RSC and the National, she, too, has directed for Clwyd and at the University of California, Davis. Admittedly women like Phyllida Lloyd, Katie Mitchell, and Fiona Laird have now joined the ranks of directors at the two national theatres so that a degree of balance has been maintained. Director Jude Kelly has made the West Yorkshire Playhouse a phenomenal success. Just as one is aware of young women directors actively pursuing their careers, one must also acknowledge an older group of women who really paved the way for young directors: Sue Parrish, Julia Pascal, and Susan Todd among them. While these women certainly paved the way for a new generation of women directors, they remain transitional figures. And, of course, one is aware of the anti-establishment director, Joan Littlewood, now living in Paris and Buzz Goodbody, whose career was cut short by her tragic suicide. It is to these women, most of whom did not achieve the recognition or success they deserved, that young directors owe a debt of gratitude.

Several of the women articulated those problems, probably unique to women, which can be obstacles to a career. Sue Sutton Mayo emphasises the choices and responsibilities of marriage and motherhood. 'One of the primary reasons why women find it so difficult to succeed in the theatre has to do with biology. Now this is probably true of all professions but in theatre, where the hours are so erratic and long and where the commitment is so total and intense, it seems enhanced somehow. Trying to do that and raise a family and be the woman in that situation is very difficult.' Mayo speaks of a time in her career when it probably would have been wise to move to London and establish herself as a freelance director: 'I think this is something that happens certainly to married women with children at any rate. What I should have done then was move to town and start to use these connections that I'd made there. I'd met Peter Hall, I'd got to know Peter Gill, I could phone Trevor Nunn, I'd got to know quite a few people. However, I had a family in Manchester, I didn't particularly want to live in London, so I came back to Manchester and experienced a tremendous lull. I think I directed two shows in the next two years. Because I'd had such a big taste of what it was I wanted to do, not to have the chance to do it was appalling. I met Nick Hytner [Associate Director of the National Theatre and known for such productions as *Miss Saigon* and the National Theatre's revival of *Carousel*] while he was working at the Royal Exchange, Manchester, and he didn't really have any idea what I was talking about. He just kept saying, "But you had these chances and you just let them go?" And I said that I didn't really perceive of them as chances at the time because they weren't realistic options in my life. Oh, I suppose many women, of course, who are much braver and stronger than I, do exactly that. Just go and do it. And I have so much admiration for them. But I couldn't do that. I've always felt really that as passionately as I feel about my work, my children actually are the most important thing in my life. And their well-being is paramount. And I know that I have chosen not to take chances because I felt that it would be wrong for them. I don't mean they stop me. I mean that was my own choice; that's the real issue.' Killick, too, has made choices because of two children, and Nancy Meckler reflects on the period in her life when she was raising two sons: 'I didn't work full time. I wasn't in television. I think if you're in television you often have to have a full-time job. I didn't run a theatre either. So, until my youngest was eight, I really only did odd productions, I wasn't working full time which made it not that difficult. It was only difficult when I was actually directing a play.'

Di Trevis expresses some of the same thoughts but adds her concerns about the problems of ageing. She says, 'I've had wonderful chances. What I feel is that if you fail – and I failed on the main stage at Stratford a number of years ago with *Much Ado about Nothing* – it matters more if you're a woman. I have a suspicion that women have to seem to be very, very good, that their work is judged more harshly than a man's. I think the men work more and can be judged by the whole scope of their career. I know the men work more than I do because I like my life and I wanted to have children, which was quite an interruption to my career. It wasn't discriminatory, it was simply biology. And we don't have role models, we women of my generation. We have Joan Littlewood. I'd rather like to grow up to be Joan and when I'm old go off and live with a Rothschild! I really feel it will be very interesting to see how it goes for me as I become a post-menopausal woman because I think the idea of *young* women and *young* men forging ahead as directors is acceptable but I wonder whether the old witch syndrome might come into it. I'm very interested to see if attitudes towards me will change, whether I'll be characterised as the old dragon.'

These points are well taken: a woman's work, if she takes time off for a family, must be judged on the basis of a much smaller body of work than a man's; and with our emphasis on youth culture, we are more accepting and encouraging of the talents of the young. An older director may be regarded as more harridan than dynamo. On the other hand, sometimes charismatic talented male directors have meteoric rises on the basis of a relatively small body of work, whereas successful women directors have had steady painstaking rises, establishing a large body of work that ultimately cannot be ignored. These are merely examples that indicate that the road to a directing career for a woman may be fraught with dangers.

Several of the directors mention the fact that they do not work as frequently, intensely, or at the relentless pace pursued by male colleagues. This idea is expressed very positively by Julia Bardsley who says, 'I think being a woman gives you a sort of freedom. I can sort of float through my directing life not really having to structure a career. A man, on the other hand, might feel he needs to get further, achieve this position, make this amount of money. I feel being a woman lets you off the hook in a sense. I have to support myself, I have to live, but I don't have to look at things in a terribly structured way. Ultimately, being a woman, I can put things in perspective and say, "Really, it *is* only theatre." It's not that I don't take it seriously, but I know how to take the pressure off. I think that's a feminine quality.'

Invariably in the discussions with the directors the subject of discrimination arose. It is interesting to me that very few of them feel any prejudice against them as women directors – or if they do they have managed to turn that perception into a positive attitude. These are not women who waste any time feeling sorry for themselves.

As Sarah Pia Anderson says, 'I might have been [discriminated against] and not been aware of it because I'm not thinking about that as a protective device. So I just don't dwell on it. If I did spend more time thinking about it, maybe I'd understand certain situations better. But I think it probably balances out. I've been fortunate to get the advantages of being a woman when it's been politically expedient for various reasons to have women [as directors]. I have in certain situations perhaps been the token woman.' On the whole Anderson believes that men are highly visible in the profession in part because men enjoy working together and tend to think of other men for jobs before they consider women. 'It sometimes isn't even a conscious thing, but it is still very much a male club whereby if you don't innately understand the rules, you just don't exist. You're invisible, you're other. But I think it's also difficult for men in lots of ways. A female director was speaking to me recently about how lonely it is to be a director, thinking that was because she was a woman. But I think that loneliness exists for both men and women. It's just the loneliness of being in a position of responsibility. It's tough for everyone.'

Anderson's main sources of work at a certain period of her career had been British television, in particular *The Bill* interspersed with classical theatre in the United States. Her last play for the RSC had been *Mary and Lizzie* by Frank McGuinness which received a mixed critical reception. 'And I kept asking to do classical work at the RSC and the National, and there was no response whatsoever. And when I was asked to do it in America, I thought, "Well, that's what I'll do." ' She now regards this period of her life as time when she was able to seize new opportunities and new avenues of exploration. Little did she know then that the attention showered on her 1994 and 1995 directing of 'Inner Circles' for the Emmy Award winning mini-series, *Prime Suspect*, would be instrumental in securing an active career in American film and television. Besides the *Prime Suspect* success, there was the knowledge of her theatre work, and the opportunity to teach on a regular basis for the University of California, Davis. It was a vital lesson, she says, in learning to 'be open and receptive to opportunities that are offered rather than holding onto false expectations'. Anyone, male or female, Anderson maintains, 'who sustains a long career in the dramatic arts, may need to realise that sometimes you think you're going to do one thing and suddenly the wind's blowing in a different direction. You must learn to go wherever you feel creative and productive.'

Similar attitudes about the climate being ripe for women directors and about men choosing to work with men are reflected in Phyllida Lloyd's responses, but she adds insightful comments about women's lack of aggressiveness and the absence of role models in the profession. 'I don't think women are discriminated against as directors in the country particularly. I think it's just as possible for a woman who has the aptitude to direct as it is for a man. I think there are certain pressures on institutions to employ more women that works to the advantage of some of us who have come at a good time. I do think it's an extremely competitive field to break into and that women tend to be less willing to thrust themselves to the forefront than men. I don't know if this has parallels in education: who are our role models in academia? What's the ratio of female to male professors? The big national institutions are almost entirely run by men. There was a significant appointment at the National Theatre of Genista McIntosh, as Executive Director there, a wonderful role model for all women working in theatre administration.

'I think there is a tendency of male directors to look for little mirrors of themselves when they're looking for assistants, which I don't always think helps women get that training. But all through my work experience I haven't felt disadvantaged in any sense by the fact that I am a woman.'

Sue Sutton Mayo tells an anecdote about being forced to take a tough line with a male actor who was *not* responding well to a woman in a leadership role. While directing Dickens's *Christmas Carol*, she had an actor who was habitually late to music rehearsals. The musical director on the project was a woman who, while she did not have a great deal of theatre experience, had enormous potential. The male actor, on the other hand, was more experienced and very well trained. Mayo could see that tension was developing, so she called the actor in and listened to his excuses about not being able to help it if the train didn't come. Mayo snapped back, 'I don't want that crap! I can see what's going on. You get to those music calls and you get there on time! She is the musical director; you are not!' Mayo believes that the tardiness excuse was in fact symbolic of a deeper problem: the man's response to a woman in an authority position. At any rate the actor was never late again, and the relationship ultimately sorted itself out.

Irish director Lynne Parker, while she does not face discrimination, feels that she does have what is probably an equally challenging problem – being taken seriously. Rough Magic is an equal opportunity organisation whose director has been a woman since its inception. 'But', Parker states, 'I'm aware that in established theatre or commercial theatre in Ireland it's still a little surprising to see a woman take control. Most of the directors in Ireland are men, and I don't think they would be comfortable with a woman in any position of authority.' While Parker believes that for a long time she was not taken seriously, she now feels she has been welcomed into both the Abbey mainstage and the Gaity by Patrick Mason and Ben Barnes respectively. 'There's an assumption that you're all very well in your little company in your little theatre space but you'd never be able to hack it in the big theatres. And what people don't take into account is that it's actually harder to put on theatre on a low budget in a theatre that leaks and where the lights don't work. You have to be more skilled and more inventive than you would if it was all laid out for you. No, I don't feel discriminated against as a woman; in fact, I think there's a climate in which it's almost an advantage. I wouldn't have felt that ten years ago. I must be grateful to my sisters, my older sisters, who have laid the tracks.'

In 1993 Garry Hynes was clearly responding to many pressures surrounding her tenure at the Abbey. I believe she was feeling a sense of rejection if not downright discrimination, but as she points out it was probably more complex than merely being an issue of gender. 'First, I am a woman but there was a previous female artistic director who was here for only about eighteen months in the early seventies; second, I haven't grown up within the Dublin Irish theatre tradition; third, I come from the west of Ireland, literally outside of Dublin.' Hynes believes all of these factors combined to make her something of an outsider. And she maintains she would never say that sexism doesn't exist. 'I used to say that for years, and then I realised it was a very easy thing to say because I had established myself and because of who I was among a group of peers, and therefore it was very easy. If I had to train or become a director by breaking into the traditional theatre, I realise that I would have had a much rougher ride.'

Perhaps the most committed feminists of the group are Brigid Larmour and Annie Castledine. Larmour recalls her experiences at the RSC in Stratford when in 1984 she put together a proposal for her, Annie Castledine, and Di Trevis to take over The Other Place in Stratford, an idea that met with great verbal support but total inaction. 'I'd been successful at my job of assistant director, they liked me, and I'd been very supportive of all of them. I started out in all innocence and good faith, and then I realised what was happening. I decided to do something about it, and perhaps later on other women were able to benefit from it. After I had written this proposal and, in fact, more when I was leaving the RSC, a couple of the associate directors, to whom I had copied this memo, came into my office and said how they realised they had been unthinkingly sexist. Some of them spoke about Buzz Goodbody at that time, and there was a sense of sadness, regret, and perhaps shame. And that was extraordinary. And, indeed, a little way down the line things did change quite radically – certainly for a while. There was clearly a certain amount of changing of hearts and minds. There was also a lot of pressure from me, Fiona Shaw, Juliet Stevenson, and others, and from Christina Burnett at the Directors' Guild which culminated in women being invited through the doors of the RSC to make their own work. I think it's something that runs through the history of feminism: that everyone owes something to the people who have gone before.'

Actors like Juliet Stevenson and Fiona Shaw brought pressure on the RSC in the mid-1980s for a greater awareness of women's concerns. Larmour acknowledges fellow director, Annie Castledine, as one who has never ceased to fight for women's status in the theatre. Castledine herself says, 'I think we're very patronised by male directors.' She recalls receiving a note from a male director that was obviously designed to be very complimentary. 'But it came from a huge and superior distance. I was being patted on the head with "Not bad, not bad". I didn't respond. I just let it go and got on with it. But that happens all the time to women directors and practitioners by male directors. You've got to be very strong if you're going to survive at all and if you're going to continue to be invited by the men, because it *is* the men who are offering the jobs. True a woman, Helena Kaut-Howson, asked me to do a production at Clwyd, but usually all the work I do is because I'm invited by male directors to do it. So I do have an ambivalent relationship with them – because we're saying, "Yes I would like to do that. Thank you very much." And we're saying, "Why aren't you really empowering more of us, beyond a cosmetic, tokenistic way." '

Castledine says, 'I feel fairly harshly on the whole towards my fellow women directors because I think they're paranoid and neurotic about their position in what is basically a male preserve. They don't see it as part of the joy of being colleagues. I judge them harshly because I expect more of them. There are fraternities of wealth and position from the outside world that infiltrate the theatre. These fraternities, on the whole, exclude women on the basis of gender, class, and age. Sometimes a director becomes a man/woman and joins the fraternities. Some women take a very strong masculine approach to career and work. They could advance projects outside their own endeavours but are reluctant to do so, reluctant to extend their energies to enable other women.'

Certainly both Annie Castledine and Annabel Arden have expressed their commitment to fellow women directors when they have, on several occasions, decided to co-direct. Arden says that people assume she does the movement work and Castledine the text work, which could not be further from the truth. Speaking of *India Song*, Arden says, 'We didn't separate our functions. Annie was very important in creating the movement, and I had a lot to do with text. I run around more than Annie does, but she sees what a movement should be. She's very articulate, and I know what to do with text although I haven't done as much as she. That's a very interesting thing about co-directing. People always try to define what the function of each person is – as if you could. It's as close as a really good love affair. How do you say what the function of each lover is?'

If there are problems with women directors either obtaining work or being recognised for the work they do, several of the directors offered suggestions, one being networking among women. Again Castledine affirms the fact that women don't help one another. 'We've not learned to network. Maybe we don't want to network. Maybe we refuse to learn to network. Maybe we need to enable one another a little bit more. I don't think we talk together as much as we should, we women directors. It is possible to create an opportunity to do so but none of us will take that responsibility. We're all too busy to start with, but we should really come together to talk about our practice.' Sue Sutton Mayo agrees with Castledine: 'We don't talk to each other very well at all. I think we're a bit frightened of each other, and there's the whole thing about work being scarce, and the stakes are so high.'

While she was head of the Abbey Theatre, Garry Hynes was in a position to hire other women directors. Deborah Warner created her *Hedda Gabler* there in 1991, and Katie Mitchell directed Maxim Gorki's *The Last Ones* at the Peacock early in 1993. Both Brigid Larmour and Annabel Arden have hired Annie Castledine for Contact and Complicite respectively. As Nancy Meckler says, 'I don't know that I have got a very defined perspective towards feminism. I've never felt any particular need to make an effort to work with women for political reasons or feminine reasons but in the last ten years I've begun to notice that in fact I really do work better with women, and so now I make much more of an effort to work with women.' Meckler has recently been co-directing with Polly Teale at Shared Experience Theatre. It should be noted, too, that Meckler was very helpful to Deborah Warner in securing

Arts Council funding when Warner established her Kick Theatre Company.

Another way in which women can support other women in the theatre is in the choice of play. Any number of the women directors speak of the importance of selecting plays that, while not written by women, have very strong female characters. Hynes says, 'There is an emotional involvement with women characters that comes from deep within my own experience.' Nancy Meckler agrees, stating, 'I began to realise that the plays I was choosing to do almost always have a very strong female protagonist, and I was ignorant enough not even to realise that in the early days, but plays like *Antigone* and *The Duchess of Malfi* were chosen very much for those reasons.' Sarah Pia Anderson is drawn to Ibsen's strong women: Rebecca West in *Rosmersholm* and *Hedda Gabler*. She has also directed Shaw's *St Joan*.

Similarly, Katie Mitchell asserts, 'I'm constantly reading plays, both new plays and classical plays, and I suppose the plays that do attract me tend to be epic, bleak, with incredibly challenging and difficult emotional journeys for the characters, and often driven by female protagonists. That isn't always possible when you're looking at the classical canon, but wherever possible I try. When it comes to that, I go out of my way to put flesh on some very bad bones which represent some of the female characters in classical drama. About five years ago, I wanted to do *Women of Troy*, and that was a direct response to what I had heard and seen about what was happening in Lithuania when the Russians invaded with their tanks, and this play seemed to speak for those women.'

A very strong feminist perspective was applied to Complicite's *The Winter's Tale*. Annabel Arden says, 'We interpreted it – how could we do otherwise given Annie [Castledine] and myself – from a very female point of view. We have a real psychotic in Leontes. He's not a woman hater per se but something in his imagination about his own sexuality, Hermione's sexuality, his own deep connection with the fear of being out of control and that she is uncontrollable – all turn him into a destroyer of all that is female. That is what happens in the first three acts, and then it all gradually turns over and around and comes back through the fourth and fifth acts. It is truly a tale of winter, an enormous cycle; it goes down, down, down, down into the depths of absolute barrenness which Leontes creates, and then the season turns to spring with the amazing scene of Antigonus, the baby, the bear, and the two shepherds.'

In her passion for commissioning new plays at the Traverse Theatre, Jenny Killick recalls, 'I was trying to commission plays with strong central roles for women, where they are not simply being – as they are in Shakespeare certainly – adjuncts to the main action. I found this so releasing in many ways. I'm keen to see plays with women driving and motivating the action.' The second play by John Clifford that Killick commissioned for the Traverse was a Faust story with a female Faust titled *Playing with Fire*.

Even more prevalent than those directors who seek strong female characters in the plays they choose to do are the women who are concerned with encouraging and supporting women playwrights. Several of the directors have, in fact, developed or attempted to develop programmes specifically for women writers. For example, Garry Hynes, while at the Abbey Theatre, asked 'Why is it that we have no significant women writers of the same calibre as men?' Because of this Hynes was committed to doing at least one play by a woman in the Abbey's season of new plays and selected Marina Carr's *The Mai*, which Hynes herself directed. 'I am concerned', she says, 'and wish to nourish and encourage and bring forward and promote women in the theatre.'

Yet Hynes was sceptical of a more formal involvement because of an experience that had an interesting backlash. 'We had a series of playreadings in 1991 which drew criticism from women who questioned why, if the plays were good enough to read, were they not good enough to stage? It made me uneasy.' While this experience made Hynes reticent about a more aggressive programme of plays by women, she nevertheless observes, 'I think the position of women hasn't improved anything like as much as people think it has. No, I don't! I think it's very easy for us in the theatre – because we are after all in a liberal, educated, cultured, middle-class environment – to think that the norms and mores of our world are those which apply universally, and they absolutely do not. My life, as an artistic director – university-educated, middle-class, who has had an enormous amount of success – is about as different from somebody who was born on the same day and in the same year as me and who lives not ten miles from here as it can be. Sometimes, I think, the theatre threatens to get locked into its own perceptions, is in danger of performing to an audience that sees itself only in terms of its own image, and judges itself only by the standards of what it thinks of itself. All that I find incredibly dangerous.'

Also striving to promote the work of women playwrights in Ireland, Lynne Parker created an initiative for new plays. Parker credits the scheme to her executive producer, Siobhán Bourke. Both Pom Boyd and Gina Moxley, who have acted for Rough Magic, have now had plays produced by the company. In 1994 Boyd won a Stewart Parker award for her first play, *Down onto Blue*. After its Rough Magic premiere the play was invited to Los Angeles for a public reading staring Judy Geeson and Alfred Molina. Rough Magic specifically commissioned Gina Moxley's *Danti-Dan*, which was also performed at the Hampstead Theatre in London. 'We're really having to look for women to write', Parker maintains, 'and that is the case throughout Irish theatre.' The well-known names in Irish writing – Tom Murphy, Brian Friel, Frank McGuinness – are men, not women. 'I'm curious to know', Parker questions, 'why women don't write. Of course twenty years ago, the question could also have been, "Why aren't women directing?" Now we are finding that more and more women are directing. I think it's just a slow evolution. The fact that women are being commissioned at this stage may mean that in another ten years things will have balanced out. But we feel it's important to take an initiative to encourage people to do this, because it's so much about confidence and feeling that there is a forum for you to work in. In my opinion the best place to offer that kind of process is a company like ours with its own structure: tightly controlled, small, flexible, and open. I think that's the most fruitful atmosphere or environment for any writer, male or female, to work in. That doesn't completely answer the whole thing because you can't just establish a process and then expect a result at the end of it. I mean it's not a sausage factory! You have to rely on there being people who have the inspiration and vision to write plays, and you can't legislate for those people. So what we're hoping to do is offer that opportunity, but the writers have to have the initiative, the ability themselves. So luck will play a very large part. What I would offer is some kind of instinct or intuition as to who might be able to make a play. That's why I picked on Gina Moxley. Just thinking of her as an actress and a writer of sketches, I knew she had a play in her. When I offered her the commission she practically fell over on the ground and wagged her tail in the air and behaved like a total child because no one had ever suggested to her that she could do this. She was delighted.' Speaking before Moxley had completed *Danti-Dan*, Parker said, 'and if she does produce something rather good or if she doesn't, well, I think it was a very, very good attempt. But I *do* believe she can do it – and I don't think I'm any more qualified than anyone else to decide who is capable – but I have the experience now to start. I wouldn't have been able to do this four or five years ago. Now I think I can.' Indeed, it would seem that belief and encouragement were ingredients needed to help launch Moxley's new career. Perhaps, a volume such as Heidi Stephenson and Natasha Langridge's *Rage and Reason* (Methuen, 1997), will serve to inspire women playwrights. Yet as Stephenson and Langridge point out, 'Women dramatists still need directors to champion their work.'

Brigid Larmour, while at Manchester's Contact Theatre, was striving for a fifty-fifty split of plays by men and by women during a season. 'It's not difficult', she says, 'to have half the writing you present, whether its classics or other plays, by women writers. It can be done.' So Larmour chose something like Liz Lochhead's *Mary Queen of Scots Got Her Head Chopped Off* as a new play and Timberlake Wertenbaker's version of

Oedipus as a classic. 'It's not impossible to have something like an approximation of real life. But', Larmour concludes, 'I don't beat my breast if it doesn't always work out.'

Several of the directors speak enthusiastically of women's work that they had done or are planning to do. While working at the Traverse, Jenny Killick worked with writer, Amy Hardie, to develop a play titled *Noah's Wife*, the Noah story set in Africa. The thesis, according to Killick, deals with the fact that Noah's wife doesn't want to go on the ark and considers it wrong that a small group of people should save themselves at the expense of an entire nation. 'The most lyrical writing in the play is when Noah's wife goes on the deck at night and has this extraordinary soliloquy about the bones and the bodies bumping against the side of the ark as the ark drifts through a sea of carnage of the people left behind. It was the politics and the poetry that really inspired me. It was a sort of peak of my work there [at the Traverse], the height of what I was hoping the theatre could do.' Killick and Hardie are currently collaborating on several film scripts, one of which is about a British woman who was jailed for leaving her two-year-old daughter alone at home when she went to work. Caught in a poverty trap, unable to afford child care, she felt she had no option. Killick is quick to add how much she enjoys working with Hardie.

Although Julia Bardsley maintains that she doesn't actively seek out the work of women, she maintains she's interested in good work and does not particularly care whether it's by a man or a woman. Bardsley has worked with writer and director Polly Teale on a piece called *Fallen*, which is a solo work about an Irish, Catholic woman accused of killing her baby. 'I'm not', Bardsley asserts, 'specifically searching for women's issues or plays by women but I am interested in the woman's perspective.' Bardsley also did her own adaptation of *Frankenstein,* in which Mary Shelley was the principal character who watches her own creation as it is taken over by men of science and as it represents what the director calls 'a masculine desire for abnormal creation'.

At the Library Theatre, Manchester, Sue Sutton Mayo staged

Ravings: Dreamings, by Kay Adshead, author of *Thatcher's Women*. 'What she's come up with', Mayo explains, 'is a play about the re-imagination of matter. She's suggesting that the capitalistic system and indeed all male-dominated systems have failed us – when you look at the Eastern block, or you look at communism, or you look at capitalism. She posits in the play that these systems have failed because they uniquely use the maleness in us, our male side. She says that we all have been party to this male system, and the time has come for us to use the female in us in order to imagine the future. It's not about a society dominated by women; all of us – men and women – must learn to use the female.' And Mayo confesses, alluding to basic Jungian theory, that the men to whom she relates most effectively are men in whom their female side is very well developed.

Beyond these individual examples of directors exploring the work of women lies the genuine pioneering commitment that Annie Castledine has made to women's plays. Not only has she edited Volumes 9 and 10 of the Methuen series, *Plays by Women*, but she has, during the past ten years, devoted herself largely to workshops and initial productions of women's work. She says, 'You wake up one day and you say, "Look at all I've done – Brian Friel, Phil Young, Peter Nichols," whatever – and you realise you have a desire to use the things you've learned to the advantage of all these women I know who are rattling around. It was just that. It was getting politicised about it but not in a necessarily aggressive way, just wanting to do it. I thought it was time that women's voices should be heard from our main stages. And why not? Especially since we make up so much of the audience, so much of the population. And I thought, our voices are not being heard. But, you see, women get used to their voices not being heard. I even began to think that *women's* perceptions about how we are were as valid as *men's* perceptions about how we are! It takes a long time for that penny to drop, doesn't it?'

So Castledine tries to do at least two productions a year of plays by women playwrights. For example, at the West

Yorkshire Playhouse she did a production of Sarah Daniels's *Masterpieces* which Castledine considers the playwright's first really exciting piece of work. In her first season at the Derby Playhouse, Castledine directed *The Innocent Mistress* by Restoration writer Mary Pix, *The Children's Hour* by Lillian Hellman, and *Sunday's Children* by Gerlind Reinshagen. The rest of her time she devotes to nurturing the writing of women. When I told Castledine how much she was admired by so many of the women directors I met, she was genuinely touched and said, 'That gives you an immense sort of strength to continue with the choices you've made and not to hunger for whatever it is that some people enter the theatre for or even pursue the theatre for. Oh, yes, I think I made an internal decision . . . I'm not sure if it was a tremendously extroverted decision . . . I don't think I could have articulated it clearly, but I obviously *did* make it as soon as I realised that a lot of women in this country and in Europe were not being given a fair chance to develop their writing, I mean to *develop* their writing. I've made it my business to do that, just to do it. So plays like *Tokens of Affection* by Maureen Lawrence, and *Self Portrait* by Sheila Yeger would never have appeared, never have materialised, had those women not been offered workshop opportunities.' Castledine told me that even while she was working during the winter months of 1993 at the Dartington College of the Arts, three burgeoning women playwrights came every weekend to Totnes where on Saturdays their plays were read and on Sundays explored through workshops. Back in London, Castledine works with women playwrights in workshops at the Actors' Centre, and in the summer of 1993 she directed *Carrington*, a new play by Jane Beeson at the Chichester Festival Theatre – a play that Castledine helped develop through workshops hosted by Southwest Arts over a period of two years. Similarly, her 1997 production of *Goliath*, adapted by Bryony Lavery from Beatrix Campbell's book, was produced by Sphinx Theatre Company and grew out of a workshop endeavour. In her programme note for *Goliath*, Sphinx Artistic Director, Sue Parrish, writes, 'There is scarcely a woman writer writing in the theatre today who has not worked with the company, either as Sphinx or as the Women's Theatre Group, or who has not been touched by its pioneering activities.'

Besides the encouragement and putting the work 'on its feet' in workshops, I asked Castledine about her dramaturgical process – how she actually helps a talented writer whose work may be raw and in need of shaping. Castledine maintains that the vessel, the form, is what must be discussed and explored. Content is rarely the problem; most women, Castledine says, have so much content. 'So it's not about content; it's about form. And that's a very hard and classical and rigorous notion. All the work I do is actually on awakening a sense of and an idea of the architecture of a play, and how the architecture will carry the meaning – the metaphor you're going to use within which your content can live and be sustained. You know, that rock strata: how levels of meaning are so important.' If, Castledine suggests, the form cannot *contain* the play, it will not allow the playwright to say what she wishes to say. In other words, the architecture must support the building. Too many inexperienced playwrights write films instead of plays. 'You can't have great hunks of textbook being read aloud by a character. You must have action and it must be highly theatrical. You can't have blackout, blackout, blackout. So what's happening in the blackout? You've got somebody moving about. I mean, come on!' In a workshop situation with the author there observing and entering into a dialogue with the director and actors, the playwright can see when a moment or a scene doesn't work. 'It's an immense process,' Castledine concludes.

Only one of the directors spoke of yet another way in which women can be supported in the theatre: through what is sometimes called cross-gender casting. Brigid Larmour says, 'It's possible to have something like an approximation of real life in the way you cast plays. I mean by that that when you are doing these great classics you can look for characters which could be women. You don't have to have women playing men. We've recently seen actresses playing Richard II and King Lear as men, but what I've been doing for years is to re-imagine the characters as women. I cast Prospero as a woman and Escalus in *Measure for Measure* as a woman so that the actresses were able to bring themselves and their femaleness into the world of the play – not to make any particular feminist point or to talk about what their femaleness is. It's simply that's who you are, and there are quite a lot of us in the world, and I'd like to see quite a lot of us on stage. There are all sorts of ways you can make the theatre a bit more like life. Which is not to say that one makes a quota or that you pervert the meaning of the play. It's just so easy to make adjustments. And I don't think I can bear to go to see too many more plays where you've got twelve men and two women who come on for one scene and then go away. It's gone on far too long.'

Larmour supported her own theory when she decided to do *The Tempest* with a female Prospero. 'What pleases me about casting a woman in this part is that Prospero is powerful and difficult, neither bad nor good. So often in classical theatre, a woman must play either good or bad. A man gets to play human and complex, flawed, and redeemed.' It came to Larmour like a blinding light: this person is an intellectual, who has a child who is difficult, who is able to create magic, who is concerned with ageing, who is ambivalent about letting her daughter go, letting her become a woman. 'All of those things have the most amazing resonance when spoken by a woman.' Larmour used the first scene of the play as an example of how a female Prospero worked. 'That first scene is often incredibly hard for everybody, but particularly for the audience because you have a grand old man of the theatre talking and at his feet you have a pretty girl listening. But once you have a mother-daughter relationship to play with, the kind of layering that went on was fascinating.' The whole first act depicted this beleaguered single mother with her difficult family, Miranda, Ariel, and Caliban. Larmour ended the show with Prospero's line, 'This thing of darkness I acknowledge mine.' Prospero opened her arms to embrace Caliban. Although afraid that he was going to be punished again, he allowed himself to be embraced, knelt at her feet, and she maternally embraced him to her belly. 'It was an image of acceptance and reconciliation that was both maternal and almost sexual. Having accepted him, she set him free and left him with the island as she spoke the epilogue. Here was something young audiences could identify with: the single mum struggling, the mother-child conflicts that can be so strong at age sixteen, and yet the complexity of love and forgiveness.'

There was one question that I asked almost every one of the directors. In some instances – Annabel Arden and Sue Sutton Mayo, for example – we ran out of time, and the question never got asked. To others the question was an annoyance, but all of the responses are none the less both interesting and thought-provoking. And the reader must be reminded that these are opinions and are presented as nothing more than opinions. There is nothing to suggest that a male director might not exude these same attributes. The question was this: what are your qualities as a woman that inform and aid your work?

Sarah Pia Anderson says, 'It has to do with being able to change shape, to do with a certain adaptability, very caring, nurturing qualities in a way. Very often we have to work with difficult, complicated people, whether they be actors, lighting and camera people, composers, designers, and I think of my female side as being able to deal with the ego problems of the personalities I work with. The masculine side I always think of as being more confrontative and less tolerant. I suppose we idealise the female, but I think there is a sort of nurturing side to it. But a negative female quality, lack of self-esteem, comes into it. I've always had that, but I recognise it, and I try to work with it.'

'I'm not very interested in status and power for its own sake,' Julia Bardsley states. 'I'm interested in making the work and trying to make an environment where the work can happen. I'm not interested in titles or in being the head of something for its own sake. The only reason I would want power is to enable me to make certain decisions for myself for the work. That attitude towards power is different for women maybe. For me I feel it's different.'

A childlike quality is the characteristic of herself as a woman that Annie Castledine feels makes her a more effective director. 'A bit of a child. Incredibly optimistic. Knowing pain but not destroyed by it. Not at all bitter. Very passionate. Temperamental. Not temperamental on an unstable day by day basis, but very passionate if moved. Volcanic, eruptive. An anarchic sense that I don't mind going to the very edge, and I'll take the consequences. In relationships with actors, I'll say, "I didn't believe that" or "that was a moment that was totally unredeemable" and not be frightened of the consequences, with the hope that the framework in which I'm working is secure enough and passionate enough and forgiving enough to be able to take it. I don't like small talk, and I will very rarely know about the home life or social life or any part of the life of the people I work with – except that life that is actually in front of me in the rehearsal room. I really like people to leave all their side effects of life outside the door of the rehearsal so we can be totally focused on the piece of work we're dealing with.'

Castledine likes to surround herself with colleagues whose work is rigorous but exciting. When I asked Castledine if she didn't believe that men did this as well, she responded, 'Yes, I think they do actually. Trevor Nunn surrounds himself with people who can nurture, support, service, inform. He will have – or did when I worked with him – a wonderfully developed idea of his mise-en-scène before he ever comes into the rehearsal process. So consummation is going to be the most important thing for Trevor Nunn, not process. No matter what happens in the rehearsal room it will come out bull's-eye if his advance planning of the mise-en-scène is correct. I don't despise that, although I don't ever do it. I do think a certain knowledge of the mise-en-scène is quite useful, although I will also take huge risks in not having any planned music and trusting that the dynamic between the music director and myself will work and we can actually create the score during the rehearsals. Again it's a huge gamble. I like to do that. I like to live quite dangerously on that level. So there's always an element of fresh surprise.'

Garry Hynes was more sceptical of the question although her response was not dissimilar to Castledine's. 'I could say women are better collaborators, blah, blah, blah. I think all of that is probably true. But I'd be wrong to say I am this way because I am a woman. I am this way because I am a person. It's always an emotional process for me in the theatre. I am not the kind of director, for instance, who can go in with a game plan, a war battle plan, and marshal a thousand people on the stage in seventeen different sets. Hell on wheels is what I would consider that! I would run a mile from that! I have no tolerance in that area, and I don't think it's something I want to do. I also think probably as a woman – but also for other reasons having to do with who I am – I am not able to accept what may be the first meaning of something. This is what it looks like it is, but is it that? What is happening on the surface may not be necessarily what is happening at all. I want to get at that.'

Brigid Larmour's response to the question is very straightforward. 'I think that as a woman it's very easy for me to integrate my intelligence and my feelings. And it is very easy for me to create the environment in which everybody feels safe, and they can emotionally take their clothes off and know that I am not going to tread on that. And it's very easy for me to collaborate with people, and it's very easy for me to lead people without making them feel diminished. There are plenty of men who have these qualities but perhaps more women. I don't know. I do know that subjectively I feel it's less of a problem for a woman. And I partially think the distinctive quality of my work as a director is because of the way I look at the world, and I look at the world through the eyes of a woman – without choosing to. And I choose to look through the eyes of a feminist and that makes for a particular quality of my work.'

Probably the most succinct response is that of Phyllida Lloyd, who says that her strengths as a woman that she brings to her craft are 'Being a good listener. Not craving power particularly. Being a good collaborator. Being prepared to admit you're wrong. Having a strong sense of irony (I don't know if that's a female quality), just having a sense of humour. There's a sensitivity to people. But these are just human qualities.'

'I feel like I can't be quite as straightforward as I'd like to be,'

Nancy Meckler asserts, 'or as blunt speaking as is natural to me. In America I could probably be more blunt and people wouldn't find it offensive, whereas living in England I know that people do think I'm a bit blunt, and bluff, and gruff. It can be misinterpreted. So it's a problem of being American and a woman. It means that sometimes I have to be polite when actually I just want to get on with the job.' At the same time Meckler says she sometimes has difficulty confronting bullies and having it out with them.

'On the question of women directors and myself as a woman director,' Meckler continues, 'I do believe that many women are particularly sensitive to what is happening internally to the people they are with. Often women are sensitive to others' emotional needs to a fault. In directing it can be useful and helpful if you realise that an actor is frightened (and therefore not functioning well). They may appear arrogant or belligerent or overly intellectual. But if you have a sense of what is really bothering them, it helps to get past it. However, one can be caring and nurturing to extremes. Actors can take advantage of your sensitivity and awareness and demand more and more time. When kept in balance, this awareness can be a strength. But if you are too obliging, an actor's personal needs can begin to overshadow and take priority over the work on the floor. I also feel this awareness, this ability to see underneath the surface, understand character, and have a three-dimensional understanding of what makes people tic and the complexities of human behaviour – all are vital to directing.'

'Oh, dear, I don't know,' began Lynne Parker. 'Practical common sense, but I don't think that's exclusive to women. It has been very difficult for me to take myself seriously. I always felt I was going to be found out. And to some extent that's still the case. It's taken me this long to realise that the things I'm going to be found out for aren't that important. And this is probably my worst defect as a director: my academic knowledge of theatre is far too sketchy. I haven't actually studied enough; my knowledge of plays is superficial. But I'm getting cheeky enough in my old age to realise that doesn't actually matter, that people come to the plays who know a lot less theatre than I do.'

The final responder to my query was Di Trevis whose wise answer provides a fitting conclusion. 'I would like to say really that I don't have qualities that are particularly womanly because, you know, it's very difficult to define what are your womanly qualities. I've always been a woman, so I find it very difficult to imagine what it would be like to be other than myself. And then, if one goes the other way and one lists qualities that are not thought of characteristically as women's qualities, then you become entirely sexist and patronising and you say, "I have a masculine mind," or something equally ridiculous. So I don't really know that there are womanly qualities that I bring to the work that are different from men. Although I'm often told that I treat actors well. I don't think that's having to do with being a woman; I think that's to do with having been an actor. That doesn't mean to say I'm easy on them; it doesn't mean to say my actors like me. My aim is not to be liked, my aim is to do good work. I guess I can't look at a woman's role in a play without bringing something of my own experience to it. All the usual things – women's nurturing qualities, women's caring, intuitive qualities – I just think men develop these qualities too and women can lack them.'

Are there surprises in these brief self-evaluations? Probably not. But one point is very clear: the women are certainly able to realise that those qualities that are traditionally thought of as women's qualities – compassion, a spirit of collaboration, willingness to admit error, emotion, intuition – can be just as much the man's province as the woman's. Most of the women would agree that all human beings have their male and their female sides, both of which need to be nurtured and developed for success in directing. It is interesting, too, how many of the women doubt themselves or lack confidence in their own abilities.

These, then, are the directors' thoughts on how they may help and support one another; through networking, appreciating and supporting one another's work, encouraging plays by women and plays that have strong female characters. One point in this support system that women need to bear in mind is expressed by Lynne Parker when she says, 'Directors hire actors, and directors hire playwrights. Directors are the key. It's a very interesting time for women in general in Ireland. Women are becoming power in a way that hadn't been before. It's quite exciting. There has been a bit of anti-feminist backlash in recent years – things like twenty years from now women will have taken over and men won't get a decent break in the world. Twenty years! What is that when compared to the whole history of mankind? There is still room for unrepentant feminism, and we can't afford to sit back and be complacent.'

With a similar note of caution, Brigid Larmour states, 'Being cynical, I think the fact that you have more women directors visible in regional theatre in this country at the moment is connected with the fact that working conditions are so poor. You will always find that we're allowed in at the bottom rung. I worry perhaps that some women think that the battle is won and that because they've got to the top it must be possible for everybody to do that if they're good enough, and I worry because I don't see that the work of men is being changed by the work of women. I don't see men casting in the way that women cast, and I think until there is change in the culture brought about by the presence of all of us working, we can't afford to assume that the playing field is level – because it's a long way from level. Boards of directors are largely male, and financial decisions are largely male. Women playwrights are ludicrously under-represented in the large companies, in fact in all companies. And I think women are in a dangerous time because of this stupid phrase, post-feminist ... as though feminism is accomplished, achieved, finished.' To assume – because a certain number of women merely take their place in the world without the need to make a huge point of it – that the status of women has really changed, is false, Larmour believes. Many women's theatre groups are struggling or have collapsed. There is less solidarity, less collectivity than there was in the early days of the movement.

It is my decision to end this chapter with the words of Di Trevis, who herein expresses the hardship, the struggle, the hope, the fears, the doubts, and the ultimate joy of being a woman director on the brink of the millennium. 'I've spent much of this year working on a stage version of *Remembrance of Things Past*, adapted from Pinter's screenplay. This is being given a workshop production at the National, so that we can begin to discuss its viability for a full-scale production. I worked on it originally with students, four afternoons a week for four months. I nearly turned the project down but was attracted by the thought of working and having time for the rest of my life. To my utter amazement, I found that for the first time for years I felt truly creative, unpressured, free. My pleasure in the work is such that it communicated itself to Harold Pinter and Trevor Nunn, both of whom were enthusiastic, warm, and welcoming. I feel at the height of my powers.

In 1998 I went with my family to California where as well as directing Odets' *Awake and Sing* at Davis, I devised a show called *Happy Birthday, Brecht* with a group formed with some of my American students, Trevis and Company, for Brecht's centenary. The show was performed at the Artaud Theatre in San Francisco, and raised money to send pianos to Cuba where the embargo has meant that even their pianos, lacking tuners and spare parts, have deteriorated. I think Brecht would have enjoyed the notion that his birthday was celebrated by the gift of a piano to Havana: "To Fidel from Bert – a birthday present". I've also been able to start an ongoing series of workshops for young actors in Havana.

'I realise that all that is very much in a convention of what readers expect and the impression so-called successful people would like to give. Idea after idea, project after project rolling effortlessly into a rosy future. But I wonder whether it is really at all like most women's real experience of a long working life in a highly competitive field.

'The truth is that I rarely feel I have a career in the sense that other people seem to. I can remember a turning point. In the year that I had a one-year-old child, I directed the opera,

Gawain, at Covent Garden, followed by *Arturo Ui* at the Olivier. Afterwards I sat down and thought, "Well, so I've survived Covent Garden and the Olivier! What do I do now? More plays? More operas? Where? At the National? At the RSC? Abroad?" And then I began really to think about my aims in life. Was anyone going to offer me any more than this ad hoc life moving from one isolated project to another, always wondering if this productions were my last? A vista stretched before me. In my mind's eye I saw actors whom I loved, rehearsal rooms, technicians, first nights. I loved that life, but was it all I wanted? I could feel that the struggle to prove oneself was never going to abate. I was never going to feel that I had made it. Where should I go? What did I want? And then I realised I could not think of any of the major companies as my home. Their directors gave me no sense that they could give me any continuity of development. At the same time the thought of stopping made me vertiginous.

'I have always been completely ignored by the theatrical establishment – a good thing, you might think – never having received an invitation to any event other than those at which my fellow women acknowledge me. Any woman who has spent a few weeks at home with a child knows the terrible unreality that past achievements quickly assume. Did I really do that? It is even more intense when your province is the theatre – the most transitory of the arts. I still look at photographs, indeed even read this book, and find it hard to believe that it was I who accomplished those things.

'Everyone is keen for advice on how to start and establish a career. Perhaps as our generation begins to grow older, we should give some thought to how we tackle the long term, for a long life in the theatre is bound to have its vicissitudes, its periods of staleness, and restlessness.

'What I envisaged has happened, and I, for several years, all but abandoned the major companies. They moved on. There is an insatiable desire for the new, the undiscovered. Although I worked again at both the National and the RSC, I felt little sense of belonging or developing. They reflected their times.

They were selling a product. We produced it. Most of the men had their eyes enviously on the world of the musical where fortunes could be made. Or the movies. I saw them in the corridors of their theatres, standing as if on stepping stones, waiting to jump. And I couldn't help thinking that the girls have, after all, never been one of the boys. And what if you are not a girl, but a woman of nearly fifty with quite other preoccupations?

'So I made a different agenda for myself – trying not to define it all so much – a mish-mash of travelling, writing, directing, teaching, learning to ice-skate with my daughter, trying to get off the treadmill and find value in my life whether my name was on posters or not. Recently I was honoured by the legal profession with an invitation to dinner along with other luminaries of the National Theatre to the Inns of Court. I had to remind myself why I was there. Is it only me who thinks of herself as a name on an out-of-date list? And yet when I step into my rehearsal room this September and see the empty space in front of me, and the faces of my actors, I know I will have a real sense once again of being where I belong.'

Without deprecating men in any way, women must continue to work together, support one another, believe in one another, and grow in confidence, self-respect, and mastery of craft. With no negative feelings towards men, these women are valuing or learning to value themselves as women working in a field that until very recently has been the province of men.

CHAPTER 9

Theatre is a light

In almost all of the discussions with British women directors, I invariably asked three questions towards the end of our meetings: who were or are the directors who have influenced or inspired you; where do you see yourself in five or ten years; and what is your vision for the theatre? Certainly, on the second and third questions, the answers were as varied and diverse as the women themselves. This is in part true of the first question as well; however, almost every one of the directors acknowledges her indebtedness to Peter Brook.

Several of the women acknowledge the influence of theatre directors but add film directors to the list of important influences on their work. Sarah Pia Anderson names Peter Brook and Trevor Nunn as theatrical inspirations. Growing up with both Brook and Nunn, Anderson finds them to be really consummate directors, capable of handling both large and small-scale productions, capable of spectacular failure as well as success. Sometimes a particular contemporary director or production has also been very influential: Declan Donnellan's work at the National, Stephen Daldry's production of J.B. Priestley's *An Inspector Calls*, and Robert Lepage, 'whose daring theatrical imagination, fusion of ideas and narrative, is always inspiring'. Anderson adds to her list of contemporary influences such groups as Theatre de Complicite and Cirque du Soleil. Simultaneously, however, Anderson acknowledges her debt to Ingmar Bergman, Luis Buñuel, Jean Cocteau, John Cassavetes, Federico Fellini, Louis Malle, Martin Scorsese, Steven Spielberg, Andrei Tarkovsky, as well as several women: Sally Potter, Jane Campion, and German director Margarethe von Trotta.

Like Anderson, Julia Bardsley adds film makers to her list of directors who have influenced her work: Wim Wenders, Atom Egoyan, Lars von Trier, David Lynch. She says, 'I've been inspired by the choreographer Pina Bausch, Robert Wilson, and also by Robert Lepage's early work. He's a French Canadian; his work is highly theatrical and very contemporary. He infuses it with magic and technology.' Bardsley particularly admires Lepage's *The Dragon Trilogy* and *A Midsummer Night's Dream* at the National, which she found to be a very clear interpretation. 'But', Bardsley continues, 'I'm much more influenced and excited by film and the visual arts than I am about the theatre. I've just begun to discover the work of experimental film makers Len Lye, Stan Brackage, and Michael Snow and am constantly turning to the images and writings of visual artists like Bill Viola, Antonio Tàpies, Anselm Kiefer, Joseph Beuys, and Joel-Peter Witkins.' As has already been mentioned, a great influence on Bardsley's work is Michael Chekhov. 'He's my hero. His books have been my bible. I think it's the most instructive, brilliant writing about the actual techniques of performing. But', Bardsley adds thoughtfully, 'Tadeusz Kantor has to be the most influential of all.'

Several of the women have been particularly inspired by the work of other women. Annie Castledine named Phyllida Lloyd and Sarah Pia Anderson as two women whose work has inspired her. Castledine has travelled frequently to Europe and acknowledges the influence of German directors, Peter Stein and Ruth Berghaus, the latter long associated with the Berliner Ensemble and heir to the Brecht aesthetic in Germany. Berghaus is particularly noted for her *Danton's Death* in 1989 and her *Ring Cycle* at the Frankfurt Opera. Of contemporary directors in England, Castledine speaks highly of Mike Alfreds, a strong influence and a close colleague and, of course, the man she assisted at the RSC, Trevor Nunn.

Like Castledine Garry Hynes's first impulse is to mention the work of a woman – Deborah Warner. 'I think she's a visionary of the theatre,' Hynes says, 'I think she's extraordinary and a real professional.' And although Hynes never saw Peter Brook's work, she is inspired by his writings and what she has read about him. She concludes, 'I find myself admiring most directors who take any kind of risk. I think once a director takes a risk – as long as there is a basic expertise and rationale under it – it's always interesting. Taking a risk and doing something anarchic for the sake of effect is crazy. I hate theatre that is just simply a reproduction of things. I think it denies what theatre is. I enjoy the opportunity of watching the novel, the unique working.'

A third director to speak first of women directors is Brigid Larmour who speaks highly of Annie Castledine. 'She's very bold, and she goes her own way. She goes for it, and she's got a very strong visual sense. She always has a very clear thing that she's trying to do with a play. I admire Di [Trevis] very much as well. There's a very precise, delicate, and crafted quality about her work which I like, and I adore Phyllida Lloyd's work: her *Way of the World* and her *Pericles*, which was savaged by the critics.' Larmour was moved by this rarely performed Shakespeare in a number of ways: the humanity of it, the transcendence, the boldness of the staging, and the contemporary vision which she never allows to become glitzy or shallow, the strong choices with ethnicity and gender. Larmour admires Terry Hands for his craft and Trevor Nunn for his heart and says that it was their work at Stratford in the seventies which really inspired her about theatre and fed her love of Shakespeare. She assisted Hands for those years during her apprenticeship with the RSC. Of course, she expresses great admiration for Peter Brook, especially his film of *King Lear*. She says that his book, *The Empty Space*, has profoundly influenced her own work with Shakespeare Unplugged.

Because of her interest in directing for opera, Annabel Arden names Peter Sellars, who she believes has completely changed people's perception of opera, and New York-based director, Rhoda Levine, who has staged many twentieth-century operas for the New York City Opera and Glimmerglass and who is a founding director of Play It by Ear, the improvisational opera group at American Opera Projects. 'Another person, of course, who is completely inspirational is John Eliot Gardiner, because he is a conductor who is practically a director. If you have a good partnership with your conductor, then it's a perfect co-director team. It's difficult for conductors because they're not always stage people. You have to find a conductor who is a theatre person. I thought I was picky about diction, but Gardiner is an absolute devil. It's nonsense when artists say they can't sing and articulate the words. It's a question of work.' Finally Arden credits her movement teacher, Monika Pagneux, who often comes from Paris to work with Arden's singers on an opera production. 'You have to introduce movement with a master,' Arden maintains.

Eastern European directors have had a tremendous impact on Jenny Killick, her mentor and inspiration being Andrzej Wajda whom she met through the Traverse when that theatre brought his staging of scenes from Dostoyevsky's *The Idiot* to Scotland. 'I had my head blown off!' Killick exclaims. 'Absolutely to this day the complete theatre that I would aspire to. As a guru figure I have a Russian, Anatoly Vassiliev, a great innovator, whom I met through my work at the Traverse. A lunatic. Really mad. But he runs a studio in Moscow, and people are sent from all over Russia, from all walks of life, to study and create with him. The work I saw in the studio was so sensory, very erotic but not pornographic. You get this burning sensation from the actors. Both men – Wajda and Vassiliev – achieve extraordinary performances, and I think this is at the heart of what I'd like to achieve.'

Like Killick, Katie Mitchell has studied and learned from Eastern European directors, also naming Wajda and film maker, Andrei Tarkovsky, as particular inspirations. Mitchell also singles out the great Swedish film director, Ingmar Bergman, as a major influence on her work.

Also drawing from European directors for inspiration, Phyllida Lloyd names Ariane Mnouchkine and Theatre du Soleil whose work she saw both in Paris and London. 'There's a kind of phenomenal scale, awe-inspiring, monumental power of the work. Peter Brook – I'm not saying that every production of his that I've seen lately I've necessarily thought was going to change my life but the exploration, the way he's gone on exploring, challenging, not being set in his ways. When other directors have set on cosy patterns and regurgitate old productions in old ways, Peter Brook is a kind of eternal student. I'm fond of the work of Mike Alfreds, who was trained in America at Carnegie-Mellon University. He's a director who has a quite rigid process: a long rehearsal period, an enormous number of improvisational exercises, and none of the scenes are ever blocked. In other words every night the actors can change what they're doing, and there are a large number of points of concentration exercises so that you get this accumulation of detail, wealth of texture, and relationships between the actors. I've also been very inspired by a lot of work that comes from Eastern Europe. It has a lot to do with companies that have continuity within the system. God knows that will all be changing now. But it's very inspiring going to what was Soviet Georgia and seeing these groups of actors working together who have been together for fifteen years in a company. They've married each other and these tiny tots are running around the rehearsal room. It's just an amazing situation.'

Sue Sutton Mayo names Phyllida Lloyd and Trevor Nunn as directors whose work she admires. Nancy Meckler names Peter Brook and Joseph Chaikin, saying, 'I've always admired Peter Brook enormously, particularly for his non-intellectual approach – because I believe in and am interested in theatre which is emotional, which elicits an emotional, gut response from people. And although I'm full of admiration for productions which are intellectually dazzling, I'm not really interested in making that kind of theatre – stimulating the intellect almost to the exclusion of the emotional life of the audience. I was very inspired by Joe Chaikin's work in theatre, which I saw when I was younger. It meant a great deal to me, and I was desperate to understand how they did what they did and imitated a lot of their work in order to try to find out how they had done it.'

In a similar way, Lynne Parker says that she admires the work of Robin Lefevre more than any other director because she is unable to see how he does it; she cannot see his technique.

Parker also greatly admires Garry Hynes and says, 'At her best she is the best.' Parker maintains that Hynes's production of O'Casey's *The Plough and the Stars* was thrilling because it was so strong and so clear. And going full circle, when I asked Di Trevis the directors she most admired, she answered with a single word, 'Brook.'

The second question I asked most of the directors in the last stages of the interviews – where do you see yourself in five or ten years? – elicited a great variety of responses. Annabel Arden values the focused and intense physical training and the ensemble experience she has gained through her years of working with Theatre de Complicite but she is finding immense pleasure in exploring new areas, in particular the world of opera, that so beautifully moulds her interest in text, drama, voice, language, and movement. A review in *The Times* of *The Return of Ulysses* expressed this synthesis when it said, 'Annabel Arden's production perfectly integrated the musical and dramatic elements – everyone on stage is immersed in the meaning of words and notes, and conveys that meaning to the audience.'

Like Arden, Di Trevis is comfortable working within her present framework – both the Royal Shakespeare Company and Royal National Theatre – but seeks to intensify what she does there. 'With this new year, I'm entering a new phase of my life, I feel,' Trevis begins. 'I've had nine years of motherhood (work mixed with motherhood) and now I feel that my child is a little more independent. For the next few years I really want to do a lot of Shakespeare and classical work. That's my ambition and where I want to devote my energies. I want to have done the major Shakespeare plays before I stop working; I have another fifteen to twenty years, so I've got to get on with it. That starts a completely new phase of my life, and I'm really looking forward to that. I just hope I can go on working steadily now and that there won't be too many interruptions.'

So many of the directors dream of working with a small, intense, and intimate circle of actors. Garry Hynes evaded my initial question about where she would like to be in five or ten years by saying, 'I've no idea. I never project my future. I've never been able to. Some people would say that's a problem, of course. I absolutely don't know where I'll be.' Nevertheless Hynes continued, sketching a kind of dream for her own future: to be involved in a collaborative process. 'That is all I ask for in life, and obviously I'd like to have some success in doing that. I would like to be working with a group of people I like working with, who I find inspiring, and who would have a similar opinion of me. So there is a mutual sharing process going on. There is nothing that gives me more pleasure, nothing.'

A similar dream is expressed by Sue Sutton Mayo who states, 'My own individual aim is to have a group of actors with whom I can work over and over again. That would be my ideal. If somebody said to me, "Here's three million pounds, go and do what you want with it," I'd find a space, and I would find actors because, you see, I just adore actors. They are gods to me really. I don't know how they do it. The idea of being able to form a group with them, to work with them, to get to know them, to create a *modus vivendi*, and to tackle work after work after work together. To me it's just a dream!'

Some of the freelance directors dream of having their own companies. The Traverse Theatre wanted Jenny Killick to see the theatre into its new building, but she found the time right to try her hand as a freelance director and in the field of television. I asked Killick if she might consider returning to the Traverse, to which she responded, 'No. It's a young person's place and always has changed its artistic director every four years. You see, I was there five and one-half years. It's a place that thrives on young energy and change.' Killick admits that, with two young children, she is not available, emotionally or creatively, to be directing at the moment, but were she to have her own theatre one day, she envisions it in this way: 'The place I would want to run is, I suppose, more mature and would utilise the experience that I have now in terms of commissioning. I'd want a rigorous commissioning policy. I'd try to inspire some degree of theatricality in the writing – poetry, passion, and breadth of vision – and not just try to describe the world as it is, which television does brilliantly. Let's have plays about big ideas, breadth of vision, imagery. The actors would have to act like Wajda's actors, presenting plays of such poetry and scope – by a living author – that they would just enchant an audience and give so much pleasure! Of course, it's shooting for the moon, but that's what I'd like to do.'

'I'd like to have much more continuity in my work,' Phyllida Lloyd explains. 'I think I'm gravitating to the point where I'm ready to make a bigger commitment of some kind – to a place or an ensemble. A building can be a huge albatross – most are under economic siege – but I'd like to spend some more time on the road. The opportunity to work abroad is a wonderful thing. I'd like to work less often but better.'

Lloyd continues to explore her place in the contemporary theatre when she says, 'I think the theatre in this country is in a muddle, rapidly losing its status as an unrepeatable live event. The collapse of public subsidy is of course catastrophic and affects everyone. No one running a subsidised company can afford to take a risk. They have first to consider whether a project will be a hit, whether it's the right "package" – all language one would have associated three years ago, even, with the world of the commercial theatre. So less risks are taken and the next generation finds it less and less enticing. The well-made play in the formal theatre building is not a seductive prospect for many people; certainly not young people. The future seems to be outside these monolithic buildings, perhaps in places where plays don't usually occur. Perhaps theatre will become less about plays and more about theatrical "events". I'm not sure for how much longer the text can reign supreme in this country. It may be that by making it our god, we have failed to notice how rapidly the changes in communication in the world have affected people.

'In some respects', Lloyd continues, 'I feel I have lost my moorings as a director. I've consistently avoided the challenge of running a theatre company and find myself asking, "Who do you serve?" Of course I have relationships with theatre and opera companies and passions of all kinds in various stages of development but I do find it difficult to see a proper shape to my career.

'I do very much enjoy my work in opera. There are vexing aspects to the structure of organisations – singers being paid to perform but not to rehearse and so forth, but it's a medium with a massive unexplored potential and incontrovertibly a live event. In the theatre I have found it harder and harder to find the igniting spark for the well-made play on the large stage. Recently I've begun working with actors and contemporary dancers on fragments of plays and poems. Small things with big possibilities.'

Very different from Lloyd's aspirations, but no less ambitious, are those expressed by Julia Bardsley. 'I've never seen my life in terms of career at all. That's how all my work has been – it just sort of happened. Something comes up, you do it, it moves you somewhere else, and makes you think about something else. Each move has helped me focus on what it is I really want to do and how I want to do it. I think my ideal would be to have my own space, a flexible working space that wasn't just about theatre but that would include studios for composers to work in, where artists could make work. It would be totally devoted to exploring the creative process.' Bardsley also aspires to an educated audience, one that is willing to try new experiences, one that thrives on new ideas, new approaches, one that is attuned to a different way of seeing things or of seeing new work. Bardsley believes strongly in the ability to educate and develop audiences. She recalled seeing a production at the Body Politic in Chicago performed by a Russian company. 'It was a strange, dark play with violence and rape, presented in Russian with available translation on head phones. What was most strange', Bardsley relates, 'is that the audience was made up primarily of elderly women who had subscribed to a season without knowledge of what they were going to see. My initial reaction was, "What an inappropriate audience! God, this is going to be disastrous!" But their comments afterwards were fascinating. They were seeing something they wouldn't ordinarily see. They were challenged and somehow managed to meet that challenge.'

Bardsley's company would be one with continuity, working together over a long period of time. 'Ultimately the quality of the work becomes better and better the longer you work with people; with long-term relationships you can push things further, whereas if you start with a new company every time, it's like going back to square one again. You have to find your shared vocabulary; you have to find out how you work together. That takes time.'

In our most recent conversation, however, Bardsley adds, 'I've been in a very reflective mode for the past three years. I haven't made any theatre. I've had my exhibitions and have been working on the film. It's been a lot of thinking and reading and looking and digesting. I'd like my work to infiltrate abroad. I've never done that, and I have a yearning to take my work into Europe. But primarily, I've been searching for the form that I can, the form in which my ideas can be articulated and lived and experienced by people. Theatre has been my life, I can't deny it, but now I must cut through the rubbish that exists within the theatre, find what's really valuable in it for myself, take those parts and put them into another configuration – perhaps a fusion of visual art, theatre, and film. I must find the nub of it that will release the work.'

It is interesting that a number of the women who work as freelance directors seem to long for their own theatres. Yet when I first met Brigid Larmour at the Contact Theatre in Manchester she was dreaming of working as a freelance director. However, she said at the time, looking towards the future, 'I think I will still be doing Shakespeare.' And doing Shakespeare she is! Her Shakespeare Unplugged, associated with the National Theatre, has inspired her to begin work on a book about the process. She is in discussions with the National about ways of addressing the crisis in classical theatre training, perhaps through setting up a young ensemble company. She hopes to continue her association with Mayfair Theatres as Creative Development Adviser to help open the West End to new voices and to forge a collaboration between the commercial and the subsidised theatre by commissioning new writings because she believes 'there is a revival in the fortunes of new writing in the British Theatre'. In the same project she's interested in encouraging new producers into the fray. Reactivating both her television work and her international career are also priorities. But for the present Larmour is thrilled with the development of Shakespeare Unplugged.

Annie Castledine's aspiration is very straightforward and direct. 'I'd probably like to be taken into the National Theatre, and not necessarily to direct a lot. I think my real dream is to direct about two productions a year and have a wonderfully long rehearsal process and invite an enormous number of my European collaborators — physical theatre collaborators, for instance — into that rehearsal process and do something really splendid but also to have, eventually, the resources of an institution so that all the work one wants to do and all the enabling one wants to do as far as women writers are concerned can take place. Eventually, you've got to have the power and resources behind you to do it. And I would love to do that.'

Two of the women, Sarah Pia Anderson and Lynne Parker, are particularly interested in branching out into film. When I first spoke with Anderson she said she found the British film industry almost non-existent. 'We don't make films any more,' she said at that time, 'I don't think we have any in England that aren't funded by American money or made by Americans. I'm depressed and angry about the fact that we don't [make films]. People say, "But it's always been like this here; there's always been a problem funding films and getting them made." ' Now Anderson is more positive. She believes there is a resurgence of interest in film in England. Part of this change, she believes, is due to the new British government openly supporting the film industry. Yet she believes it is sales from abroad that keep the industry alive. 'The British film industry today needs to be creating something people want to see in different parts of the world, so it becomes a new British way of opening out to the world.' Anderson also applauds the new emphasis on the work of independent film makers. 'I think I got very, very tired in the theatre. With film I could bring together everything I've learned: how to deal with actors, how to work with light and sound. I'm beginning to learn about lenses and photography and how one can achieve certain effects in order to tell a story. I find working with a camera, constructing the whole thing to be very satisfying.'

With her usual sense of humour, Lynne Parker muses, 'I could have given theatre up [in five years] and gone to teach history somewhere, or I could be making film, or I could be at the Abbey, or I could be desperately trying to make a living as a jobbing director in England. I really don't know. I think if I could keep control of it I would be still running Rough Magic, but I'd be very interested in going into another medium, which is film. I think anyone who didn't want to make a film is daft at this stage of the game, and the Irish film industry – after having been dormant for so long – is just ready to take off. In some ways working in the theatre at the end of the twentieth century is somewhat nostalgic.'

Katie Mitchell's vital aspiration would seem to revolve around her love of research and travel. 'It's crucial that as directors we should continue to learn and develop our skills. So I tend to combine directing productions with travel, travel not only associated with research projects specific to the production I'm working on, but travel that also takes me to different countries to look at different ways of working. For example, I went to Japan to observe the work of Tadashi Suzuki, which was a real education. I also like to travel to countries just to look at different cultures, political situations, economic situations. So recently I've been in Italy, Munich, Belgrade, and Montenegro.' Mitchell is convinced that such experiences provide a vital aspect of our learning process.

Another individual note was expressed by Nancy Meckler, the only one of the women who has seriously weighed a teaching career for her future. In our first interview Meckler confessed, 'The last year or two I've suddenly felt myself less ambitious, which amazes me. I never thought I would stop having this hunger to direct plays. And I keep fantasising about teaching – which is something I've always loathed. I seem to want to pass things on; it's like I want to give something back, and I'm still trying to find out how to do that.

'My dream ending would be to have a small theatre somewhere that just did a season every summer, just one or two projects that I really enjoyed. Something like that and maybe doing some teaching and finding a way to teach. The truth is I teach a great deal in rehearsal but that doesn't give me a method for teaching people outside of rehearsal, which is something I would have to develop. I'd be interested in teaching directing and introducing people to basic concepts. I tried it once and realised that I would need to spend a lot more time working out my approach.'

In contrast to our first interview several years ago, Meckler more recently said, 'I find it difficult to say what I would like to be doing in five years. I've reached a watershed in my life because I'm now over fifty-five and my children have left home. I have two sons who both look like they're going to work in theatre. I've taken a bit of time off from directing because for the last five years every project has overlapped. I've done two films and five productions in that time, which is crazy. Although I'm still running Shared Experience, I have almost nine months where I'm playing more of a producing role while trying to think clearly about the future, but I haven't reached any conclusions. Teaching still holds an attraction, but I'm not sure how to make that work as I've always found it unsatisfying in the past.

'I'm taking time to develop pet ideas,' Meckler continues, 'for example, an idea to create a children's music piece.' Meckler envisions an archetypal story like Noah's Flood that might tour the country. Children's choruses could train in each city and become part of the production there. 'Which means', Meckler says, 'it would bring the community in to see their own children creating a piece. It's that sort of thing you need time to think about and research. If you're doing other projects you just never get past putting it down on a piece of paper. I'd also love to find a film script that I felt a personal connection with.'

We come now to the third of the questions that was consistently asked at the end of each interview: what is your vision for the theatre? At times it was asked in a different way: why do you do what you do? Or with crises in Bosnia and the Middle East, for example, why is the theatre important? But the women responded to the question passionately, articulately, and thoughtfully. These reactions are presented here as much in the women's own words as possible.

'Oh, to give us back our faith in ourselves!' is Sarah Pia Anderson's justification for what she has chosen as her life work. 'The theatre's always been a place where I've been put back in touch with a part of myself that I have come to understand. Theatre is real human beings moving around in front of you being other people and giving you back an experience that is yours; giving you a sense of worth. I suppose I want the theatre to reflect social and psychological issues that have meaning in people's lives today. That can be Shakespeare or it can be the newest playwright. I want to be touched by it; I want to encounter something on stage that will enable people to go through the next twenty-four hours of their lives feeling better about things, feeling enhanced and fed by it. I want them to come back, see more, and think it's important. I have a desire to share that. I don't think theatre has a particular social function that can be analysed. People can get something from *Carousel* or they can get something from Edward Bond. You can't legislate so that one is better than the other, more worthy, more rich. I think we can equally enjoy both, and we're fortunate that we have a choice. I have always felt moved, and excited, and touched by the theatre, and I just want that to happen for other people. Like any art form, it's there to help you, there to give you what you already have actually. You've read a book or seen a painting a hundred times, but then you suddenly see it anew because it's touched a different part of you. That means you can see the great works – *King Lear* or *The Winter's Tale* – time and again. Something new is revealed to you because they are so complex. How do you know until you've lived part of your life what they're all about? That's what I don't want *ever* to lose.'

Like Anderson, Julia Bardsley does not consider herself a political director except, perhaps, in a marginal way. 'The process of theatre', she muses, 'is lumbering and laboured, and it's difficult to respond to issues. The process is not immediate like television.' Bardsley refers again to Robert Lepage whom she finds very social, capable of fusing theatricality with contemporary issues. 'I don't think my social aim is about political issues – although in a way everything *is* political because everything one does is about the human condition. Even the way one stages something is a political statement, a testing of the status quo.' Bardsley maintains that she is more interested in making artistic and aesthetic statements – new approaches to old works, new ways of looking at the theatre – than in trying to present and deal with the problems of the world.

Annie Castledine answered the question more from a personal point of view, perhaps because she had already dealt at length with her quest to further the work of women playwrights and the perception of women in the theatre. When I told Castledine how many of the other women directors spoke of her with such respect, she responded, 'That's very nice of them because we have to admit that I am not successful, not successful in worldly terms. I am a high achiever, so I do like to succeed. I very, very much want to create moments of absolute theatrical joy if at all possible; and we all know that the conspiracy of circumstances needed for this – the glories of text, the glories of the performer, the design, everything fusing into one wonderful whole – is a continuous quest. Well, I'm on that quest. Yes, I want to be a great director, whatever that means. I want to be very good. I want to be very, very good indeed.'

Expressing her personal quest in a somewhat different way, Garry Hynes says, 'I think boredom is the greatest sin in the theatre. I think to bring a group of people in and sit them down and bore them is unforgivable. I think it's extraordinary what we're given: six hundred people have paid to come in and let us do what we want with them. I think that's an enormous power; the theatre is potentially enormously powerful.' There is also, Hynes maintains, an incredible energy among all the artists working in the theatre and among performers and audience, and the release of that energy is exhilarating. 'I think the world is a cruel, dark place. I think theatre – whether it's two people in a room or 700 people in a national theatre – is a light of some kind. It may be just a match, but a light it is. The more society is at the edge – economically, in terms of war, starvation, anarchy, corruption – the more crucial it is that theatre exists.'

Jenny Killick agrees with Hynes about the condition of boredom in the theatre when she says, 'We've got to do theatre that makes people want to stay. They can't leave, they are just riveted.' Many old plays are, to Killick, dogmatic; and she remains, as she says, 'Joan of Arc-ish' about new works. She wants the audience spoken to by someone living, actors who are totally comfortable with what they are saying, who want desperately to communicate that play and to tell that story. 'That's rare now, that sense of urgency, that need to communicate, I wish that new plays were more central to our culture, that we had confidence in ourselves to believe in what we've got to say. I think it's incredibly important – the now. We lack confidence in our ability just now, and that's undermining the health of our culture. I would like to see the primary creative person in the theatre be the writer, and people would flock to the theatre to hear what he or she has to say. It's a dream, but I feel if I were living in a culture where that was happening, it would be a healthier culture all around: more confident, more creative, more imaginative. And everything would flow from that in terms of politics and society.

'So I feel slightly in exile because the whole establishment of British theatre is obsessed with the director, the director's concept, so a secondary creative person is being put in the centre. That's off balance; I don't think it's as dynamic as saying, "The centre of the event is the words, the story." I don't mean any disrespect, but we go to the theatre to see Nick Hytner's *King Lear*. Where's Shakespeare? It isn't a very comfortable situation. A comfortable situation is one in which the play-wright wants to tell a story so he or she says, "Come to the theatre tonight" and we, all the secondary creative people like the director and designers, say, "Wow, let's communicate it with energy!" I hate to sound evangelical, but I think that's a wonderfully healthy theatrical concept, and it's been marginal-ised from the Thatcher decade on. I think her influence, politically and culturally, is to be totally shored up by the past. And I think we're better than that; I think people have more to offer.'

Like Killick, Brigid Larmour laments the status quo of much of contemporary British theatre and incorporates that concern into her statement of her theatrical vision. She laments the appalling working conditions, the wages, the inadequate rehear-sal spaces, the brief periods allotted technical rehearsals. The problems of being at a regional theatre are accentuated by what Larmour calls the snobbish and 'Londoncentric' theatre critics. On the positive side, however, she says, 'There are so many people who are so talented and so idealistic who work in these circumstances. People are committed; they believe in the work.' Larmour's office at Manchester's Contact Theatre was next to the wardrobe room and two doors from the shop – all a part of the vision in which there was no separation between the production and performance areas of the theatre like that which exists in the large institutions. Larmour believes that there are too many West End type theatres doing fifties sort of theatre in a nineties environment. She would like to see more subsidy given to regional theatres and small-scale touring companies than to antiquated and safe offerings. With the huge increase in audiences for film and for television, Larmour believes the only justification for theatre is in its *difference* to cinema and video. 'So all the work I do', she concludes, 'is non-naturalistic. It's theatrical writing, in the tradition of Sophocles and Shakespeare; it's not plays set in a living room with realistic dialogue because you can see that in television or the cinema. The roots of theatre are collective and imaginative and original; that's what we have to commission and produce and concentrate on: work which is physical and theatrical, which uses space and place and language interestingly. I also have a vision of theatre which is representative of society, representative of the possibilities in society, which means non-racial casting and non-gender casting.

'There is a sort of intensity in the collective experiences that I think is very important, particularly in a culture that is increasingly agnostic if not atheist. The proportion of people in this culture with religious beliefs is falling. I think it's very important that there is a place where you can have an intense feeling with a group of other people, that it isn't about which side wins – that's what you get from sport – but is about being touched and moved. Sometimes you're doing plays which ask questions about us and about our lives. Sometimes it's plays that ask big questions, plays that don't come up with answers but that say there is more to life than politics and entertainment.'

On a more cautionary note Phyllida Lloyd states, 'What one does can be any number of things – a call to arms, a plea for tolerance, an evening of downright silliness – as long as it makes some difference. The power of the theatre is a mysterious one; it's impossible to be precise about its effects but the importance of its being live, a coming together of people to experience something that will never have been and never be the same again, is enormous. There are more and more reasons not to leave one's house to join a group of strangers to hear a story told in public. Now that people can disappear into a technological world for experiences both frivolous and profound, the theatre has to be very sure about what it can offer as an alternative.'

Sue Sutton Mayo is also fervent about the potential of theatre. 'I believe', she says, 'so passionately in the power of theatre, in the healing power of theatre, in the educative power of theatre, in the spiritual power of theatre that I just want to share that with people.' Nancy Meckler, on the other hand, states her need to do theatre in highly personal terms when she says, 'I wanted to express physically and in three dimensions my feelings about all sorts of things . . . that thing of needing to make one's inner life somehow concrete, to make it live in space and time, to allow other people to experience it. I think that's an impulse that probably a lot of us do have, whether we decided to pursue it is another thing. My hunger and my need have lessened recently, but I still enjoy doing it enormously.'

'A theatre environment where we all set ourselves impossibly high standards and fight very hard to realise those standards' comprises the vision of Katie Mitchell. 'An environment where there is a very vibrant and vivid exchange between practitioners in all forms, from the avant-garde through to the mainstream.' Enlarging her vision, Mitchell says, 'It would be very good indeed if people from all countries who are working in the theatre could see each other's work, share ideas, share projects in as open a fashion as possible. There's so much to learn from the ways in which different political systems or different cultures can bring different ways of working in theatre, different ways of looking at theatre, different productions. And in an increasingly nationalistic climate, I just think that the more exchange of ideas, thoughts, projects, people, visions between practitioners of different countries the better.'

Di Trevis, on the other hand, finds profound value in the theatre's ability to validate one's own experiences. She says, 'As a young woman, from a virtually bookless working-class background in Birmingham, my experience of the theatre was that it gave me a vision of the whole world, it allowed me to study my own culture and gave me freedom in my mind to have a vision that went beyond my immediate physical surroundings. That's why theatre fascinates me, because it's subjecting the major culture that you're in, putting it under a microscope and examining the sub-cultures that make up this major culture, and I think that's very freeing to people's minds. So that's what I'm in theatre to do: to rescue people from group thinking, to make them see that their own experience is worthwhile, that their own pain is tragic and that their own joys are the essence of comedy . . . that their lives are important.'

Often very pragmatic in her responses, Lynne Parker says, 'Sometimes we really have to ask ourselves why we do this because in this world there are an awful lot more useful things that one could do. We could all be out in Somalia or Bosnia trying to save lives. I think it's important to save lives but it's also worthwhile to respond to the part of us that needs to be fundamentally and profoundly silly. The theatre is capable of being profoundly silly, and it's only by giving air to that sense of humour and sense of the ridiculous that we can keep imaginatively and mentally healthy. I think a lot of serious political problems are created by people who have ceased to be able to ridicule themselves, who take themselves too seriously, or who are trapped in ego. By setting up situations where you can bat your eyes, laugh at yourself, visualise ideal situations, the theatre provides a huge outlet for sanity. I mean that's the basis of art, isn't it? That there has to be some light and humour as a part of life. Meaning becomes functional: there has to be an element of joy in what we do; otherwise there's nothing. Whether theatre is savage or anarchic in its humour, it is giving expression to that kind of joy, that kind of emotion and sensual pleasure. It's what living is about; otherwise it's just existing.

'My ambition', Parker continues, 'is that I produce the kind of show that isn't boring to a single member of the audience for one second. That sounds really dumb but I believe it's the hardest thing of all, and I may never achieve that. What I would like to do is, like sex, get people turned on. I want to turn the audience on and make them feel lust, rage, love, hate; I want theatre that makes people feel. But if you're going to turn people on, you've got to be prepared to annoy them as well. You've got to embrace controversy.'

The directors' passion – those who have inspired them, their dreams for themselves and their own careers, their visions for the future of the theatre, and their constant questioning as to why they pursue this elusive, demanding, agonising work – is no doubt something that changes almost daily with each of the women. Economic factors, the highs and lows of their own careers, the stability and moral stance of the global community itself become key factors. But it is abundantly clear that all of the women strive for excellence, for the best work that they can do, for a greater and more meaningful theatre. So often the women's words remind me of a phrase used by my own theatrical mentor, Frank M. Whiting at the University of Minnesota, who used to say that what we are striving for is the best possible production of the best possible play. These women want to touch lives, to give meaning to lives, to expand perception of what our lives and our lives in relationship to others can be.

Just do it

A number of the directors offered advice to young women who might be considering entrance into this difficult, demanding, and elusive profession. As we talked, an awareness existed in their minds that they might be helping a new generation of women directors. Sarah Pia Anderson says, 'Keep doing it. It doesn't matter where or with whom because I can only advocate what happened to me, that I was given the opportunity to practise, and I gradually got better at it. Without that, I wouldn't. There's a lot of talk about directors' training, and I'm sure it's good; it's just that I didn't do it in that way.' Regarding her career as a whole, Anderson says, 'My ambition is to be able to continue what I am doing. In any career there are ups and downs. Cynicism, hopelessness, feelings of failure afflict even the strongest temperament. Be graceful about the disappointments and happy about the upswings. Hand in hand with the insecurities go tremendous satisfactions. So enjoy the success. Everything is transient.'

Annie Castledine, herself trained as a teacher and consistently evidencing the qualities of a fine teacher, advises 'that the young woman knows a lot about plays and texts and has been to the theatre a lot. If she were very, very talented academically, she might want to go to university and pursue theatre whilst there. (Go to Cambridge; there are wonderful opportunities for making theatre, and you enter a privileged elite which makes your entry into the theatre world very possible.) If she were not that academic, I would suggest she go to the Bristol Old Vic, and do a director's course in a theatre school. Then I would suggest she become an assistant director. I mean there are so many young people who are wonderful and having to do such a lot of unpaid work as assistant directors! But sometimes that pays off, really materialises into something successful for them. I love working with assistant directors, and I do usually have one on a production. Eventually you have a whole family of assistant directors. I would ask the young woman what kind of director she wanted to be, place her in the right institution [to further her education and training], and from there send her off to work with a good director.'

While Garry Hynes, unlike Castledine, suggests that she has no idea how to train a young director, she also observes, 'I tend a little bit towards the "get out there and do it" school. I suppose I say that because I think what I did was the right thing. Obviously you can learn a lot technically by being a stage manager, and all those kinds of things, and clearly it's a way in. But I believe that the more potential directors can interact with actors and get themselves involved, the better. So much of it is the ability to create a sense of purpose, lead a group of people, and create the kinds of circumstances in which a group of people will then go on to create. An awful lot of those things are about personal skills in some way. And then finally it's about having a vision of something: it doesn't matter what that vision is, whether it's good, bad, or indifferent. But if you have a sense of what that is, and if you can communicate that to a group of actors, designers, directors, writers, then that's what being a director is, really.'

When asked about confidence in women directors, Brigid Larmour offered this advice: 'It depends on the person. I think it's all to do with if you can make up the rules: being a director is whatever you want it to be; it doesn't have to be like any of the other directors. Women do often suffer much more deeply from confidence problems than men, and I think we tend to fall into groups: those who do [have a confidence problem] and those who concentrate so hard on overcoming the problem that something of humanity is lost along the way. This thing about confidence is very depressing, and I think it often happens very, very early in childhood. I think the important thing is that you can do it; you can do whatever you want; and it doesn't matter if you get it wrong.'

Larmour touches on what may be a universal experience of capable young women when she tells of an encounter at the RSC in Stratford in the early 1980s. Always an excellent student, both in her progressive school and at Cambridge, Larmour never questioned that she could direct if she chose to do so. 'Towards the end of my first year at Stratford [as an assistant director], a production slot became vacant. There was me and there was a man. We had done a festival together; he made a lot of noise and I did a lot of work. He got offered the slot to direct and I went, "what?" They never even discussed it with me. Now in retrospect, I realise that I should have been making more noise, of course, but I thought just doing the job was enough.' She had grown up 'in the belief that men and women were equal, that the battles were over and won, that there was a level playing field – and then came to earth with a thud!'

Implicit in Larmour's anecdote is a fact now well substantiated in feminist theory: that we are so used to accepting a man's knowledge, superiority, expertise, and confidence that we may be guilty, however unaware, of sexism. A woman colleague and I have so often observed how often in faculty meetings time limits are placed on our remarks but not on those of our male colleagues, how often our overlooked suggestions, when rephrased and articulated by our male counterparts, are met with approval. The point here is not the oversight but the need for young women directors to find their voice, their confidence, and their strength to fight for their place in the theatre.

The final bit of advice, so positive and so upbeat, was offered by Di Trevis when she affirmed, 'I hope lots of women do it because it's a wonderful job. I think that even more than Deborah [Warner] I'm the one who has been asked more questions about being a woman because I'm slightly older, the first woman here [at the Royal National] to have a company, and I was the one who went off and had a baby, and came back again. I just hope that it becomes not unusual.'

Specifically relating to young women as potential directors, Trevis says, 'Well, they've just got to do it; they've got to direct even if it's only five mates in the church hall. Just do it! Because nobody's going to make it happen. There's a Chinese saying, "A cooked chicken never flew in through the window." Or, as I often say to young women starting out on any difficult career, nobody is going to knock on the door and say, "I hear you want to be a director (or designer/writer/artist); can I help?" You have to communicate this wish to people, and what is more, as I have often learned the hard way, you have to go on and on and on reiterating the wish, the intention, the idea throughout your career. Also no one can help unless you are specific and realistic. You have to ask for something that is entirely logical, feasible, and within their power to grant. I am reminded of a story about Dorothy Parker whose lover or husband had just died and as she came out onto the steps after the funeral, her face distraught and tear-stained, a friend rushed up to her and said, "Dottie, Dottie, what can I do? If there's anything I can do, day or night, please just ask." "In that case", said Dottie, "run along and get me a pastrami on rye – mustard, lettuce, and no mayonnaise." That is, I'd rather meet someone for five minutes, even if it's a matter of them speaking to me in a foyer after a show than receive a totally unrealistic request to be my assistant from someone I've never met and whose work I've no chance of seeing. It's the same when I am formulating plans and ideas and putting them to other people.'

I must confess in conclusion that this has been a great labour of love and learning. I hope that, even though I have taken great liberty in arranging the material, and in sometimes formalising – or simplifying – spoken speech into written language, I have remained true to the spirit and intent of the women's comments. I have used direct quotations so extensively for two reasons: first, I so often felt that the women expressed the thought or idea far better than I could; second, I hope this technique has enabled us to have a glimpse of the personalities of the women and a sense of the spontaneity of their thoughts and observations.

Julia Bardsley had written me a fairly formidable letter prior to our first meeting in which she said, 'If you want to arrange an interview please ring . . . and we'll see what can be arranged, although I must add that I will be very busy and immersed in the production [*Macbeth*].' Naturally, I pictured a strong presence and certainly someone not overly eager to meet with me. But the person who greeted me at the stage door of the Leicester Haymarket Theatre was clearly a very friendly and a very young woman in blue jeans and a sweater. I was so surprised by her youth that I said something like 'I'm sure I'm older than you imagined, and you are certainly younger than I imagined'. There was nothing off-putting in her demeanour or attitude towards me. In fact, there was nothing formidable in the way any one of the women greeted me or responded to my endless questions over a period of several years. Each is in her own way extraordinary and I carry vivid first impressions of them all.

Here is an essence of those impressions. Phyllida Lloyd answered all of my initial questions with such care and thoughtfulness. I was struck by her calm, her poise, and her intelligence. I've already mentioned Julia Bardsley's youth. I was also impressed by her eclectic artistic vision and her daring. Sue Sutton Mayo ended our interview saying, 'I could talk to you all day.' She immediately seemed like an old friend and the ease of the conversation and the similarity of our situations – both people who got late starts after being at home with small children for several years – created a warm bond.

Just as I had been struck by Bardsley's youth, I was surprised at how petite and yet how feisty and tenacious Garry Hynes seemed. Lynne Parker was funny and witty and a tremendous individual. Brigid Larmour impressed me as a passionate feminist and also a woman of tremendous intellectual gifts. When I sat across from Annie Castledine in front of the fire at the Old Forge in Totnes, I was aware that I was in the presence of an uncompromising woman of indomitable energy, tenacity, and idealism.

After a full day at the television studio, Sarah Pia Anderson came to see me at my not-very-glamorous hotel room in London. I responded keenly to her honesty, depth, humility, and thoughtfulness. Jenny Killick had just tucked her little boy into bed when she greeted me in her home. Her energy and vitality and verve were infectious, her commitment to new plays compelling. Di Trevis and I almost missed each other. I never received her letter agreeing to our interview but happened to meet her at the National Theatre. She did not meet with me then because she was going home to be with her daughter. We saw each other the next day. I responded to her quiet and calm dignity, the absolute clarity with which she expressed her ideas, and the sharpness of her rehearsal process.

I first met Annabel Arden in Oxford where she was acting in *Street of Crocodiles*. Thoughts and convictions poured from her in rapid torrents of words, and I knew that she believed in herself and in her future as an artist with intense passion. Katie Mitchell's intelligence in the work I saw at the Abbey Theatre inspired me, and I observed her sitting at the back of the theatre. She remains the only one of the directors I have never interviewed face to face. Yet I am grateful that, once she agreed to talk with me, she insisted on honouring that agreement. Finally there was Nancy Meckler, whom I finally met several years after an initial taped interview. I so deeply appreciate the candour, honesty, seriousness, and integrity with which she answered my initial queries without the support of any kind of give and take dialogue.

By now I have met some of the women two and three times. Our dialogue has spanned several years. Children have been born, partnerships severed; jobs and fortunes have changed. I have been able to follow their careers and see their work. Yet my responses to the women have remained remarkably consistent and true to those first impressions, and the women, in turn, have continued to be remarkably tolerant of me. I maintained in the Introduction to *Taking Stage* that this was not a text book; yet I have never in all my years of training learned so much about directing as I have from these women. Not only do impressions of their dignity, intelligence, and thoughtfulness live in my consciousness, but also I am enriched by the wisdom each of them imparted to me.

By way of summary, I can mention a few of the concepts that stay constantly with me. From Sarah Pia Anderson I learned the willingness to choose difficult works, works that are not immediately accessible, and then bring them to light with clarity. From Annabel Arden it was the sheer intelligence and the unabashed joy and belief she finds in her work. Julia Bardsley gave me courage for the work: to dare to explore, to seek new avenues of expression, to constantly challenge one's own creativity. Annie Castledine shared the idea of having every actor at every rehearsal, improvising, helping to solve the problems of the production. Garry Hynes offered the idea of the amazing transforming quality of the individual and the material in the rehearsal process. Jenny Killick pointed out the dichotomy between being an artistic director of a theatre and a director of plays.

Through Brigid Larmour I was encouraged, in casting and in play choice, to allow the theatre to represent life and not just a western, patriarchal view of life. Through Phyllida Lloyd I learned about dignity in the rehearsal situation, the need for consistent mutual respect, sharing, and consideration. Through Sue Sutton Mayo I learned the value of having everybody in the rehearsal room learn to work beyond ego, through Lynne Parker the value of balance and humour in the rehearsal situation.

One of Nancy Meckler's great lessons was the subtle psychology of the director-actor relationships, that a frightened actor may appear resistant or belligerent. Katie Mitchell shared with me the value of meticulous, detailed research and the importance of exchanges among people and theatres of different cultures and nations. Di Trevis taught me the importance of exploration of values like weather, time of day, climate conditions, customs and rituals that may lead the director into the text.

From the women collectively I learned even more profound truths: that women in the profession can be nurturing, open, collaborative, giving, willing to admit error; that the rehearsal is the centre of the experience, for it is there that we discover how to do the play; that women are visionaries and ground breakers striving towards a new and free theatre, unfettered by the bonds of realism and literalness; that courage, endurance, and tenacity are not the province of men alone; and that kindness, decency, respect, and caring can be key concepts in a theatre that is too often regarded as crass, cold, and unfeeling. If there is one word that seems to flow consistently through these pages, that word would be collaboration. These women have taught me above all to regard the rehearsal, design, and production processes as a non-threatening and rewarding collaboration among artists who share a vision, a hope, and a purpose.

So, with Di Trevis, I admonish the women reading this book to 'just do it' – through university training, through conservatory training, through experience – just do it! Perhaps in another ten years we will see balance between women and men theatre directors commensurate to the population balance in the world itself. It is my fervent hope that this book will lead the members of our profession and the theatre-going public to realise just how qualified, capable and productive women directors are. It is time now that women directors of every nationality take their place beside their male counterparts in the world's theatre.

Current Biographies

Sarah Pia Anderson was born in Hertfordshire, England, did her university training at Swansea in English literature, and worked as a stage manager at the Traverse Theatre in Edinburgh and at the Royal Shakespeare Company before being awarded an Arts Council bursary to train as a director at the Sheffield Crucible. She directed Franz Xaver Kroetz's *The Nest* at the Bush in London in 1986 and made her RSC directing debut with *Indigo* in 1987, the same year her distinguished production of Ibsen's rarely performed classic, *Rosmersholm*, was seen at the National Theatre and later at La Mama in New York. Anderson's other American work has included *The Winter's Tale* at the Shakespeare Festival Santa Cruz; *The Recruiting Officer, The Crucible, The Three Sisters, The Rover* and *In Exremis*, a project with Howard Brenton – all at the University of California, Davis; Schiller's *Mary Stuart* and Shaw's *St Joan* at Washington, DC's Shakespeare Theatre (formerly the Folger). In 1994 Anderson collaborated with American actor, Kelly McGillis, on Ibsen's *Hedda Gabler* at the Roundabout Theatre in New York. Anderson has also been successful directing for television, after accepting an intensive thirteen-week course offered by the BBC in 1981. She has directed numerous plays for television including those by Howard Baker, Robert Holman, and Anne Devlin. She was the first woman to direct one of the award-winning Granada Television *Prime Suspect* episodes starring Helen Mirren. Sarah has taught at the Royal Academy of Dramatic Art and the Central School of Art and Design. She is currently a tenured Professor in Dramatic Art at the University of California, Davis. Her television work in

Los Angeles includes *Nothing Sacred* for ABC (winner of a Peabody Award and a Prism Award), *Profiler* and *ER* for NBC. Most recently she directed *Plastic Man*, a four-hour television drama starring John Thaw, for ITV.

Annabel Arden, co-founder with Simon McBurney and Marcello Magni of Theatre de Complicite, presents a unique vision. Among her favourite directing projects with Complicite have been Dürrenmatt's *The Visit* (*Time Out* Award for Best Director and Olivier Award nomination for Outstanding Achievement, 1988) and Shakespeare's *The Winter's Tale*, 1991, the latter co-directed with Annie Castledine. The two directors worked together again in the fall of 1993, on Marguerite Duras's *India Song* at Theatr Clwyd. Arden attended Cambridge University where she read English literature and involved herself in extensive experimental theatre work. Upon graduation, Arden and seven other artists, including Gloria founders Leah Hausman and Neil Bartlett, who now runs the Lyric Hammersmith, and the film maker Annie Griffin, banded together to form a socialist, feminist collective which was called the 1982 Theatre company for the year of its founding. The collective performed two major works, Brecht's *In the Jungle of Cities*, and a Latvian work titled *The Silver Veil* by the Poetess 'Aspasia', 1905. According to Arden, 'It was a political, poetical, operatical sort of a thing. And we stated it as a Spectacle for Now. It was a lot about our own history, our own personal history. We all came from different countries; we were all trying to make sense of our positions as artists, as aspiring artists at the end of the twentieth century, war, women, democracy, and it was pretty extraordinary as a show when I think back to what we did. And it was about ensemble; it was absolutely about ensemble.' It was at the end of that adventure that Theatre de Complicite was formed in 1983. A noteworthy recent production, with Arden as actress and McBurney as director, is *The Street of Crocodiles*, 1992–99, based on the work of Polish writer and artist, Bruno Schulz. While Arden still acts with and teaches for Complicite, she has recently been devoting herself to the staging of operas: *The Magic Flute* and *The Return of Ulysses* for Opera North, Gounod's *Faust* (Stadttheater Luzern), *Leonore*, Beethoven's first draft of *Fidelio* with John Eliot Gardiner and L'Orchèstre Revolutionnaire et Romantique and Zemlinski's *The Dwarf* for the Teatro Comunale in Florence. In 1998 Arden worked with Candoco, a group of disabled and able-bodied dancers in one company, and translated *Mickey La Torche* by Natacha de Pontcharra for the Royal Court Theatre.

Julia Bardsley comes from a theatrical family. Not only did she have a great-uncle who was an early television actor but her mother was an actress who ran a drama school in Worthing. Bardsley did a degree in Performance Arts at Middlesex Polytechnic, a programme that suited her eclectic interests in all of the arts. It wasn't until her final year that she tried her first directing. That enterprise, *Cupboard Man*, an adaptation of Ian McEwan's short story, won Bardsley the RSC Buzz Goodbody Directors Award and an Edinburgh Fringe First Award. In 1985, with Phelim McDermott, Bardsley formed dereck, dereck Productions and did considerable work in London's fringe theatre before assuming joint Artistic Directorship of the Leicester Haymarket Theatre where she has directed productions of Kroetz's *Dead Soil*, Lorca's *Blood Wedding*, Eliot's *The Family Reunion*, Shakespeare's *Macbeth*, Andrew Poppy's chamber opera *Baby Doll*, and her own adaptations of Zola's *Thérèse Raquin* and Mary Shelley's *Frankenstein*. In 1993 she was named joint Artistic Director of the Young Vic where she directed her own adaptations of Zola's novel, *Thérèse Raquin* and Shakespeare's *Hamlet*. Since 1994 Bardsley has been concentrating her artistic talents on visual arts and film. In 1996 she had her first solo exhibition, titled *The Error Display* at Chiltern Street, London. She was a 1997 recipient of a Wingate Scholarship, awarded to research artificial memory theatres. In 1998 she collaborated with Aldona Cunningham on a photographic installation, *Twelve Stages of the Alm*. She has just completed work on her first film, *Snow*, and is about to start work on [12]/stages$_2$, a film/video project with Aldona Cunningham.

A display of her new work, *Punishment & Ice Cream* opened at The Gallery, St Pancras Way, in January 1999.

'**Annie Castledine** should be head of the National Theatre someday,' was a sentiment expressed by several of the directors. Annabel Arden said, 'Annie was a real inspiration I must say. She's taught me a great deal. She's a superb director. What I find extraordinary is that she's really too hot for the main stages and the main artistic men directors to handle. Mainly because she is a serious radical thinker.' Annie Castledine, currently a freelance theatre and BBC director, has served as an Assistant Director at the RSC, Associate Artistic Director of Theatr Clwyd, and as Artistic Director of the Derby Playhouse. In London she has directed for the Royal Court, the Gate, the Greenwich Theatre, the Young Vic, and the Lyric Theatre, Hammersmith. She is in frequent demand at Theatr Clwyd, the Contact Theatre, Manchester, Chichester Festival Theatre, and West Yorkshire Playhouse. Castledine has made a deep commitment to contemporary plays by women and to that end is the editor of *Plays by Women*, Volumes 9, 10 and 11, 1991 and 1993 and 1999, published by Methuen. In her introduction to Volume 9, Castledine writes that the work in the series proves '. . . that women can write, that they can tackle classical themes and create plays which transcend time and place and be acknowledged Great. Yet this exceptional work is marginalised or neglected altogether.' Castledine exerts tremendous energy helping these female voices find an audience. Along with Stephen Daldry, Castledine is responsible for producing, publishing, and bringing to the public the plays of Marieluise Fleisser who was both a protégée of and a talent exploited by Bertolt Brecht. It was not until 1960 that Fleisser's unique voice was heard outside of Germany. In 1994 Castledine became a Producer in Development for BBC television drama and in 1995 directed *Henry IV* for BBC television. Also in 1995 she at last directed at the Royal National Theatre in London, staging Euripides' *Women of Troy*. Working with co-director, Marcello Magni, Castledine directed *Foe*, adapted from the novel by J.M.

Coetzee for Theatre de Complicite in 1996. She considers her
directing, with Annabel Arden, of Marguerite Duras's *India Song*
at Theatr Clwyd as one of her most rewarding directorial
experiences. Her 1997 production of Bryony Lavery's *Goliath* at
the Bush Theatre met unanimous critical acclaim. In 1998 she
directed *Hymn to Love*, which was much lauded for its
innovative look at the use of music and verbal text. It played at
the Traverse at the Edinburgh Festival and at the Drill Hall and
was broadcast on Radio 3 in January 1999. She enjoys working
at the Royal National Theatre Studio and is currently engaged
in a project, *Spoonface Steinberg*, with Kathryn Hunter and
Marcello Magni

Garry Hynes was born in Ballaghadereen, County Roscom-
mon, and graduated from University of County Galway where
she earned a BA degree in English and History. 'But basically I
spent the whole time involved in drama society matters.' Hynes
stayed on at the university to earn a diploma in education that
qualified her to teach in second-level institutions. But in 1975
she left the academic world to establish the Druid Theatre
Company with, she says, very little money and no prospects.
Ultimately Druid became a vital part of the life of Galway and a
vibrant new force in Irish theatre. Hynes states, 'I directed
almost entirely for Druid until 1986 so my entire life was
devoted to it. Then in 1986 I began to feel the need to get some
experience outside of Druid and also to open up Druid to other
people. So the first production I directed was *Whistle in the Dark*
by Tom Murphy at the Abbey Theatre, and then I did almost a
production a year for the Abbey as a freelance director until
1991.' In 1988 and 1989 Hynes directed Etheridge's *The Man of
Mode* and Wertenbaker's *The Love of the Nightingale* for the
Royal Shakespeare Company. She became Artistic Director of
the Abbey Theatre in Dublin in January of 1991, making her
debut with O'Casey's *The Plough and the Stars*. In 1994 Hynes
returned to Druid Theatre Company and resumed her role as
Artistic Director. There she began an ambitious programme of
new works by such notable playwrights as Billy Roche, Marina

Carr, Niall Williams, Frank McGuinness, and Martin McDonagh. In 1997 Hynes directed a McDonagh trilogy – *The Beauty Queen of Leenane, A Skull in Connemara,* and *The Lonesome West* – which was co-produced by Druid and the Royal Court, where Hynes is an Associate Director. Garry Hynes won a Tony award for Best Director of a Play for *The Beauty Queen of Leenane* when it transferred to Broadway in 1998.

Jenny Killick achieved a position of authority very early in her career. Just after college at the University of London and a brief apprenticeship at Riverside Studios, she was granted a Scottish Arts Council Director Traineeship at Edinburgh's famed Traverse Theatre in 1983. By 1984 she was directing award-winning productions at the Traverse, and in 1985 was named Artistic Director, making her the youngest artistic director in Britain and the first woman to hold that position at the Traverse in its twenty-five year history. Killick says, 'It was a fantastic opportunity and experience very, very young. I was just twenty-five when they gave me the artistic directorship.' Killick gained a reputation as a daring experimenter and a champion of new plays, one of the most successful of these being John Clifford's international hit *Losing Venice.* Since leaving the Traverse in 1988 Killick has worked as a freelance director, at the Royal National Theatre, Bristol Old Vic, Leicester Haymarket, University of California, Davis, in the West End, and in television where, like Sarah Pia Anderson and Annie Castledine, she was trained by the BBC. Her first major directing assignment was a new political series about policemen being investigated for crimes, titled *Between the Lines,* which won a Royal Television Society Award for Best Drama Series. From 1995 to 1997 she continued working at the BBC as a Development Executive for the Independent Commissioning Group, becoming Series Editor for *Screen Firsts,* short film acquisitions for BBC2, and then Series Producer for *Brief Encounter,* a series of 35mm short films introducing new directors, writers and producers, co-produced with Channel 4. She has two young sons.

Brigid Larmour has a degree in English and Economics from King's College, Cambridge, where she both acted and directed. Her professional training involved working as an assistant director with the RSC from 1982 to 1985. According to Larmour, 'I worked there for three years and I did quite a lot of pressurising while I was there on behalf of women directors. In fact, I put a proposal together which involved Di Trevis, Annie Castledine and myself taking over The Other Place, which both Terry Hands, who was effectively running the company, and Trevor Nunn said was a terribly interesting proposal and that they'd set up a meeting when they were both free, and this went on for months and months and months – and nothing ever happened.' Larmour does feel that the initiative she and others began has ultimately proved at least partially successful. (Katie Mitchell is now Artistic Director of The Other Place in Stratford-upon-Avon.) As a freelance director, and as Associate and later Artistic Director of the Contact Theatre, Manchester – a post she held from 1989 to 1994 – Larmour remained committed to non-traditional casting and aimed to programme approximately one-half of the Contact repertoire to represent 50% of the population. At the Contact she directed such plays as the premiere of Charlotte Keatley's *My Mother Said I Never Should* and *The Singing Ringing Tree* and the English premiere of Liz Lochhead's *Mary Queen of Scots Got Her Head Chopped Off*, as well as commissions by James Stork, Tyrone Huggins, and Kevin Fegan. In 1991 she wrote and presented a documentary for the BBC titled *Half the Story – The Role of Women in the Arts*. On leaving Contact in 1994, she trained with and directed for Granada TV. Larmour has a particular passion for Shakespeare, and in recent years has evolved a distinctive method and performance style through a series of promenade touring productions for the Royal National Theatre, which she has called Shakespeare Unplugged. She is currently writing a book about this work, which has included two productions of *The Tempest*, with a female Prospero, as well as *Henry V* and two productions of *Twelfth Night*. She has taught and directed extensively at universities and drama schools both in the United

Kingdom and America, including Southern Methodist University and Juilliard. In 1998 Larmour was appointed Artistic Director of ACT Theatre Productions, a new production development company attached to Associated Capital Theatres, one of London's two major West End theatre management groups.

Phyllida Lloyd studied English and Drama at the University of Birmingham, and there realised that she wanted to be a director. Upon graduation, she says, 'I went straight from university to work on the studio floors of the BBC. At the time this was the start of a well-trodden path to becoming a director in television.' At the same time Lloyd began directing plays on London's fringe and to apply for Arts Council Trainee Director bursaries. On her third attempt, she was successful and went to the Wolsey Theatre, Ipswich. In 1986 she became Associate Director of the Everyman Theatre, Cheltenham, and she has also served as Associate Director at the Bristol Old Vic and the Royal Exchange, Manchester. Lloyd made her RSC debut with *The Virtuoso* at the Swan Theatre, Stratford, and also directed Ostrovsky's *Artists and Admirers* at The Pit. Among Lloyd's most celebrated works have been her Royal Court productions of John Guare's *Six Degrees of Separation* starring Stockard Channing and Terry Johnson's *Hysteria* (also at the Mark Taper Forum in Los Angeles). She directed *The Threepenny Opera* for the Donmar Theatre, *Dona Rosita The Spinster* for the Almeida Theatre, and four productions for the Royal National Theatre: *Pericles, What the Butler Saw, The Way of the World* and *The Prime of Miss Jean Brodie*, both with Fiona Shaw. She has directed a number of opera productions: *L'étoile, La Bohème, Medea, Gloriana* and *Carmen* for Opera North; and *Macbeth* for Opéra National de Paris. She is currently preparing *The Dialogues of the Carmelites* for English National Opera and *Mamma Mia!*, a musical based on the songs of Abba.

Sue Sutton Mayo, currently the producer of Channel 4's *Brookside*, has left theatre for television. Previously a resident director at the Library Theatre, Manchester. 'The Library Theatre', Mayo says, 'is absolutely unique. It's the only theatre in the country which is totally owned and run by a local council.' Mayo left school at sixteen and worked at various jobs and then after five years came to Manchester to train as a teacher of drama at what is now Manchester Metropolitan University. She taught for a year, married, and formed a Theatre-in-Education company until, with two children of her own, she decided to stay at home and devote herself to their upbringing. A weekend jaunt with a friend to Stratford to see *Nicholas Nickleby* and a subsequent fan letter to Trevor Nunn resulted in a job with the RSC. When the RSC tour ended, Mayo returned to Manchester. She says, 'I was a dresser at the Palace for a while, I stage-crewed, I did some flying, really just about everything. Not terribly well but I did it.' Mayo began to direct at the Library Theatre on their lunch-time series of new plays. It was there that she first directed Valerie Windsor's *Effie's Burning,* which ultimately enjoyed considerable success in London. The Library Theatre's Artistic Director, Chris Honer, invited Mayo to be an occasional director and subsequently a resident director at the Library Theatre. 'He didn't like the idea that people just visited the company, directed and moved on. Chris has a desire to have a team around him. So he approached me and asked if I would like to become resident director. And he asked me to do three shows a year and to hang around in between and to become part of the management team really.' Recent productions are *A Christmas Carol*, Ibsen's *Ghosts*, and a production of Kay Adshead's play, *Ravings: Dreamings*. Subsequently Mayo has moved into television work, initially directing and currently producing *Brookside*. 'I love it' says Mayo 'but occasionally miss theatre with a passion that knocks me sideways. One day I'll definitely go back.'

Nancy Meckler is unique among the women for two reasons: first, she is by birth an American, although she has been a part of the British theatre scene since 1968; and second, while she has often worked as a freelance director, she is Artistic Director of a

London fringe theatre that calls itself Shared Experience Theatre. Meckler graduated from Antioch College in Yellow Springs, Ohio. 'I participated in all things theatrical there although I didn't particularly want to be a drama major because I always felt that somehow a more liberal education would be more useful to me. But in my last two years there I did major in drama partly because the department was very small, and they really needed people like me to make a commitment.' After graduation, Meckler, determined to be an actress, took a year programme at LAMDA (London Academy of Music and Dramatic Art) and then returned to the United States where she attended a Master's degree course in dramatic theory and criticism at New York University. There she studied with Richard Schechner and was inspired by the innovative experimentation of Joseph Chaikin. In 1968, Meckler returned to England and was a founding member of Freehold, a theatre company whose production of *Antigone* was performed at the Edinburgh Festival and various festivals on the Continent. Landmark productions or Meckler include Pam Gems's *Dusa, Fish, Stas and Vi*, first at the Hampstead Theatre and later as a transfer to the West End, and *Uncle Vanya* with Ian Holm and Nigel Hawthorne, again at the Hampstead Theatre. In 1981 Meckler was the first woman to direct on the main stage of the National Theatre with her production of *Who's Afraid of Virginia Woolf?* Meckler has directed at the Bush, the Almeida, Leicester Haymarket, and the Royal Court as well as at regional theatres in the US. In 1987 she directed Wendy Kesselman's drama, *My Sister in This House* for Monstrous Regiment, Leicester Haymarket Studio, tour, and the Hampstead Theatre. In 1994 she made her debut as a film director with an award-winning cinematic version of the same story titled, *Sister My Sister*. In 1988 Meckler became Artistic Director of Shared Experience Theatre where recent award-winning successes have been *Anna Karenina*, *Mill on the Floss*, and *War and Peace*, the last two co-directed with Polly Teale. The *Guardian* has said of her work, 'Nancy Meckler is one of the few directors in this country with the guts to encourage her company to go beyond naturalism into larger than life expressionism.' Her most recent film is *Alive and Kicking*, written by Martin Sherman and released in June of 1997. At both the Hamptons Film Festival and the London Film Festival, *Alive and Kicking*, with Antony Sher, Jason Flemyng, and Dorothy Tutin, was presented Audience Prize for Best Film. In 1998 *Anna Karenina* played in the Brooklyn Academy of Music's Next Wave Festival in New York.

Katie Mitchell, probably the youngest of all the directors included here, began directing school plays at 16, an activity that continued at Oxford University where she served as President of the Oxford University Drama Society. Determined to give herself approximately three years of apprenticeship, Mitchell first typed scripts at the King's Head Theatre in Islington. She then joined Pip Broughton's small-scale touring company, Paines Plough, for a year. After that she says she was lucky enough to become an assistant director at the Royal Shakespeare Company for two years, assisting such notables as Cicely Berry, Ron Daniels, Adrian Noble, and Gene Saks. Mitchell also assisted three distinguished women directors – Garry Hynes, Di Trevis, and Deborah Warner. A key event in Mitchell's career occurred when she received a Winston Churchill Memorial Trust Fellowship to research directors' training and rehearsal techniques in Eastern Europe. In the late 1980s Mitchell founded her own company, Classics on a Shoestring. The first three productions she directed for that company at the Gate Theatre – Gorki's *Vassa Zheleznova*, *Arden of Faversham*, and Euripides' *Women of Troy* – won *Time Out* awards. Among Mitchell's recent successes are Thomas Heywood's *A Woman Killed with Kindness* (1991), Solomon Anski's *The Dybbuk* (1992) and Ibsen's *Ghosts* (1993), all for the RSC. Mitchell received rave reviews with her *House of Bernarda Alba* at the Gate Theatre in 1992, and she made her Abbey Theatre debut in the winter of 1993 with Maxim Gorki's *The Last Ones*. In 1994 she directed *Rutherford and Sons* at the National, and in 1995 Ernst Toller's *The Machine Wreckers*. Mitchell, who has been an Associate Director at the RSC, is deeply committed to new productions of rarely performed classics and overlooked or forgotten masterpieces. In 1996 she won the Evening Standard Award for Best Director for her production of *The Phoenician Women*. In 1997 she directed epic medieval plays under the collective title of *The Mysteries* at The Other Place in Stratford, *The Creation* dealing with the creation of the world and the human race, and *The Passion*, concerning the life and death of Jesus.

Lynne Parker was born in Belfast and educated at Trinity College, Dublin. In 1984 she became co-founder and Artistic Director of Rough Magic Theatre Company. Early work for Rough magic includes *Nightshade* and *Spokesong* by Stewart Parker, *Decadence* by Stephen Berkoff, *The Country Wife* by William Wycherley, *Top Girls* and *Serious Money* by Caryl Churchill, *Aunt Dan and Lemon* by Wallace Shawn and *The Dogs* by Donal O'Kelly. She was nominated for a Harveys Theatre Award in 1988. Since 1990 she has directed the work of her colleague Declan Hughes, notably *Digging for Fire* and his adaption of *Farquhar's Love and a Bottle* which won the Time Out Award in 1992. For these shows and her production of *Lady Windermere's Fan* she won the Bank of Ireland/Arts Show Award. She has worked with a number of companies including Druid, Tinderbox, Opera Theatre Company and 7:84 Scotland, and she was an associate artist of Charabanc for whom she adapted and directed Lorca's *The House of Bernarda Alba*. Most recent work includes *Euripides' The Trojan Women* (Peacock), Helen Edmundson's *The Clearing* (The Bush Theatre, London), Shaw's *The Doctor's Dilemma* (Abbey), Synge's *The Playboy of the Western World* and O'Casey's *The Silver Tassie* (The Almeida Theatre, London), Jimmy Murphy's *Brother's of the Brush* (The Arts Theatre, London) and O'Casey's *The Shadow of a Gunman* (Gate Theatre, Dublin). For Rough Magic she has directed *New Morning* by Declan Hughes, *The Way of the World* by Congreve, *Down Onto Blue* by Pom Boyd, *Hidden Charges* by Arthur Riordan, *Danti-Dan* by Gina Moxley, *Northern Star* and *Pentecost* by Stewart Parker, which won the Dublin Theatre Festival

Appendix

Award for Best Irish Production. Most recently she directed Declan Hughes' *Halloween Night* at the Donmar Warehouse, April de Angelis' *Playhouse Creatures* for the Peter Hall Company at the Old Vic, *The Importance of Being Earnest* for the West Yorkshire Playhouse and *The School for Scandal* for Rough Magic at the Gaiety Theatre and on tour. For the 1998 Dublin Theatre Festival she directed *Love Me?!* by Arthur Riordan for the Car Exchange's CarShow.

Di Trevis is the only woman who had a career as an actress before becoming a director. Born in Birmingham, Trevis read social anthropology at the University of Sussex and then joined Glasgow Citizens' and Sheffield Crucible as an actress. Trevis says, 'I love the theatre and I love the acting process, but I felt that I was temperamentally very unsuited to being an actress, being subject to vagaries of the career, vagaries of casting, loss of control over one's life. I felt it was really like being a woman twice over, that in society women are struggling all the time against a feeling of powerlessness and then, in the very job I did, it was further powerlessness. It made me unhappy, and I suddenly realised that there was something else I wanted to do in the theatre where in a sense I could take control of the whole vision.' In 1981 Trevis served as an assistant to Peter Gill at the National Theatre and went on to direct at a variety of fringe and regional theatres before becoming a regular at both the National and the RSC. In the 1993–94 season Trevis directed for both national theatres: *Elgar's Rondo* by David Pownall at the RSC's Swan Theatre in Stratford and *Inadmissible Evidence* by John Osborne at the Lyttelton Theatre of the Royal National Theatre in London. Trevis has directed for both the Scottish Opera and the Royal Opera House, Covent Garden, and she has recently directed several productions for Theatr Clwyd. In 1998 she directed Clifford Odets' *Awake and Sing* at the University of California, Davis, where she has twice been Granada Artist-in-Residence. In the same year she formed Trevis and Company and devised *Happy Birthday, Brecht*, to celebrate the Brecht centenary. The show played at the Artaud Theatre in San

Francisco and raised money to send pianos to Cuba and to set up a scholarship for a Cuban pianist to study in London. Trevis and Company now plan a season of Brecht and Beckett for touring in the US and Europe. Di Trevis has also started teaching a series of workshops for young actors in Havana. She has just completed an adaptation of *The Remembrance of Things Past* with Harold Pinter for the Royal National Theatre.